GARDENING WITH
FOLIAGE FIRST

GARDENING WITH
FOLIAGE FIRST

127 dazzling combinations that pair the **beauty of leaves** with flowers, bark, berries, and more

KAREN CHAPMAN AND
CHRISTINA SALWITZ

Timber Press
Portland, Oregon

To our gardening
friends—past,
present, and
future—whose
passion for plants,
the landscape, good
wine, and chocolate
sustains us.

Karen & Christina

Pages 2 and 26: Nestled among the fern-like foliage of false spirea, this weathered Italianate urn becomes a striking focal point.

Pages 5 and 55: An explosion of foliage and flowers is accented by a colorful spiral obelisk.

Photo, design, and location credits appear on pages 325–327.

Thanks are offered to those who granted permission for use of photographs but who are not named individually in the acknowledgments. While every reasonable effort has been made to contact copyright holders and secure permission for all materials reproduced in this work, we offer apologies for any instances in which this was not possible and for any inadvertent omissions.

Published in 2017 by Timber Press, Inc.

The Haseltine Building
133 S.W. Second Avenue, Suite 450
Portland, Oregon 97204–3527
timberpress.com

Printed in China
Book design by Kristi Pfeffer

Library of Congress Cataloging-in-Publication Data

Names: Chapman, Karen (Landscape designer), author. | Salwitz, Christina, author.
Title: Gardening with foliage first: 127 dazzling combinations that pair the beauty of leaves with flowers, bark, berries, and more / Karen Chapman and Christina Salwitz.
Description: Portland, Oregon: Timber Press, 2017. | Includes bibliographical references and index. | Description based on print version record and CIP data provided by publisher; resource not viewed.
Identifiers: LCCN 2016021287 (print) | LCCN 2016018329 (ebook) | ISBN 9781604697834 (e-book) | ISBN 9781604696646 (pbk.)
Subjects: LCSH: Foliage plants. | Gardening.
Classification: LCC SB431 (print) | LCC SB431 .C492 2017 (ebook) | DDC 635.9/75—dc23
LC record available at https://lccn.loc.gov/2016021287

A catalog record for this book is also available from the British Library.

CONTENTS

INTRODUCTION
Sensational Scenes, Expansive Ideas, and Original Thinking

What do you get when you let two designers loose in a nursery? A car filled to overflowing with a wild assortment of trees, shrubs, perennials, and more. It is a given that you will not be able to see out of the rear window, and you should expect to have plants on the seats, on the floor, and in cup holders. It is only when plants are precariously balanced on the dashboard that we think we may have enough.

But these are not just any plants. The majority will be an outrageous selection of foliage plants with enormous tropical leaves jostling feathery grasses; stripes, spots, and splashes alongside bold solid colors from vibrant orange to deepest purple. Tucked in here and there will be some flowering plants. Experience has taught us that these truly perform, either with a reliably long bloom time or interesting leaves as well as flowers.

As designers, speakers, and coauthors, we have gained a reputation for being entertaining as well as inspiring and for sharing our expertise in a way that is easy to understand. We encourage and challenge each other, which brings out the best in both of us. This, in turn, provides readers with a much broader range of ideas than either one of us could accomplish alone. Together we have fun while we walk you through our design process, which puts foliage first, then adds a final flourish to take the scene from predictable to exceptional.

THE FLORAL SEDUCTION
When you go to the grocery store, you probably have a plan (or at least a recipe) in mind. But how often do you take a shopping list to the nursery? Without forethought, you are headed for disaster—it is too easy to get seduced by all the colorful flowers so prominently displayed. On impulse, you grab one of this and one of that, and when you get home that collection of pretty blooms never quite translates into a glossy magazine image. It is just a wild kaleidoscope with no cohesive sense of design—or, worse, the blooms fade, and you spent a lot of money on a short-term burst of glory. What went wrong?

You may have chosen plants that are individually beautiful, but did you consider whether they look good together? Is there a visual connection between them? Or perhaps you succumbed to the display of blooming annuals and perennials, the enticing photographs promising an abundance of flowers in summer. But how many months do you need to wait for the plants to reach that stage—and how long will they bloom? If you focus on the flowers without considering the foliage, you may end up with a disappointing mélange of midsize green leaves for much of the year, not a unified, well-designed look. It is far more effective, and attractive, to start with foliage.

TAKING THE NEXT STEP
After building a foliage framework, we show you how to layer in flowers or other artistic elements to add the finishing touch. We take the mystery out of the design process and explain what makes a combination successful. If you follow our ideas or use them as a springboard for your own creations, you will feel like we are your personal design coaches.

In this book, we demonstrate how quickly and easily you can assemble plants that reflect your personal style and suit the largest border or smallest container. We teach you how to make strategic plant choices, clarify why certain plants are great investments for year-round interest, and explain how every element will help you achieve a cohesive look.

INSPIRATION FOR ALL SEASONS, SITUATIONS, AND SETTINGS

Our ideas go beyond the typical summer growing season. The book is divided into two main sections—Spring and Summer, Fall and Winter—both of which feature design schemes for sun and shade situations. You will be able to create a true four-season garden that will work for your style and design challenges. Are you still trying to outwit the deer? We feel your pain, and have included Beauty Without the Beast just for you. Looking for something to add winter interest to your cold-climate garden? We were inspired by Serendipity and we think you will be, too. Do you prefer a hot, spicy color palette? Sassitude is sizzling hot. Need ideas for a fall container? Pumpkin Spice Latte is just one of the flavors on the menu.

We scoured gardens from British Columbia to Arizona and Florida to Washington State to find designs to delight, inspire, and embolden you to try new ideas, new plants, and new ways of looking at plant combinations. There are ideas for small patio containers to large sweeping borders, and everything in between. Each combination includes an explanation of how it works. Many of our favorite plants have multiple periods of significance, so we also discuss how each component evolves during the year and offers ideas on how to extend the season of interest even further.

New gardeners will quickly gain confidence as they learn how to select plants that work together, as well as how to identify the details that create a strong foliage picture frame for the flowers on which they may have initially focused. Intermediate gardeners will learn how to transform their gardens from a jumble of collectors' plants to a carefully composed design, while those with many years of dirt under their fingernails will be inspired by a fresh twist on old favorites—plus exciting new introductions that will spark the imagination and help you craft unique creations.

CREATING A FOLIAGE PICTURE FRAME

You don't need to be a horticulturist or an artist to learn how to design. Careful observation of the smallest detail will help you transform a group of plants on a cart in the nursery into a memorable vignette: your foliage picture frame. Begin with an inspiration plant that drives you wild with excitement. Maybe it is one you have loved and used a number of times, or perhaps it once intimidated you. Whether you are choosing a tree, a perennial, a shrub, or a succulent, look at its key features first.

Far more than just an evergreen shrub, this variegated English holly (*Ilex aquifolium* 'Argentea Marginata') offers the gardener shades of deep green, creamy yellow, and even a rosy winter blush to use as design inspiration.

DESIGN INSPIRATION FROM COLOR, TEXTURE, AND FORM

Imagine putting a leaf under a spotlight. What design cues are revealed? Look at color first—is the underside of the leaf different from the upper surface? Are there distinctive veins? Is the leaf variegated? If so, what are the different colors? Does the leaf have a subtle margin?

Or perhaps that spotlight is coming from behind the leaf, like the backlighting we employ in photography. Many leaves appear translucent and suggest a new color. For example, purple smoke bushes may be purple in the shade but warm hues of rosy red as light streams through the foliage. As we learn to search for and identify these color cues, we can use them as a jumping-off point to build our design.

When we discuss texture in plants we are considering two key elements: first, the surface area of the leaf, which may have a bold, medium, or fine texture, and second, whether it feels smooth, rough, bumpy, or velvety. We can combine these features in different ways to create high contrast or a quieter pairing.

Light also affects how we see texture. Shiny leaves will reflect light and thus appear brighter and with more highly saturated color. Foliage with a matte surface will absorb light and appear less intense.

Recognizing the form of a plant will help you create interesting pairings. Prostrate, mounding, and columnar are just three of the many possibilities. We see gardens and containers every day that are perfectly nice to look at, but lack attention to the use of form and miss the opportunity to create an exceptional scene. If you learn to identify and use a variety of shapes and forms in your landscape and containers, you will add visual excitement to your own compositions. Try punctuating a mostly flat planting scheme with a surprising vertical element, or introducing a broad swathe of low-growing grasses in front of a tapestry of mounding shrubs.

Backlit by the evening sun, the foliage of this smoke bush (*Cotinus coggygria*) changes from dusky purple to warm orange-red.

The glossy foliage of the Tequila Sunrise mirror plant (*Coprosma repens* 'Tequila Sunrise') reflects light.

Dinosaur kale (*Brassica oleracea* 'Lacinato') has leaves that are leathery and bumpy to the touch.

Mirjam arborvitae (*Thuja occidentalis* 'Mirjam') has a perfectly mounded form without pruning.

MAKING THE DESIGN CONNECTION <- ->

Once you identify the unique features in your inspiration plant, it is time to highlight them. The easiest place to start is with color. When we offer garden advice to our clients or audiences, we frequently use related ideas for pulling designs together. For example, when furnishing an empty room, we might start with a fabric swatch, a throw pillow, or piece of art as color inspiration for the rest of the combination. You may be putting together an outfit for an event and begin with a pair of shoes, a piece of jewelry, or a favorite top. Making the design connection with plants is exactly the same process.

Suppose your inspiration plant is the sun-tolerant Spitfire coleus (*Solenostemon scutellarioides* 'Spitfire'), which boasts a luscious shade of crushed raspberry with unusual taupe markings. To highlight this unexpected detail, try pairing it with Orange King coleus (*S. scutellarioides* 'Orange King'). This was never one of our favorites because of its odd dirty mustard color, but as soon as it is partnered with Spitfire it makes sense, as the dominant color of Orange King is the same as the secondary hue in Spitfire. In addition, the raspberry tones in Spitfire are also repeated in the veins, margins, and underside of the Orange King foliage. We refer to this tight visual connection as a color echo, a feature that highlights our inspiration plant perfectly and is also a great building block for developing more extensive plant combinations.

Perhaps you are inspired not only by the color of your feature plant but also its texture. The large silver-spotted leaves of lungwort (*Pulmonaria* species) are distinctly rough, almost bristle-like. Planted adjacent to the soft ferny foliage of Silver

Mound wormwood (*Artemisia schmidtiana* 'Silver Mound'), this tactile quality is highlighted while the silver note is repeated in both perennials.

If you're like the magpie who is attracted to shiny things, you will love Spellbound coral bells (*Heuchera* 'Spellbound'). The plant has oversize metallic foliage in a luscious shade of medium purple, and each leaf sports distinct darker violet veins. To draw attention to both these features, try pairing it with Ruby Glow spurge (*Euphorbia amygdaloides* 'Ruby Glow'): the velvety dark purple leaves echo the deeper tones in the coral bells, while its matte surface contrasts with the highly reflective foliage of Spellbound, creating a magical combination.

If you're a detail person, you might be fascinated by foliage patterns that form unique and individual combinations, similar to a quilter piecing together fabric like a puzzle. The narrow silver-blue ribbons of foliage with a creamy white edge on Silver Swan spurge (*Euphorbia characias* 'Silver Swan') layer together in an unexpectedly elegant way with this ruffled Henna coleus (*Solenostemon* 'Henna'). The hot chartreuse, copper, and burgundy foliage of the coleus make for a spicy trio in this combination. The blooms of the small white alyssum (*Lobularia maritima* 'Snow Crystals') and lemon-lime felted leaves of Limelight licorice plant (*Helichrysum petiolare* 'Limelight') round out and pull together this finely detailed patchwork.

- -

The tight color echo between Orange King and Spitfire coleus (*Solenostemon scutellarioides* 'Orange King' and *S. scutellarioides* 'Spitfire') is a great starting point for a design.

Contrasting texture while repeating the color silver in lungwort (*Pulmonaria* species) and Silver Mound wormwood (*Artemisia schmidtiana* 'Silver Mound').

Spellbound coral bells (*Heuchera* 'Spellbound') echoes the color of Ruby Glow spurge (*Euphorbia amygdaloides* 'Ruby Glow') while contrasting leaf size, shape, and reflective qualities.

An intricate patchwork of foliage and flowers featuring Silver Swan spurge (*Euphorbia characias* 'Silver Swan'), Henna coleus (*Solenostemon* 'Henna'), white alyssum (*Lobularia maritima* 'Snow Crystals'), and Limelight licorice plant (*Helichrysum petiolare* 'Limelight').

PULLING IT ALL TOGETHER

The final step is an opportunity to add something unexpected, such as a piece of glass art or a colorful flower. Or you may simply develop a monochromatic theme to include additional foliage and flowering plants. Often these elements will have a color echo with some other design component, but with experience you will learn how to use a wild card that at face value has nothing in common with the other plants. For example, in Citrus Splash we show you that the level of color saturation between the two elements makes them perfect partners, even without any specific color echo. Winter designs take considerable creativity to think beyond evergreens, so we will show you how to use berries, seed heads, and colorful branches as layers to enhance your design.

Our aim is to convey our passion for great garden design by sharing inspirational ideas, and to teach you how to layer together the design elements so you are successful every time. Whether you want a floral extravaganza, a classic look, or something clean and contemporary, it all comes down to designing around foliage.

HOW TO USE THIS BOOK

This book is divided into two main growing seasons: first, Spring and Summer, and second, Fall and Winter, each of which is subdivided into sections for growing in sun and shade.

Every juicy combination has a fun title and offers a large glamour shot, plus an explanation of why it works and details of how the design will mature to reach its pinnacle of perfection. The foliage framework includes individual plant portraits and easy reference details about what each needs to thrive, followed by the finishing touch, which may be anything from flowers, thorns, berries, or twigs to a specially selected piece of garden art that completes the scene. These combinations may have as few as two plants or as many as ten.

KEY TO THE PAGES

Understanding your growing conditions is one key to design success.

SITE This indicates how much sun or shade the combination requires to thrive. Observation is key, as an area that receives full sun in summer may be significantly more shaded in winter months. We refer to four variations:

Full sun: At least 6 hours of direct sun each day.

Partial sun: Between 4 and 6 hours of direct sun, with protection during the hottest part of the day.

Partial shade: Morning sun only, often on the eastern side of the house.

Full shade: Less than 2 hours of direct sun, with some filtered sun during part of the day.

SOIL Soil can vary enormously from dry sand to wet, sticky clay and everything in between; it also fluctuates across the country and within a single garden. Understanding what your soil is like and growing appropriate plants is the first step toward successful gardening. If you are new to plants, seek out local expert advice to help you gain confidence. We use the following terms to describe soil types:

Average: Many gardeners refer to this soil as loam. Typically it is rich and dark, crumbles easily, and retains moisture while still allowing water to percolate through.

Well-drained: Soil does not stay saturated even after heavy rains.

Moisture-retentive: Such soils are often rich in organic matter or have been mulched well with compost. Even after prolonged high temperatures these soils do not completely dry out, but they are not waterlogged.

Potting soil: These can vary widely in content, price, and quality. Ask an experienced local container designer for a recommendation based on the plants you want to grow and what is available in your area.

ZONE The USDA hardiness rating system provides gardeners a way to determine which plants will survive in their geographical location based on the average annual frost-free days and minimum winter temperatures. The lower the zone number, the colder the winter temperatures. Individual plants within a combination can have different hardiness ratings, so in the headnote we provide the zones in which all the plants will survive (except annuals), but we also give specific hardiness information for the individual plants. Like all avid gardeners, we are not put off simply because a label suggests that a fabulous shrub may die in our Seattle winters—we will try it anyway. A little research at your local nurseries may help you find a perfect hardy alternative to an otherwise tender plant. Local knowledge of microclimates is invaluable. To see temperature equivalents and to learn which zone you garden in, see the U.S. Department of Agriculture Hardiness Zone Map at planthardiness.ars.usda.gov/PHZMWeb/. For Canada, go to planthardiness.gc.ca. For Europe, go to uk.gardenweb.com/forums/zones/hze.html. For the UK, search for "hardiness" at rhs.org.uk.

SEASON This refers to the seasons of visual interest that the combination provides. If all plants listed die to the ground in winter, the season is listed as spring through fall. If some key structural elements remain—such as interesting twigs, berries, or an evergreen shrub—then it is considered year-round, even if annuals are included.

A SPECIAL NOTE ABOUT FALL AND WINTER CONTAINERS

When designing containers for spring and summer we are mindful of the heat and light tolerance of each plant, given that temperatures even in temperate climates can rise above 90°F, quickly scorching plants that are not true sun worshippers. With lower temperatures and shorter days in fall and winter we can take considerable liberties with our plant

COMMON GARDENING TERMS

Even the most novice gardener must be familiar with certain words and terms to create successful foliage combinations.

annual A plant that completes its growing cycle in one season and then dies (such as coleus). For simplicity, we refer to any plants that would survive winters only in zone 10 or warmer as annuals, even though many are suitable as houseplants or thrive in more tropical conditions.

perennial A plant that may be deciduous or herbaceous but comes back each year (like coneflower).

herbaceous A plant that dies to the ground in winter but re-emerges in spring (such as hosta).

deciduous A plant that loses its leaves in fall but retains its twiggy structure through winter (like spirea).

semi-evergreen A plant that may lose a proportion of its leaves in prolonged cold winters but will grow fresh foliage in spring (such as abelia).

evergreen A plant that keeps its leaves year-round (like camellia).

selection, including a sun-loving conifer in a partially shaded porch or a variety of coral bells that usually needs afternoon shade in a more open aspect.

The beauty of container gardening is that nothing has to be permanent. You can easily move smaller containers from one location to another and transplant the plants to another pot or into the landscape as season, style, or growth suggests.

The guide to placement for fall and winter container designs takes into account what will give you the best results for that combination during that season. Note our suggestions, as well as individual plant details for ongoing care.

INVASIVE PLANTS

Some of the plants featured in this book may be invasive in your area—please consult your local Cooperative Extension or County Extension Office, or check the USDA website. We suggest substitutions for some and offer alternatives for any that are especially problematic. Your selection will be based on the attribute you are looking for, as well as your climate. A local nursery professional or trained horticulturist will be able to assist you.

Barberry (*Berberis* species) These thorny deer-resistant shrubs are available in many colors, sizes, and shapes, from tall fountains to low mounds. Consider varieties of weigela (*Weigela*), fringe flower (*Loropetalum*), or ninebark (*Physocarpus*) instead.

Mexican feather grass (*Stipa tenuissima*, also sold as *Nassella tenuissima*) This soft, airy evergreen grass moves in the breeze but reseeds readily. Consider moor grass (*Molinia*) or blue grama grass (*Bouteloua gracilis*) for a similar look.

Parney's cotoneaster (*Cotoneaster parneyi*, *Cotoneaster lacteus*) Evergreen foliage and fat clusters of red berries make this popular in many areas, but where it is invasive you may be able to substitute toyon (*Heteromeles arbutifolia*).

Italian arum (*Arum italicum*) A shade-loving perennial with lush foliage and seasonal berries that looks beautiful but spreads rapidly by seed and underground corms. Native Jack-in-the-pulpit (*Arisaema triphyllum*) has similar shaped flowers and berries, or one of the hardy cyclamen (*Cyclamen coum*, *C. heterophyllum*) or barrenwort (*Epimedium* species) may provide alternative foliage interest.

Western coltsfoot (*Petasites palmatus*) Proof that a native can also be invasive, this herbaceous perennial will quickly overtake other plants if the conditions are right. Rodger's flower (*Rodgersia* species) or some of the large hostas, like Sum and Substance, may be better choices.

Darmera (*Darmera peltata*) Native to shady streamsides in parts of the Pacific Northwestern United States, this herbaceous perennial can quickly outgrow its space and its welcome. Astilboides (*Astilboides tabularis*) behaves better and has similar foliage and plume-like white flowers.

Yellow flag iris (*Iris pseudacorus*) This eye-catching perennial can quickly choke out native wetland species. Siberian iris may be a better choice; Butter and Sugar (*Iris sibirica* 'Butter and Sugar') has soft yellow and white flowers.

DEER DISCLAIMER

Trying to outwit deer is a lifelong challenge for those of us who live in deer country. Just when we think we understand their preferences, they develop a taste for something new. Although it is true that deer will eat anything when hungry enough, we suspect they can read price tags. They always seem to eat the most expensive specimens.

Then again, there are levels of deer resistance. Deer will eat some plants to the ground every year, will moderately graze others but leave enough that it is still worth growing them, and will rarely, if ever, touch certain plants. Some plants that are considered deer resistant lose new growth and/or flowers to deer, although the less tender parts of the plant stay safe. Taste also varies according to region and the age of deer (young ones really will try anything).

In the Pacific Northwestern United States we can indulge our passion for colorful foliage by selecting from an abundance of *Heuchera* and *Heucherella*. However, our favorites may not thrive in the humid south or extreme cold of the Midwest. We asked Dan Heims, president of Terra Nova Nurseries Inc., to share his expertise and experience to help you substitute varieties as needed. These recommendations are based on performance at regional test facilities, and they are his personal favorites for health, vigor, and hardiness in those areas.

	SOUTH	PACIFIC NORTHWEST AND BRITISH ISLES	MIDWEST	COLOR	COMMENTS
HEUCHERA VARIETY					
Autumn Leaves	●			ruby red	needs heat
Bella Notte	●		●	black	tough plant
Black Taffeta	●	●		black	ruffled leaves
Blondie		●	●	toffee	compact, repeat bloomer
Cherry Cola			●	red-brown	
Electric Lime	●			lime	
Fire Chief	●	●	●	vibrant red	
Forever Purple		●		purple	
Galaxy	●			red	multiple shade changes
Glitter			●	silver	black veins
Green Spice			●	green, silver	deep red veins
Lime Ruffles		●	●	lime	
Marmalade		●	●	amber	raspberry underside
Peach Crisp			●	amber	
Peach Flambé		●		orange, red	fabulous in full sun
Shanghai			●	silver, purple	tough plant
Southern Comfort	●			peach	
Spellbound	●	●	●	purple	metallic sheen to large leaves
Sweet Tart			●	lime	compact, repeat bloomer
HEUCHERELLA VARIETY					
Brass Lantern	●	●		gold, red	
Buttered Rum		●	●	caramel	
Copper Cascade			●	copper	vigorous trailer
Honey Rose			●	coral	
Redstone Falls	●	●	●	copper	vigorous trailer
Solar Eclipse	●	●	●	yellow, cocoa	
Solar Power	●	●		yellow	dark red markings
Sweet Tea	●			copper	lush and full
Tapestry	●			green	dark center

COMBINATIONS FOR SPRING AND SUMMER

Captivating Combinations for Bright Locations

BAD HAIR DAY

SITE **FULL SUN**   SOIL **AVERAGE, DRY**   ZONE **8**   SEASON **YEAR-ROUND**

Between the tufty hair on the pineapple lilies and the disheveled orange dahlias, this looks like quite the pajama party. Wine-colored barberry echoes the dark spotting on the stems of the pineapple lilies, while golden Korean fir plays to their lighter notes. This foliage combination is attractive but unremarkable until the aptly named Bed Head dahlia is added in the background, adding a fun splash of color.

HOW THE DESIGN GROWS

The golden foliage of the fir will be a year-round highlight, with the bright new growth and clusters of yellow flowers of the barberry adding spring interest. In summer the dahlia and pineapple lily provide summer color with foliage and flowers. The merrymaking continues through fall, when foliage of the Concorde barberry will turn from wine to scarlet and tiny red berries become visible on the thorny stems. As the clumps of pineapple lily and dahlias mature, this party will only get more colorful.

FOLIAGE FRAMEWORK

Golden Korean fir (*Abies koreana* 'Aurea') This broad upright conifer has pale yellow needles in spring that mature to a softer green, creating a dramatic backdrop for the blue-purple cones. Grows to 4–6 feet tall in zones 5–8.

Concorde barberry (*Berberis thunbergii* f. *atropurpurea* 'Concorde') There are many purple-toned barberries, but Concorde stands out for its reliable mounding shape, rich blue overtones, and slightly larger foliage. Add yellow spring flowers, red berries, and great fall color and this becomes a garden-worthy three-season shrub. Grows to 3 feet tall and wide in zones 4–8. **CAUTION** Before planting, make sure barberries are not invasive in your area.

FINISHING TOUCH

Pineapple lily (*Eucomis comosa*) Fat flower spikes emerge from succulent rosettes in summer and support the strange pineapple-like flowers. This perennial needs well-drained soil. Grows to 2 feet tall and wide in zones 8–10, but will survive in zone 7 with winter protection.

Bed Head dahlia (*Dahlia* 'Bed Head') Looking positively rumpled, these 4-inch orange flowers are as much fun as they are vibrant. Makes an excellent cut flower that gets even curlier in the vase. Stake the stems and add slug protection when young. Grows to 5 feet tall in zones 8–10, but you can lift and protect during the winter in colder areas.

COLOR AND CUT

SITE **FULL SUN, PARTIAL SUN**   SOIL **AVERAGE**   ZONE **6–8**   SEASON **YEAR-ROUND**

The energetic contrast of purple and gold is one of the cheeriest color pairings for early spring, when the garden is just coming back to life after winter. When you add to that fresh color duo the delightful fragrance from the violets and the unique, finely cut foliage of the fresh geranium growth, the pace of your walk down the garden path slows just a bit so you can appreciate the refined details that this combination brings to the landscape.

HOW THE DESIGN GROWS

This trio is particularly wonderful in early spring, just as the colorful bulbs are blooming, but it carries tons of personality for the rest of the year too. The curved deep green foliage of the violet with long-blooming purple flowers stands out against the chartreuse new growth on the stonecrop. As the weather warms and the bulbs complete their spring show, the geranium begins to bloom and draw all of the attention. When the landscape becomes cool and quieter in autumn, the stonecrop takes on warm tones of copper while the geranium leaves become bolder in full sun, showing an array of fall colors from gold and orange to red.

FOLIAGE FRAMEWORK

Angelina stonecrop (*Sedum rupestre* 'Angelina') As if being drought tolerant was not enough, this golden succulent is also a tough evergreen. Spreading exuberantly through the garden, it roots quite easily, making a low carpet of warm color that contrasts beautifully with darker plants. Does best in well-drained soil in full sun, but will happily tolerate average moisture in partial shade. Grows to 6 inches tall and spreads in zones 6–9.

Hardy geranium (*Geranium* species) Valued for their large, deeply dissected foliage and colorful flowers in late spring, hardy geraniums are excellent in the mixed border as well as the woodland garden. Cut back this garden workhorse after it has bloomed to rejuvenate the plant for the remainder of the growing season; this may also encourage a late-season flush of blooms. It is not unusual to get some dramatic fall color on the foliage. This unique hardy geranium is an unknown seedling, but for a similar look try Mrs. Kendall Clarke (*Geranium pratense* 'Mrs. Kendall Clarke'), which grows to 2 feet tall and 3 feet wide in full to partial sun and is hardy in zones 3–10.

FINISHING TOUCH

Western dog violet (*Viola adunca*) Fragrant 1-inch blooms on this native perennial plant bring delight beginning in April with heart-shaped leaves and an almost constant supply of bearded rich purple flowers. This hardy and adaptable plant spreads by seed and rhizomes to make a low, densely matting ground cover in full to partial sun. It is also the singular host for the threatened Oregon Silverspot butterfly. Does best in moist, well-drained soil. Grows to 12 inches wide in zones 4–10.

SMOKE SIGNALS

SITE FULL SUN, PARTIAL SUN   **SOIL** AVERAGE   **ZONE** 4–8   **SEASON** SPRING THROUGH FALL

Sometimes two plants with multiple assets are all it takes to set the garden aglow. While the smoky color scheme may be subtle, the colors shift with the seasons from softer plum and pink to intense red and orange. The glossy rose hips glow like hot embers amid the smoldering purple leaves of the smoke bush, producing unexpected sparks of bold hue. Throughout these transitions the two shrubs play off one another, their combined foliage always the perfect backdrop for the flowers and hips of the rose.

HOW THE DESIGN GROWS

From spring until fall this simple duo will add color to the garden with foliage, flowers, and hips. The young smoke bush leaves emerge vibrant burgundy, mature to a smoky plum as seen here, and transition to sizzling shades of orange and red in fall. In spring the mellow foliage sets off the spring roses, while in fall the rose hips add a punch of scarlet, a harbinger of the fiery scene to come. To extend the interest through winter, a mass planting of evergreen blue oat grass (*Helictotrichon sempervirens*) in the foreground would maintain the color scheme while introducing a new texture.

FOLIAGE FRAMEWORK

- ->

Grace smoke bush (*Cotinus* 'Grace') Grace has larger blue-toned leaves that set it apart from other purple smoke bushes. This deciduous shrub produces a hazy froth of flowers in late spring. Pruning in early spring will sacrifice this "smoke" in favor of extra-large foliage. However, even with pruning Grace will reach 6 feet in a season. This semi-translucent foliage is especially beautiful when backlit, so consider its placement carefully to take advantage of this feature. Grows to 10 feet tall and 8 feet wide (unpruned) in zones 5–9.

FINISHING TOUCH

- ->

Redleaf rose (*Rosa glauca*) Give this shrub rose some elbow room and it will reward you with a fountain of blue-tinged foliage. In spring, clear pink flowers add to the display, and red rose hips follow in late summer and fall. This rose self-seeds readily, but unwanted seedlings are easy to remove and you can hard prune the shrub to manage its size. Grows to 6 feet tall and wide in zones 2–8.

SAVVY SOLUTION

SITE **FULL SUN**   SOIL **DRY**   ZONE **5–9**   SEASON **YEAR-ROUND**

If you want drama without the dramatics, this may be your answer. Thriving in poor, dry soil and a sun-drenched site, this trio will reward you with color, fragrance, foliage, and flowers. The juxtaposition of soft and spiky textures with the alluring color scheme of silver, blue, and yellow creates a memorable combination. All three plants are deer resistant and drought tolerant, making them a wise choice for many landscapes.

HOW THE DESIGN GROWS

Although the sea holly blooms in early summer, the papery seed heads can last well into winter in some climates. Late summer will see the remaining plants flowering, and although the mullein may deteriorate the evergreen yucca will look good throughout the fall and winter. This combination will change frequently as new yellow mullein seedlings mature to replace those that have died.

FOLIAGE FRAMEWORK

– →

Yellow mullein (*Verbascum epixanthinum*) This perennial may be short lived, but those huge, fuzzy silver leaves are worth it. Even if this never flowered it would add architectural interest to the border, but the 3-foot-tall woolly yellow spikes in summer complete the scene. Mullein needs very well-drained soil and a hot, sunny site. Grows to 3 feet tall and wide in zones 5–9.

– →

Color Guard yucca (*Yucca filamentosa* 'Color Guard') A deer-resistant, drought-tolerant, and low-maintenance spiny evergreen shrub also known as Adam's needle. In summer mature rosettes will produce a tall, fragrant flowering spike. Grows to 6 feet tall and 3 feet wide in zones 5–11. **CAUTION** Wear gloves to divide every 5–6 years.

FINISHING TOUCH

– →

Sapphire Blue sea holly (*Eryngium* 'Sapphire Blue') Metallic blue bracts are the hallmark of this tough perennial. The basal rosettes of foliage are also spiky and tinged with blue. Grow in poor, dry soil and full sun for best results; in richer soil you will have to stake the plants. You can cut back the seed heads or leave them for winter interest. Grows to 2½ feet tall and 2 feet wide in zones 5–9.

AGING GRACEFULLY

SITE FULL SUN, PARTIAL SUN   **SOIL** AVERAGE, MOISTURE-RETENTIVE   **ZONE** 6–7   **SEASON** YEAR-ROUND

A weathered Italianate urn nestles among the fern-like foliage of false spirea, and the Japanese maple repeats the pink tones of both. The dusky purple leaves of the smoke bush add depth and definition in the same way a mat does when you are framing a painting, while the informal medley of shrubs suits the rustic nature of the vessel and evokes a sense of history.

HOW THE DESIGN GROWS

While spring is a colorful highlight, summer and fall also offer special moments. First, the false spirea blooms, then all three shrubs ignite into fiery shades of magenta, red, and gold. In winter only the twiggy shrub structures remain, so adding a low-growing evergreen ground cover, such as Winter Chocolate heather (*Calluna vulgaris* 'Winter Chocolate'), at the base of the urn would help bridge the seasons.

Both the false spirea and the smoke bush benefit from coppicing in spring, a pruning practice that will help maintain the balance between the shrubs and the urn they frame.

FOLIAGE FRAMEWORK

- >

False spirea (*Sorbaria sorbifolia* 'Sem') Richly textured leaves open pink in spring, blending with shades of yellow and green as the season progresses. This deciduous shrub grows to a compact mound with plume-like white flowers that attract butterflies. Beware of letting this loose in the garden, as it is likely to send out suckers and colonize an area. A sharp shovel will keep it in check, or enjoy it in a container. Prefers full sun or light shade and moisture-retentive soil. Grows to 3–4 feet tall and wide in zones 3–7.

- >

Grace smoke bush (*Cotinus* 'Grace') One of the most striking smoke bushes for its large blue-toned purple foliage that turns red in fall. When pruned hard in spring this deciduous shrub will be more compact and have even larger leaves (albeit at the expense of the fluffy, smoke-like flowers). Prefers full or partial sun. Grows to 10 feet tall and 8 feet wide (unpruned) in zones 5–9.

- >

Beni schichihenge Japanese maple (*Acer palmatum* 'Beni schichihenge') You will not forget this Japanese maple, which is noted for its bright pink spring color. Each leaf is unique both in its shape and the degree of its green, white, and pink variegation. The stems add to the kaleidoscope and help explain its name, which means "red and changeful." Fall foliage color is magenta. Prefers full sun or open shade. Grows to 18 feet tall and 15 feet wide in zones 6–8.

FINISHING TOUCH

- >

Urn If you allow this urn to weather naturally over many years and resist the urge to brush away the moss, the Italian-style vessel will lend an air of history to the garden. In a temperate climate the frost-resistant pot can remain outdoors year-round, but in colder regions it needs protection indoors during the winter.

FIT FOR A KING

SITE **PARTIAL SUN**   SOIL **AVERAGE**   ZONE **4–8**   SEASON **YEAR-ROUND**

While the purple barberry creates a sweeping royal robe of crushed velvet, the mounding conifer is the glorious crown, resplendent in shades of copper and gold. A ruffled trim of shimmery purple coral bells adds just enough sparkle to suggest royal patronage. But no coronation regalia is complete without priceless jewels—the tiny clusters of dangling golden flowers encrusted within the barberry foliage. This combination deserves a royal visit.

HOW THE DESIGN GROWS

The spring scene shown here is but one seasonal highlight. As spring gives way to summer, the conifer will turn bright chartreuse. This bold contrast with the other plants is softened by the spikes of tiny white flowers rising above the coral bells. In autumn the barberry begins its fiery display, and as the scarlet leaves fall to the ground the small red berries become visible. Meanwhile, the Rheingold arborvitae changes into its burnished winter layer. This grouping requires almost no maintenance beyond a quick spring cleaning of the coral bells to remove winter damaged foliage.

FOLIAGE FRAMEWORK

- →

Rheingold arborvitae (*Thuja occidentalis* 'Rheingold') This colorful conifer will fit into any landscape or container, its chartreuse summer foliage turning shades of burnished copper in colder months. The natural mounding shape makes it ideal for a foundation plant as well as in a mixed border, and you can clip it for a more formal look. Prefers full sun, but also does well in partial sun and will even tolerate wet soils. Grows to 3–5 feet tall and wide in zones 4–8.

- →

Plum Pudding coral bells (*Heuchera* 'Plum Pudding') There are so many coral bells from which to choose, but Plum Pudding still stands out as an excellent performer in containers and the landscape. Rich purple foliage is overlaid with a silver network of veins, giving it a shimmery appearance—the perfect foil for the sprays of white flowers in spring. Grows to 10 inches tall and 16 inches wide, with flower spikes rising to 2 feet, in zones 4–9.

FINISHING TOUCH

- →

Crimson Velvet barberry (*Berberis thunbergii* var. *atropurpurea* 'Crimson Velvet') This is a vibrant three-season thorny shrub, resistant to deer, that opens fuchsia-red, matures to deep purple, and turns bright crimson in fall. In spring the golden flowers are especially noticeable against the dark backdrop and are followed by bright red berries. Grows to 4 feet tall and wide in zones 4–9. **CAUTION** Before planting, make sure barberries are not invasive in your area.

POCKET PRAIRIE

SITE **FULL SUN**   SOIL **AVERAGE, DRY**   ZONE **4–9**   SEASON **SUMMER THROUGH FALL**

Combine ornamental grasses with coneflowers to re-create the look of a wild prairie in the smallest space. Simplicity is key, so a serene monochromatic color scheme works best. Rather than introducing lots of different flowers, select two different varieties of coneflower. Here the subtle contrast between the classic White Swan and a more flamboyant double form creates interest without looking overdone. The result is a dreamy, naturalistic planting that moves in the breeze and attracts bees, birds, and butterflies. You can fit this design into a tiny courtyard or expand it for acreage.

HOW THE DESIGN GROWS

Beautiful in summer and fall with winter seed heads extending the interest, this planting is perhaps quietest in spring. This would be a good time to introduce ephemerals that fit with the overall design aesthetic. White camassia (*Camassia leichtlinii* 'Alba') or snakes head fritillary (*Fritillaria meleagris*) are spring-blooming bulbs that are well suited to prairie conditions.

FOLIAGE FRAMEWORK

--->

Variegated purple moor grass (*Molinia caerulea* 'Variegata') Creamy yellow-and-green variegated blades form a mounding hummock from which purple seed heads rise in summer. The overall effect is a wonderful haze that moves in the breeze. This herbaceous grass becomes dormant in fall. Prefers full or partial sun and average soil. Grows to 3 feet tall and 2 feet wide in zones 4–9.

FINISHING TOUCH

--->

White Swan coneflower (*Echinacea purpurea* 'White Swan') Drooping white petals in a classic daisy shape surround stiff copper cones. This low-maintenance, drought-tolerant perennial is a magnet for bees and butterflies, and works equally well in traditional garden design, prairie-style plantings, or containers. Leave seed heads in place to attract and feed birds in fall and winter. Does best in average soil and full sun. Grows to 2–3 feet tall and 2 feet wide in zones 3–9.

------------------------------------->

Double white coneflower (*Echinacea purpurea* variety) This coneflower has a fluffier central cone. It was a happy accident, as it was mislabeled White Swan. The variety Meringue closely resembles this beauty, with a creamy pom-pom and light green center surrounded by white rays. All coneflowers make exceptionally long-lasting cut flowers. Grows to 2 feet tall and wide in zones 3–9.

SITTING PRETTY

SITE **FULL SUN, PARTIAL SHADE**   SOIL **AVERAGE**   ZONE **6–8**   SEASON **YEAR-ROUND**

An antique steamer deck chair painted in deep red beckons you to re-energize your spirit in this garden setting with a color palette full of warmth on a cool spring day. Providing sunny color near the pond, the soft mound of sedge foliage dances gracefully in the breeze. Contrasting with the loose form of the grass is the stout arborvitae, still sporting a coppery glow from winter even as it puts on fresh golden growth, while the tower of feather-soft bright green needles on the spruce radiates the freshness of spring. The heart of this vignette is the voluminous red rhododendron, which pairs well with the chair color.

HOW THE DESIGN GROWS

Spring brings flowers and bursts of colorful new growth in this landscape right when we need it after cold, gloomy winter days. Although the sedge foliage remains bright throughout summer, the display will be quieter when the flowers are gone and the mature colors of the conifers mellow. To augment this display for the summer and fall, try adding some bold tropical drama with a red-leaved banana (*Ensete ventricosum* 'Maurelii') and Bishop of Llandaff dahlia (*Dahlia* 'Bishop of Llandaff'), which has dark leaves and bright scarlet flowers. For fall glory, 'Little Henry' Virginia sweetspire (*Itea virginica* 'Little Henry') would bring on the heat with intense red foliage just when the tips of the arborvitae begin to gain some burnished tones for winter.

FOLIAGE FRAMEWORK

- >

Bowles' golden sedge (*Carex elata* 'Aurea') Whether sited in full sun or partial shade, this semi-evergreen grass brings a notable golden glow to the garden. Trim in spring to bring out the best in fresh color and new growth. Best in average to wet soil. Grows to 2 feet tall and wide in zones 5–9.

- >

Rheingold arborvitae (*Thuja occidentalis* 'Rheingold') Slow-growing with scaly, fan-like gold foliage that turns a rich bronze at the tips for fall and winter. Its naturally upright rounded form needs minimal pruning. Best in full sun with consistent watering, but appreciates light afternoon shade. Grows to 3–5 feet tall and wide in zones 4–8.

- >

Dwarf Alberta spruce (*Picea glauca* 'Conica') The perfect cone-shaped conifer for both the formal and casual landscape. This very slow-growing, low-maintenance evergreen shrub puts out bright green new growth in spring that is incredibly soft to the touch. An excellent choice for foundation planting and containers. Prefers full to partial sun in moist, well-drained soil. Grows to 6–8 feet tall and 4–5 feet wide in zones 2–8.

FINISHING TOUCH

- >

Elizabeth rhododendron (*Rhododendron* 'Elizabeth') This very old hybrid is popular for its dependability and trumpet-shaped red blooms that can flower so heavily they hide the oval deep green leaves. This long-lived shrub prefers moist but well-drained soil in full sun to partial shade. Grows to 10 feet tall and wide in zones 6–8.

DRIPPING WITH JEWELS

SITE **SUN, PARTIAL SUN**   SOIL **POTTING SOIL**   ZONE **9–11 OR ANNUALS**
SEASON **YEAR-ROUND OR SUMMER ONLY**

The intense orange color of the gemstone carnelian invites clarity and focus, just like the orange begonia in this scene leads your eye straight to it. Pairing the cascading begonia with the tropical-looking honey bush elevates this container to a new level of sophistication, bold texture, fragrance, and color. The design and the setting combine to create a glorious scene. Color echoes from the small terra-cotta pots bring the warm tones of orange down low, where more jewels in the form of teal quartz stones wrap around the base of the pot.

HOW THE DESIGN GROWS

This dynamic container design thrives in mild climates from early summer through fall. Although the begonias are annuals, you can overwinter them in a greenhouse or a cool room indoors if necessary. The honey bush can survive outdoors as a woody shrub in warm-climate gardens, although gardeners in colder regions should cut it back as you would a perennial.

FOLIAGE FRAMEWORK

- →

Honey bush (*Melianthus major*) This tropical or tender shrub has long, serrated silver-green foliage with a unique scent that is somewhat like peanut butter. In late spring and summer it blooms with deep red flower spikes. Grows to 6–8 feet tall and 8–10 feet wide in zones 8–11 as a semi-evergreen suckering shrub, but some gardeners prefer to treat it like a perennial and cut it back every year.

- →

Mexican snowball (*Echeveria elegans*) This short-stemmed, clump-forming succulent has tight rosettes of fleshy pale green-blue leaves that are evergreen and bear long slender stalks of pink flowers with yellow tips in spring. This drought-tolerant perennial wants full sun and very well-drained, if not gritty, soil. Grows to 2–4 inches tall and up to 20 inches wide in zones 9–11 or enjoy as an annual.

FINISHING TOUCH

- →

Bonfire begonia (*Begonia boliviensis* 'Bonfire') A dramatic red-orange tuberous begonia, Bonfire cascades with a multitude of long fluted blooms and serrated deep green foliage from late spring to fall. Grows to 2–3 feet tall and wide in zones 9–11 or enjoy as an annual.

THE LONG VIEW

SITE **SUN, PARTIAL SUN**   SOIL **AVERAGE**   ZONE **4–8**   SEASON **SPRING THROUGH FALL**

The spring trio immediately grabs your attention with its fresh, sophisticated color palette, but the larger picture offers an exceptional design lesson by demonstrating how to take advantage of a distant view. When you look beyond the colorful tulips, you will notice the swathe of dark barberry foliage deep in the background that creates an exquisite color echo of the brown peony foliage. This repetition causes that longer view to become an important design element of the vignette in the foreground. Adding contrast, the variegated white oat grass up lights the base of the dark peony, while tall yellow tulips add just the right punch of refined color.

HOW THE DESIGN GROWS

Emerging tulips are the first flowers to open in this combination, just as the cocoa-colored new peony foliage develops against the white-and-green variegation of the grass. At the peak of the tulips' glory, the peony will crack open fat buds to feature large yellow double blossoms with a subtle reddish tint in the center and a light, fresh fragrance. The peony foliage matures to deep green, sustaining this rich color on its heavily dissected leaves even as it blooms in spring and early summer. As the tulips finish flowering and begin to go dormant in late spring, the peony continues its metamorphosis and leaves behind interesting seed heads that will split open to reveal shiny black seeds and provide handsome fall foliage color.

FOLIAGE FRAMEWORK

- →

Bartzella peony (*Paeonia* 'Bartzella') Large double ruffled yellow flowers shine on this unusual hybrid between a garden peony and a tree peony. Prized by collectors, this easy-to-grow herbaceous plant has a bushy, lush growth habit that does not need staking and features distinctive divided leaves and a mild fragrance from the blooms. Does best in full sun, average soil, and consistent moisture. Good deer and rabbit resistance. Grows to 3 feet tall and wide in zones 4–9.

- →

Variegated bulbous oat grass (*Arrhenatherum elatius* var. *bulbosum* 'Variegatum') This low-growing, deer-resistant perennial looks best in spring, when it forms a dense clump or white-and-green variegated foliage. Trimming it back in June rejuvenates this grass and keeps it looking fresh if it is in full sun; in partial sun this is less of an issue. Grows to 12 inches tall and 18 inches wide in zones 4–8. **CAUTION** This may be invasive in some areas; check before planting.

FINISHING TOUCH

- →

Golden Apeldoorn tulip (*Tulipa* 'Golden Apeldoorn') Symbolizing eternal happiness and perfect love, this tulip is one of the best bulbs for perennial performance, as it naturalizes well and is excellent for cutting. This golden yellow beauty can get up to 6 inches across when fully open. Prefers full to partial sun. Grows to 20–24 inches tall in zones 3–8.

BEE HAPPY

SITE **FULL SUN**   SOIL **WELL-DRAINED, DRY**   ZONE **8–9**   SEASON **YEAR-ROUND**

This may prove to be the noisiest part of the garden as swarms of bees gorge themselves on the abundant flowers. A spring appetizer of rosemary, followed by germander and pineapple lily for a summer dessert, will ensure your garden is listed as pollinator-friendly. This combination is equally exciting to the gardener, thanks to the glossy strap-like foliage of the pineapple lily, which provides a bold, colorful counterpoint to the fine-textured green leaves of the herbs.

HOW THE DESIGN GROWS

Truly a combination that keeps on giving to the kitchen and the pollinators, this trio looks spectacular from spring until late summer as each of the plants takes turns blooming. In winter, only the pineapple lily goes dormant: the evergreen germander and rosemary continue to add shades of green to the garden, while rosemary also provides fragrant foliage for cooking. Incorporate a large boulder with a shallow depression to hold water for bees and butterflies in summer and add an interesting focal point.

FOLIAGE FRAMEWORK

- →

Tuscan Blue rosemary (*Rosmarinus officinalis* 'Tuscan Blue') This early-flowering upright variety of rosemary is a popular choice for hedging as well as culinary use. Shear back by up to one third after flowering to shape the bush. The needle-like foliage of this evergreen woody perennial is wider and more aromatic than many, but like all rosemary it is drought tolerant and deer resistant. Prefers full sun and lean, well-drained soil. Grows to 2–4 feet tall and 2–3 feet wide in zones 8–11; can reach 6 feet tall in ideal conditions.

- →

Sparkling Burgundy pineapple lily (*Eucomis comosa* 'Sparkling Burgundy') A tropical-looking perennial with fleshy burgundy leaves that fade to green, then revert after blooming. The unusual pineapple-shaped dusky pink flowers appear in midsummer. These bulbs do best with average water during the growing season, but need well-drained soil to survive the winters. Grows to 2 feet tall in zones 6–9.

FINISHING TOUCH

- →

Wall germander (*Teucrium ×lucidrys*) A drought-tolerant, evergreen, woody perennial that thrives in full sun and lean, well-drained soil. It blooms in summer with a profusion of lavender-pink flowers that are highly attractive to bees, but the gray-green foliage is also ornamental and fragrant. It is no longer recommended as an edible herb but remains popular as a low hedge around vegetable gardens. Cut back after flowering to maintain a compact habit if desired. Grows to 1–2 feet tall and 2–3 feet wide in zones 5–9.

CALCULATED RISK

SITE **FULL SUN**   SOIL **AVERAGE**   ZONE **6–7**   SEASON **YEAR-ROUND**

Four herbaceous perennials, each with a unique leaf texture and bloom time, jockey for position in front of the evergreen box honeysuckle shrub. Even when not in bloom this vignette offers many shades of green, from lemon and lime to blue tones, and the burgundy chevron of the Virginia knotweed introduces contrast. The vertical spikes of deep blue spike speedwell flowers mimic the form of the stonecrop while contrasting with the layered structure of neighboring plants. Both the darmera and Virginia knotweed have a reputation for running wild in the garden, but here the calculated risk has paid off.

HOW THE DESIGN GROWS

Although rich in foliage interest, this vignette also produces waves of flowers beginning with pink and white darmera in spring, blue spike speedwell and pink stonecrop in summer, and the unusual red flowers of the Virginia knotweed in fall. This combination will require careful monitoring to prevent any one plant from overgrowing a neighbor. Individual spot watering may also be necessary, as the darmera requires much wetter conditions than average.

FOLIAGE FRAMEWORK

- →

Darmera (*Darmera peltata*) A fast-growing herbaceous perennial that needs constantly wet soil and shade, although it will tolerate full sun with sufficient water. Drumsticks of pink-and-white flowers appear in spring before the leaves emerge. Each leaf can be up to 18 inches in diameter. Grows to 3–6 feet tall and 5 feet wide in zones 5–7; often spreads much further.

- →

Autumn Joy stonecrop (*Sedum* 'Autumn Joy', also sold as *Hylotele-phium* 'Autumn Joy') Succulent blue-green foliage grows into a dome topped in late summer by flat clusters of rose-pink flowers that attract bees and butterflies. To keep it more compact, cut the foliage back by half in early spring. Grows to 2 feet tall and wide in zones 3–10.

- →

Lance Corporal Virginia knotweed (*Persicaria virginiana* var. *filiformis* 'Lance Corporal') Whether you consider this herbaceous perennial merely vigorous or an invasive thug may depend on your specific site and soil conditions, but be sure you really want it before planting. Beautiful chevron leaf markings make this an attractive foliage plant, but it also has scarlet flowers in late summer. Prefers partial sun to full shade. Grows to 2 feet tall and wide in zones 4–10. **CAUTION** Before planting, make sure it is not invasive in your area.

continued on next page

Calculated Risk continued

Lemon Beauty box honeysuckle (*Lonicera nitida* 'Lemon Beauty') An arching shrub with boxwood-like gold-and-green variegated leaves. Usually evergreen, it may lose some leaves in a harsh winter. You can use this deer-resistant, drought-tolerant shrub as a low informal hedge, but it also works well in containers, as a ground cover, or as a screen. Grows to 3–6 feet tall and 3–4 feet wide in zones 6–11.

FINISHING TOUCH

Spike speedwell (*Veronica spicata*) The variety is uncertain, but it is very similar to Sunny Border Blue. It is known for its extended bloom time from summer until fall. The tubular violet-blue flowers attract butterflies and also make excellent cut flowers. Grows to 2 feet tall and 12 inches wide in zones 4–8.

CONTAINED EXCITEMENT

SITE **FULL SUN, PARTIAL SUN**   SOIL **AVERAGE, MOISTURE-RETENTIVE, AND POTTING SOIL**
ZONE **5–7**   SEASON **YEAR-ROUND**

Why plant just one large shrub when you can fill two jumbo pots to overflowing with a colorful assortment of trees, shrubs, and perennials? You will still have room to add a tall stately grass to one side and a froth of flowering perennials at the base. Purple and gold are the predominant colors of both foliage and flowers, knitting this elaborate design together, while every element introduces a new leaf shape and texture to make a dramatic statement. Underplanting the pots with a sprawling mass of Ann Folkard hardy geranium was a genius touch, as a more demure planting of a compact variety would have lost the exciting momentum.

Contained Excitement continued

HOW THE DESIGN GROWS

In fall both the smoke bush and maple will light up the scene with fiery shades of crimson, distracting the eye from the hardy geranium as it enters dormancy. The winter blooms of the hellebores will continue the pink and burgundy tones while the tan grass blades will rustle in the breeze. After two or three years the potted plants will outgrow their allotted space and need transplanting. However, this unapologetic display of sheer exuberance is a huge success.

FOLIAGE FRAMEWORK

Red Dragon Japanese maple (*Acer palmatum* 'Red Dragon') A smaller variety of the popular Crimson Queen, Red Dragon has a cascading mound of finely dissected leaves that open bright scarlet in spring, mature to burgundy, and turn vibrant crimson in autumn. This variety holds its color well in full sun. Grows to 5–8 feet tall and wide in zones 5–9.

Sungold threadleaf false cypress (*Chamaecyparis pisifera* 'Sungold') Finely textured thread-like golden foliage grows slowly in a layered mounding habit, but you can prune to keep it smaller. New growth emerges bright gold and softens to lime green with age. This evergreen conifer prefers full or partial sun. Grows to 3–5 feet tall and 4–6 feet wide in zones 3–7.

Morning Light maiden grass (*Miscanthus sinensis* 'Morning Light') Growing as an elegant upright fountain, this perennial clumping grass has green-and-white variegated blades. Tassel-like inflorescences appear in fall and can last for many months, standing tall above the faded tan foliage, making this an outstanding ornamental grass for architectural interest year-round. Prune back to 12 inches when new growth appears in spring. Does best in full or partial sun and average soil. Grows to 4–6 feet tall and 3–4 feet wide in zones 5–9.

Royal Purple smoke bush (*Cotinus coggygria* 'Royal Purple') A popular deciduous shrub or small tree for full or partial sun, this variety sports rich purple leaves with a hot pink margin. If you do not hard prune in spring, smoky plumes appear in summer. Plant this where the light can shine through to best appreciate the translucent foliage, which turns scarlet in fall. Grows to 15 feet tall and 10–12 feet wide in zones 4–8.

Hellebore (*Helleborus* species) Although the plant tag has long since been lost, this is likely the variety Pink Frost (*Helleborus* Gold Collection Pink Frost). Burgundy stems and evergreen green leaves become the backdrop to a profusion of tall outward-facing blooms in shades of pink, burgundy, and light green, often starting in fall and continuing until spring. Prefers partial shade to partial sun. Grows to 12–15 inches tall and 2 feet wide in zones 5–9.

FINISHING TOUCH

Heather (*Calluna vulgaris*) County Wicklow would give a look very similar to this unknown variety; it blooms with pale pink double flowers from midsummer to fall on bright green foliage. Alternatively, try lavender-flowering Fritz Kirchner, which fades to white at the base. Grows to 12 inches tall and wide in zones 4–8.

Ann Folkard hardy geranium (*Geranium* 'Ann Folkard') This vigorous perennial will quickly weave its way between and over adjacent plants, its magenta flowers and contrasting chartreuse foliage creating an eye-catching display. This low-maintenance plant may benefit from a quick trim in midsummer to curb its enthusiasm to more manageable proportions. Grows to 2 feet tall and 4 feet wide in zones 5–8.

CHERRY GARCIA

SITE **FULL SUN, PARTIAL SUN, PARTIAL SHADE** SOIL **AVERAGE** ZONE **4–7**
SEASON **SPRING THROUGH FALL**

Who doesn't love a little indulgence now and then? This melt-in-your-mouth combo of dark chocolate ninebark and sweet colored clematis should definitely be on your summer dessert menu. Using the ninebark for support, the vine easily threads its way through the shrub, and its fat buds burst to reveal the fully double flowers. The two mingle so well that it appears the ninebark is blooming. Delicious.

HOW THE DESIGN GROWS

This is such a well thought-out pairing. In spring the dark ninebark foliage is the perfect foil for its prolific clusters of white flowers. As these fade, the clematis begins to bloom, its bare lower stems disguised by the shrub on which it grows. The cerise flowers are enhanced by the chocolate backdrop, the duo continuing to add flavor to the garden well into fall when the ninebark leaves turn red. In winter the bare woody stems are visible, revealing the peeling bark on the mature canes. Planting winter-blooming Cinnamon Snow hellebore (*Helleborus* Gold Collection Cinnamon Snow) at the base would accent this feature, as the fat pink buds open to reveal their cinnamon- and cream-toned flowers. To enjoy this delicious pairing each year, be sure to prune the clematis hard in late winter and thin the shrub as needed.

FOLIAGE FRAMEWORK

- →

Diablo ninebark (*Physocarpus opulifolius* 'Diablo') This large deciduous shrub offers something for every season. Dark summer foliage turns red in fall, and red seed heads follow the white flowers. Even in winter the striped bark is interesting. To control size, prune one third of the oldest canes to the ground each spring and reduce the height by half. Grows to 8–10 feet tall and wide in zones 2–7.

FINISHING TOUCH

- →

Clematis (*Clematis* 'Purpurea Plena Elegans') The ruffled double flowers are only 3–4 inches in diameter but are borne in abundance in spring and with a repeat flowering in early fall. Prune the oldest stems on established vines in late winter to the two lowest healthy buds. Grows to 12 feet high in zones 4–8.

DIPPED IN ROSÉ

SITE **SUN, PARTIAL SUN** SOIL **WELL-DRAINED** ZONE **6–8** SEASON **SPRING, SUMMER**

Many evergreen plants have a unique quality whereby they acquire a winter "blush" of color on their foliage, frequently holding on to that shade in a spectacular way. This variegated holly retained some of that winter color until late spring, when the hardy geranium began to bloom even on the new growth, making the leaves look as though they were dipped in rosé wine. The contrast in texture between the lush green geranium foliage and the spiny holly leaves is another reason this pair deserves attention. The intensity of the blue-purple geranium flowers makes this pink-and-purple combination a standout for those who have an affinity for ladylike colors but appreciate an evergreen shrub undaunted by winter cold.

HOW THE DESIGN GROWS

This pairing peaks in spring and early summer, when that special color is still showing on the holly. However, even when the holly fades to its typical creamy yellow variegation, the hardy geranium will still be a blooming garden workhorse of flower power. This low-maintenance couple does not need too much effort, other than annually pruning the holly to keep it to your preferred shape and size and pruning back the geranium at the end of the growing season. If you divide the clump of geranium every three to four years, it will keep blooming well.

FOLIAGE FRAMEWORK

- ->

Variegated English holly (*Ilex aquifolium* 'Argentea Marginata') This medium-size shrub or small tree with a conical growth habit is a showy, low-maintenance choice for the landscape. The spiny, undulated leaves are boldly outlined with creamy white margins. If there is a male holly nearby, small white flowers turn into dazzling red berries that provide fall and winter interest. Prefers partial to full sun. Grows to 15 feet tall and 8 feet wide in zones 6–9.

FINISHING TOUCH

- ->

Rosemoor hardy geranium (*Geranium magnificum* 'Rosemoor') This easy hardy perennial is a longtime landscape favorite. The dazzling violet-blue blooms grow from a foliage clump sporting palmate leaves. The foliage has been known to get tinges of lovely fall color. Prefers full sun to partial shade. Grows to 2 feet tall and wide in zones 5–8.

PIZZAZZ WITH PALMS

SITE **FULL SUN**　SOIL **AVERAGE, MOISTURE-RETENTIVE**　ZONE **8–9**　SEASON **YEAR-ROUND**

Adding style and flair with palm trees requires planning for each stage of growth, and this combination shows that level of skill. The fast-growing gold conifer paired with the deep blue-green of the young palms gives bold shape and texture, while the showy red daisies and grass have a chance to display their colors in an up-close view as the palms mature.

HOW THE DESIGN GROWS

In cool climates this combination provides an irresistible tropical ambience that lingers as long as possible before the gray days of winter. When the red sneezeweed and the Japanese blood grass are in the full grandeur of summer, they still have quite a bit of life in them. The peak for this combination would surely be in the waning days of summer and early fall. Yet even when the daisies begin to fade the drama continues: the vibrant Japanese blood grass reaches its elegant perfection in fall, the fiery tones playing off the colors and textures of the conifer and palms.

With the addition of shrubs such as oak leaf hydrangea (*Hydrangea quercifolia*) or Henry's Garnet Virginia sweetspire (*Itea virginica* 'Henry's Garnet'), the deep burgundy of the fall foliage would take this combination from summer pizzazz to long-lasting autumn glory.

FOLIAGE FRAMEWORK

- >

Gold Rush dawn redwood (*Metasequoia glyptostroboides* 'Gold Rush') This fast-growing deciduous conifer is like liquid gold. Chartreuse new growth emerges soft and fern-like: it will not burn in summer sun and turns amber-orange in fall. Be sure to water consistently in summer for best color. Grows to 50 feet tall and 20 feet wide in zones 4–10.

- >

Japanese blood grass (*Imperata cylindrica* 'Rubra') This named variety of blood grass is a much more polite perennial than its rather invasive cousin, commonly named cogon grass. The upper part of the blade turns garnet red in summer, often deepening toward burgundy as the growing season progresses. Once established it tolerates shade, poor soils, and even drought. Grows to 12–18 inches tall and 2–4 feet wide in zones 5–9.

- >

Mediterranean fan palm (*Chamaerops humilis*) The cold-hardiest of all palms is also deer resistant and drought tolerant and has a wonderful multitrunk growth habit. It has a canopy of fan-shaped blue-green leaves that work equally well in containers and landscape designs featuring desert or tropical themes. Grows to 10–15 feet tall and wide in zones 8–11.

FINISHING TOUCH

- >

Red sneezeweed (*Helenium autumnale* 'Red') Vigorous and easy, this late-season perennial brings plenty of flashy copper-red color and buckets of long-lasting 2-inch cut flowers from August to October. Grows to 3 feet high and 30 inches wide in zones 3–10.

TREASURE HUNT

SITE **FULL SUN, PARTIAL SUN**   SOIL **AVERAGE, MOISTURE-RETENTIVE**   ZONE **6–8**
SEASON **YEAR-ROUND**

There are some plants that you just have to have—and this treasure trove will get you writing up a new shopping list. Glossy black leaves of a unique daphne join a new sea holly that sports spiky golden foliage, which in turn makes the bright silver-blue of a prostrate noble fir seem to shimmer. Surrounding these collector's gems are more familiar shrubs and perennials, but in this company they are all transformed into precious jewels.

HOW THE DESIGN GROWS

As summer transitions to fall, the barberry will turn crimson and the rhododendron may contribute some red flowers to the scene. Although the daphne will lose foliage in a harsh winter and the sea holly will become dormant, the conifer and rhododendron will provide winter color, to be joined in spring by flowers on both the daphne and Ostbo's Elizabeth rhododendron. You may have to prune the conifer and rhododendron to maintain this balance of riches.

FOLIAGE FRAMEWORK

------------------------------------>

Ostbo's Elizabeth rhododendron (*Rhododendron* 'Ostbo's Elizabeth') An outstanding rhododendron with deep burgundy foliage and masses of funnel-shaped scarlet flowers in spring, often with a repeat bloom in fall. This evergreen shrub needs well-drained acidic soil and afternoon shade. Grows to 6 feet tall and wide in zones 6–8.

------------------------------------>

Prostrate blue noble fir (*Abies procera* 'Glauca Prostrata') This low-growing evergreen conifer is known for its exquisite silver-blue needles that are soft to the touch. Needs full sun and fertile, well-drained soil. Grows to 2 feet tall and 6 feet wide in zones 4–8; prune out any leaders that emerge.

------------------------------------>

Black daphne (*Daphne ×houtteana*) A coveted semi-evergreen shrub for serious plantaholics. In full sun the glossy leaves will be almost black, an exciting backdrop to the mauve spring flowers. Prefers fertile, moisture-retentive but well-drained soil. Grows to 2–3 feet tall and wide in zones 6–9.

continued on next page

Treasure Hunt continued

Bagatelle barberry (*Berberis thunbergii* f. *atropurpurea* 'Bagatelle') A dwarf form of barberry that maintains a compact mound without pruning. Deep red foliage turns crimson in fall and is accented by yellow flowers in spring. Best color in full sun but will also grow in light shade. Grows to 18 inches tall and wide in zones 5–8. **CAUTION** Before planting, make sure barberries are not invasive in your area.

FINISHING TOUCH

Neptune's Gold sea holly (*Eryngium ×zabelli* 'Neptune's Gold') A new introduction with flowers that mature to electric blue and are surrounded by bracts in shades of gold, silver, and lavender, all held high above striking gold foliage. You will definitely want to hunt for this treasure. Prefers full sun. Grows to 2 feet tall and 12 inches wide in zones 5–9.

TWIST AND SHOUT

SITE **FULL SUN**   SOIL **AVERAGE, DRY**   ZONE **7–8**   SEASON **YEAR-ROUND**

An explosion of golden foliage and flowers, spikes, and spirals aims for the sky while softer tufts of grasses and threadleaf false cypress create gentle mounds at ground level. Dancing between the two are indigo streaks of blue Caradonna sage, which repeats the spiky theme, and purple verbena, which introduces a new shape with its flattened spherical flower heads. All these pointed forms create a visual tension that is eased by the dense foliage of a variegated shrub dogwood, which also provides a solid foliage curtain against which viewers can appreciate these slender forms.

Twist and Shout continued

HOW THE DESIGN GROWS

While the photograph captures the midsummer look, there are still key elements to enjoy year-round. The variegated yucca, sedge, and conifer are all evergreen, and when the dogwood loses its leaves in fall the bright red stems will be revealed, adding to the winter display. The beauty of using a nonliving focal point, such as this colorful spiral obelisk, is that it will continue to add height, color, and form to the garden long after the annual vine has finished.

FOLIAGE FRAMEWORK

- →

Color Guard yucca (*Yucca filamentosa* 'Color Guard') When the color of other variegated yuccas begins to fade in midsummer, this brightens to a creamy gold. The foliage grows to a clump from which flowering spikes explode in summer, bearing a cluster of white blooms that hummingbirds love. Evergreen, drought tolerant, deer resistant, and low maintenance. Grows to 6 feet tall and 3 feet wide in zones 5–11. **CAUTION** Wear gloves to divide every 5–6 years.

- →

Sungold threadleaf false cypress (*Chamaecyparis pisifera* 'Sungold') This finely textured conifer resembles a golden mophead. Prefers full sun or partial shade. Grows to 5 feet tall and 6 feet wide in zones 4–9.

- →

Orange New Zealand sedge (*Carex testacea*) Evergreen olive green blades are tipped with orange, the color intensifying in fall. Grows to 18 inches tall and wide in zones 7–10.

Variegated red twig dogwood (*Cornus alba* 'Elegantissima', also sold as *Cornus alba* 'Argenteo-marginata') A four-season deciduous shrub with gray-green and white foliage that transitions to rose, apricot, and gold in fall. In winter the red stems become visible. For the brightest stems, grow in full sun and cut one third of the oldest stems to the ground in spring. Prefers moist, well-drained soil but adapts well to clay, sand, or wet conditions. Grows to 8 feet tall and 6 feet wide or more in zones 2–8.

FINISHING TOUCH

Black-eyed Susan (*Thunbergia alata*) This vine is available with flowers in shades of cream, rose-pink, yellow, and orange, but all have the distinctive black eye. These vines grow to 8 feet tall as a summer annual but can reach 20 feet in zone 10, where it is an evergreen perennial.

Homestead Purple verbena (*Verbena canadensis* 'Homestead Purple') A vigorous ground-covering perennial with large purple flowers in spring through fall. Drought-tolerant once established. Grows to 6–12 inches high and 3 feet wide in zones 7–10.

Caradonna sage (*Salvia nemorosa* 'Caradonna') Tall black stems support spikes of deep blue flowers. If deadheaded regularly, these will bloom all summer. This drought-tolerant, deer-resistant perennial looks best planted in groups. Grows to 2 feet tall and wide in zones 4–9.

WILL-O'-THE-WISP

SITE **FULL SUN**   SOIL **DRY**   ZONE **8–10**   SEASON **SPRING THROUGH FALL**

Like a ghostly mist, the silver wormwood swirls around the stiff rubber-like stems of the stonecrop. Seemingly frozen in fear, the budded flower heads strain upward, trying to escape the curling fingers of its ethereal companion. The delicate balance of contrasting textures, together with the fresh silver and pale green color scheme, adds a cool touch to the more typical saturated hues found in the late summer garden.

HOW THE DESIGN GROWS

This combination is at its dramatic peak in late summer before the stonecrop blooms, although the foliage of both plants will make fascinating companions from spring through fall. The personality will change once the rose-pink flowers of the stonecrop open, resulting in a softer, feminine look. Both perennials will die down in winter, so to extend the interest a backdrop of Northwind switch grass (*Panicum virgatum* 'Northwind') would add height, the bleached color and rustling sounds enhancing the ghostly theme and bridging the seasonal gap. For early spring, a carpet of white glory of the snow (*Chionodoxa luciliae* 'Alba') would quickly naturalize, each stem bearing a spray of five or more star-shaped blooms. As the perennials emerge in late spring they will disguise the spent bulb foliage.

FOLIAGE FRAMEWORK

- →

Canescens wormwood (*Artemisia alba* 'Canescens') One of the most beautiful wormwoods, this variety is a semi-evergreen shrub with exceptionally finely cut silver foliage that resembles curled threads and emits a pungent herbal smell when crushed. Cut back straggly growth in spring to maintain a tidier habit. All wormwoods need full sun and well-drained soil to do well, but are otherwise low maintenance, deer resistant, and drought tolerant. Grows to 18 inches tall and 2 feet wide in zones 8–10.

FINISHING TOUCH

- →

Autumn Joy stonecrop (*Sedum* 'Autumn Joy', also sold as *Hylotelephium* 'Autumn Joy') An old-fashioned favorite for the late-season border, this drought-tolerant perennial forms a mound of succulent foliage topped by flat heads of rose-colored flowers. Do not rush to tidy up in fall, as the dried seed heads are a decorative addition to the winter garden. To keep this herbaceous perennial from flopping, cut it back by half in early spring and divide every couple of years. Grows to 2 feet tall and wide in zones 3–10.

FOLIAGE EXPLOSION

SITE **FULL SUN**   SOIL **DRY**   ZONE **7–9**   SEASON **YEAR-ROUND**

From the monster-size yucca to the low-growing spurge, everything explodes skyward in this dramatic composition. Yet the contrast in texture between the feathery ground cover with the taller, broader blades also plays an important role, while the subtle colors ranging from blue-green to bronze add another intriguing layer. The finishing touch is the splash of bright yellow flowers from the Solfaterre crocosmia, a welcome softening of the strong vertical lines.

HOW THE DESIGN GROWS

The evergreen yucca adds a sculptural detail to the garden even in winter. The crocosmia and spurge, however, are herbaceous perennials, so for more early season color, try winter aconite (*Eranthis cilicica*) to lend a sprinkling of buttercup-type yellow flowers in January. The foliage of these bulbs will die down by late spring and will not detract from the main display. As the design matures, the spurge and crocosmia will multiply, bringing ever more color to the scene.

FOLIAGE FRAMEWORK

------------------------------->

Curve-leaf yucca (*Yucca recurvifolia*) There is no ignoring this striking architectural plant. The gently curving blue-green blades are evergreen, and it explodes with tall flowering spikes of creamy white flowers in midsummer. A fabulous specimen plant for full sun that is drought tolerant once established. Grows to 6–8 feet tall and wide in zones 7–9.

------------------------------->

Cypress spurge (*Euphorbia cyparissias*) While this low-growing woody perennial is attractive, it is also invasive in many areas of the United States and cannot be recommended for planting. However, the attributes that are so appealing—the fine-textured foliage and ability to grow in dry soil and full sun—can also be found in Blue Spruce stonecrop (*Sedum rupestre* 'Blue Spruce'), which is also a soft blue-green and would be a perfect substitute. Grows to 6–8 inches tall in zones 3–11.

FINISHING TOUCH

------------------------------->

Solfaterre crocosmia (*Crocosmia* 'Solfaterre') This is not your typical crocosmia. The bronze foliage sets it apart from its relatives, making it a much more exciting design contributor, especially with the rich yellow blooms. This herbaceous perennial, which grows from a corm, is also slower growing and shorter than most other hybrids. It will take full or partial sun, and although drought tolerant when established it benefits from occasional watering. Grows to 20–24 inches tall and 8–10 inches wide in zones 7–10.

SUMMER CRUNCH

SITE **FULL SUN**   SOIL **AVERAGE**   ZONE **5–7**   SEASON **YEAR-ROUND**

Feeling hungry? This imaginative combination will allow for a summer full of salads, but the garden will never look bare thanks to the ice plant's vibrant magenta flowers. The rich color is repeated in the bold ribs and stalks of some of the Swiss chard as well as the kale. This is also a textural feast, with the soft chard leaves contrasting with small succulent needles and the densely frilled, more leathery kale. Don't keep this recipe to yourself—there is plenty to share with friends.

HOW THE DESIGN GROWS

Intended to tempt your taste buds from summer through fall, this may be only a short-term culinary feast, but the addition of the evergreen ice plant will ensure there is always something interesting to look at. The peak season is undoubtedly when flowers and edible foliage and stems coincide, but when the greens are harvested a planting of bright pansies will bridge the gap, maintaining color for the colder months without sacrificing the space for next year's crop.

FOLIAGE FRAMEWORK

– →

Curly Roja kale (*Brassica oleracea* 'Curly Roja') A versatile, highly ornamental kale that you can harvest when young for salads or use for cooking. This cold-hardy variety benefits from a light frost, which sweetens the flavor. It may stand through mild winters or die back and regrow from the root in spring. Frilly green leaves and purple stems are most colorful in full sun, but kale will also grow in partial shade. Grows to 18 inches tall and wide. Annual.

– →

Bright Lights Swiss chard (*Beta vulgaris* 'Bright Lights') A great cut-and-come-again vegetable that is as tasty as it is beautiful. Brightly colored stems and ribs in shades of yellow, red, pink, and white are the hallmark of this popular variety, while the lightly curled foliage may be green or burgundy. Grows to 20 inches tall and 10 inches wide. Annual.

FINISHING TOUCH

– →

Blut ice plant (*Delosperma ashtonii* 'Blut') One of the best cold-hardy ice plants, Blut forms a low-growing evergreen mat of succulent foliage topped in summer with a dazzling display of daisy-shaped magenta flowers that open to the sun. This vigorous ground cover is reliably drought tolerant and needs well-drained soil in full or partial sun. Grows to 1 inch tall and 15–18 inches wide in zones 5–7.

NAUGHTY BUT NICE

SITE **FULL SUN**   SOIL **AVERAGE, WELL-DRAINED**   ZONE **6–9**   SEASON **YEAR-ROUND**

Some plants grow vigorously, others are described as spreading easily, and a few are downright promiscuous. Jennifer (and most other Kaffir lilies) is in the latter category, jumping in and out of beds with abandon. Thankfully this wild child plays well with her bedfellows and looks both charming and sophisticated with the silver-and-black foliage shown here. However, silver Valerie can be equally naughty. If she is too much to handle, substitute the felted silver foliage of Bella Grigio lamb's ears (*Stachys byzantina* 'Bella Grigio').

HOW THE DESIGN GROWS

This simple trio has a lot to offer from spring until fall with foliage, flowers, and fragrance all playing their part, but be ready to keep both perennials in check by promptly removing clumps that spread out of bounds. To extend this through winter, consider the elegant Japanese stewartia (*Stewartia pseudocamellia*). This deciduous tree has the most beautiful mottled bark in soft shades of gray and salmon as well as fragrant camellia-like blooms in summer that would work well with this flirty combination. The foliage turns from soft green to bronze and purple in fall.

FOLIAGE FRAMEWORK

Valerie Finnis wormwood (*Artemisia ludoviciana* 'Valerie Finnis') Thankfully a little more restrained than her cousin 'Silver King', Valerie Finnis spreads quickly but is not as naughty as her floral companion. Give this deer-resistant perennial well-drained, low-fertility soil in full sun and she will shine from spring until fall. Shear back the deeply cut silver leaves after the nondescript yellow blooms are spent. Grows to 2 feet tall in zones 4–9.

Black daphne (*Daphne ×houtteana*) This is a plant to lust after. Glossy leaves in the deepest shade of purple bring a tropical look to temperate gardens, while lightly fragrant mauve flowers in spring add drama to this semi-evergreen shrub. Does best in fertile, moisture-retentive but well-drained soil. Grows to 2–3 feet tall and wide in zones 6–9.

FINISHING TOUCH

Kaffir lily (*Schizostylis coccinea*) This variety appears to be very similar to Jennifer. It is a vigorous clump-forming perennial with grass-like foliage that is evergreen in mild winters. Clear pink flowers bloom sporadically for many months, but are most prolific in late summer and autumn. Kaffir lilies spread easily—sometimes a little too easily—so be prepared to regularly thin out the clumps as needed. Grows to 2 feet tall in zones 6–9.

GONE FISHING

SITE **PARTIAL SUN**   SOIL **AVERAGE, MOISTURE-RETENTIVE**   ZONE **6–8**   SEASON **YEAR-ROUND**

Poised above a dry creek bed, this heron is likely to go hungry, but we can enjoy his dark silhouette against the backdrop of intricate foliage textures. The naturalistic setting relies on mass planting key shrubs but showing restraint in the color palette. The light green spike winterhazel echoes the brighter foliage of the distant dogwood, while the weeping blue atlas cedar connects visually to the grays of the boulders and the deeper blue-green leaves of Ramapo rhododendron. Grass-like hummocks of daylilies enhance the illusion of a stream bank.

HOW THE DESIGN GROWS

Every season brings something new. The daylilies will soon be in full bloom, their golden trumpets blaring for many weeks. In fall the dogwood and winter hazel will turn yellow before losing their leaves. The winter transition is key, as the fiery colored stems of the dogwood will add a glorious contrast to the blue conifer. The spike winterhazel will also bloom during this season, with deep yellow flowers that dangle from its bare branches. Finally, in spring Ramapo will be covered with lavender-blue blossoms.

FOLIAGE FRAMEWORK

Spike winterhazel (*Corylopsis spicata*) Richly textured leaves turn yellow in fall, but this multistemmed shrub is best known for its fragrant yellow flowers that emerge along the bare branches in winter. Prefers moisture-retentive soil and protection from hot afternoon sun. Grows to 4–8 feet tall and 6–8 feet wide in zones 5–8.

Weeping blue atlas cedar (*Cedrus atlantica* 'Glauca Pendula') A dramatic evergreen conifer that can be trained with a tall trunk or kept lower and allowed to cascade. The branches look best when allowed to drape their short blue-green needles over boulders or water features, or used to create an arch. Prefers full sun and well-drained soil. Grows to 15–25 feet tall and wide in zones 6–9.

Midwinter Fire dogwood (*Cornus sanguinea* 'Midwinter Fire') This deciduous shrub is grown primarily for the vibrant twiggy branches in shades of red, orange, and gold that are revealed only in winter. For the best color, cut back the shrub by one third each spring; the brightest hue is always on the newest growth. Light green foliage and white spring flowers also feature. Grows to 4–5 feet tall and wide in zones 5–8.

continued on next page

Gone Fishing continued

- →

Stella De Oro daylily (*Hemerocallis* 'Stella De Oro') One of the most popular daylilies. This herbaceous perennial forms a mound of grass-like leaves and has spikes of golden yellow trumpet-shaped flowers over many weeks. Grows to 2 feet tall and wide in zones 3–9.

- →

Ramapo rhododendron (*Rhododendron* 'Ramapo') An evergreen shrub with a dense, compact habit and trusses of purple flowers that cover the blue-green foliage in spring. Site in partial shade and water regularly. Grows to 3 feet tall and 4 feet wide in zones 4–8.

FINISHING TOUCH

- →

Metal art Actually a grouping of several pieces, this heron sits among the bulrushes waiting patiently for his lunch. This artwork can stay outdoors year-round, even as the scenery changes.

IN THE SPOTLIGHT

SITE **FULL SUN**   SOIL **AVERAGE, MOISTURE-RETENTIVE**   ZONE **5–8**   SEASON **YEAR-ROUND**

As the late afternoon sun streams through the lacy maple, shafts of light illuminate the translucent purple leaves of the smoke bush, transforming them into a rosy haze. Shielded from direct sun, the maroon-tipped switch grass and dwarf conifer retain their soft blue-green hue; the contrast in color saturation is key to the success of this vignette. Rozanne hardy geranium creates an informal froth at the base of the taller plants, and the colors of the surrounding foliage highlight its clear blue flowers and prominent purple stamens.

In the Spotlight continued

HOW THE DESIGN GROWS

As summer transitions to fall, the Japanese maple turns a warm shade of orange with red highlights, stunning next to the similar autumnal colors of the smoke bush and Shenandoah grass. The soothing blue-green dwarf hinoki offsets the vibrant display, while its golden tips still add a little sparkle. Rozanne will continue to bloom until a hard frost, at which time she will go dormant until the following spring. The smoke bush will need annual coppicing in spring to keep it compact, but the remaining plants should do well without intervention for several years, after which the perennial grass and hardy geranium may need dividing.

FOLIAGE FRAMEWORK

------------------------------------→

Koto-no-ito Japanese maple (*Acer palmatum* 'Koto-no-ito') The translation "harp strings" perfectly describes the thread-like leaves of this midsize Japanese maple. In spring the new leaves emerge tinged with crimson, maturing to green and ending fall in a spectacular display of peach and orange tones. Grows to 10 feet tall and wide in zones 6–9.

------------------------------------→

Shenandoah switch grass (*Panicum virgatum* 'Shenandoah') This warm-season grass has olive green blades tipped with deep red, the color intensifying in fall. Airy red seed heads dance like tiny jewels in the late summer breeze. Grows to 4 feet tall and 2 feet wide in zones 4–9.

Royal Purple smoke bush (*Cotinus coggygria* 'Royal Purple') This deciduous shrub has purple leaves that turn scarlet in fall. Plumes of so-called smoke appear in summer, but many gardeners prefer to hard prune smoke bushes in spring, sacrificing the flowers to get larger foliage. Grows to 15 feet tall and 10–12 feet wide in zones 4–8.

Gold Fern hinoki cypress (*Chamaecyparis obtusa* 'Gold Fern') Dense branches clothed in fern-like blue-green foliage, accented with golden tips, make this an exceptional dwarf form of hinoki false cypress. Short and squat, it prefers some protection from strong afternoon sun. Grows to 5 feet tall and 6 feet wide in zones 5–8.

FINISHING TOUCH

Rozanne hardy geranium (*Geranium* 'Rozanne') A vigorous low-maintenance perennial with an exceptionally long bloom time. Grows to 12 inches tall and 3 feet wide in zones 4–9, but can scramble higher.

PUZZLE ME PERFECT

SITE **SUN, PARTIAL SUN**   SOIL **AVERAGE**   ZONE **6–7**   SEASON **YEAR-ROUND**

The best jigsaw puzzles keep you in suspense until the last piece clicks into place, and this design does just that. Fine-textured fern leaf buckthorn, paired with the fat needles of the golden plum yew, adds traditional vertical elements that contrast with the broad leaves of the luxurious banana. The looser, upright growth habit of the orange barberry is the central piece of this puzzle, adding a warm glow echoed by new burgundy growth on the red contorted filbert. The spherical forms of the ornamental onions make the unique scene all the more distinctive.

HOW THE DESIGN GROWS

Spring may be a highlight, but there is a lot more to this composition. The ornamental onions signal the apex of bold spring color, while summer brings a softening of the deep wine-colored new foliage of the filbert and turns it to rich green. When cool fall nights arrive, the hues of the barberry become deeper orange before dropping their leaves to expose tiny red berries, while the buckthorn and filbert turn warm gold before losing their leaves as well.

FOLIAGE FRAMEWORK

- →

Hardy fiber banana (*Musa basjoo*, also sold as *Musa bajoo*) With good mulching, this banana is quite hardy as far north as New England. Although it produces small inedible bananas, the lush foliage makes you feel like you should be in the islands eating tropical fruit. Requires consistent water and fertilizer in the heat of summer, and you must prune back this fast-growing colonizer each fall. Prefers partial to full sun. Grows to 12 feet tall in zones 6–10.

- →

Korean Gold plum yew (*Cephalotaxus harringtonia* 'Korean Gold') This deer-resistant, fat-needled conifer with soft gold tips grows in an upright manner. Much like its cousin the true yew, the female plant has red berries in fall that can be quite showy. Prefers partial sun or partial shade, but it can tolerate full sun in cool climates with consistent watering. Grows to 6–10 feet tall and 3–6 feet wide in zones 6–9.

- - - - - - - - - - - - - - - - - - - →

Fine Line fern leaf buckthorn (*Rhamnus frangula* 'Fine Line') This architectural plant has an upright, columnar habit. The feathery green foliage is wonderful in borders, as a hedge, along a pathway, and in containers where you need deer-resistant, adaptable plants. Turning warm gold in autumn, the leaves drop to reveal brown stems speckled with white. Grows to 5–7 feet tall and 2–3 feet wide in zones 2–7.

continued on next page

Orange Rocket barberry (*Berberis thunbergii* 'Orange Rocket') Noted for its upright growth and ruby color that turns orange in fall, like all barberries this variety is deer resistant, drought tolerant, and low maintenance. Grows to 4 feet tall and 2–3 feet wide in zones 4–9. **CAUTION** Before planting, make sure barberries are not invasive in your area.

Red Majestic contorted filbert (*Corylus avellana* 'Red Majestic') This striking form of filbert with deep reddish-purple spring growth fading to olive green in summer offers interest season after season. The curly foliage drops in fall to reveal curvy, contorted branches that are very interesting for late winter, when rosy purple catkins dangle like jewelry. Grows to 6–12 feet tall and wide in zones 4–8.

FINISHING TOUCH

Ornamental onion (*Allium* species) This striking spring bulb flowers in colors that range from violet-pink to lilac on blooms that can grow as large as a softball. Like all members of the onion family, it is naturally and blissfully deer resistant. The foliage dies back just as the bloom peaks. The seed heads are attractive to butterflies and bees, and highly orna-mental in the garden if you do not cut them back. Grows to 3–5 feet tall in zones 6–10.

MIDAS TOUCH

SITE FULL SUN **SOIL** AVERAGE **ZONE** 7 **SEASON** SPRING THROUGH FALL

Framing white spring flowers with lemon and lime foliage is a sure way to celebrate the freshness of a spring garden, while the columnar golden barberries add structure to the looser shrubs beyond. The purple blooms of Homestead Purple verbena in the foreground add an exciting contrast and ensure a long-lasting color punch that will stretch through fall. Purple and gold always look good together; they are opposite each other on the color wheel, so they appear brighter when paired.

Midas Touch continued

HOW THE DESIGN GROWS

By summer, the yellow viburnum berries will have ripened, contrasting nicely with the dark green leaves. Fall will see a transition from cool to warmer hues as the foliage of all three deciduous shrubs turns orange, red, and burgundy while the accent of purple verbena flowers will continue until frost. In winter only the twiggy structures will remain, so allow a carpet of purple crocus to naturalize around the base of these plants to add welcome early color.

FOLIAGE FRAMEWORK

- ->

Gold Pillar barberry (*Berberis thunbergii* 'Gold Pillar') The columnar shape of this deciduous shrub makes it easy to fit into the smallest garden or container, while the burn-resistant gold foliage is a true standout. The red stems add subtle contrast, as do the red-tinted new shoots. In fall the whole bush turns orange-red. Deer resistant and drought tolerant. Grows to 4 feet tall and 2 feet wide in zones 4–7. **CAUTION** Before planting, make sure barberries are not invasive in your area.

- ->

Golden Spirit smoke bush (*Cotinus coggygria* 'Golden Spirit') An easy-care multistemmed deciduous shrub for full sun or partial shade. Allow it to grow and smoke, or cut it back in early spring to forgo the flowers in favor of larger foliage. The semi-translucent chartreuse leaves turn amber, orange, and burgundy in autumn. Grows to 10–12 feet tall and wide in zones 4–8, but ultimate size depends on pruning practices.

FINISHING TOUCH

- ->

Homestead Purple verbena (*Verbena canadensis* 'Homestead Purple') This woody perennial is perfect for adding color to the front of a border. Rich purple flowers cover the prostrate stems from spring until late summer. Plant in full sun and well-drained soil. Grows to 6–12 inches high and 3 feet wide in zones 7–10.

- ->

European cranberry bush (*Viburnum opulus* 'Xanthocarpum') Lacecap-type white flowers cover this deciduous bush in spring, ripening by late summer to clusters of yellow berries that often persist well into winter. The lobed maple-like leaves turn shades of orange in fall. Thrives in moisture-retentive soil in full sun to partial shade. Grows to 6–8 feet tall and wide in zones 3–8.

BEAUTY WITHOUT THE BEAST

SITE **FULL SUN**   SOIL **AVERAGE**   ZONE **5–8**   SEASON **YEAR-ROUND**

Deer are notorious for having fickle tastes, but in most gardens they would leave this combo alone.
Layers of evergreen and deciduous foliage provide the perfect picture frame for the lilies. Try this
fragrant, sunny vignette as a privacy screen or a backdrop for darker colors.

HOW THE DESIGN GROWS

This combo changes with the seasons, getting better each year, and always offers something of interest. Peak season for this trio is midsummer, when the lilies are in full bloom, but the golden locust tree will partner with the evergreen conifer from early spring to late fall.

To expand the combination while keeping to the same buttery color scheme, grow a carpet of spring-blooming old-fashioned English primroses (*Primula vulgaris*) as a ground cover under the tree. Fall would be the perfect time to introduce some fiery reds and oranges to contrast with the softer yellow shades. Grace smoke bush (*Cotinus* 'Grace') would be an ideal candidate for such a role, as it is a dusky blue-purple for most of the year but turns vivid scarlet in November.

FOLIAGE FRAMEWORK

- >

Golden locust tree (*Robinia pseudoacacia* 'Frisia') Stand under the golden canopy of this translucent foliage to feel bathed in sunshine—even on a cloudy day. Deer shun this fast-growing deciduous tree, which has fragrant white flowers in spring and is remarkably tolerant of poor soils. Grows to 30–50 feet high and 20 feet wide in zones 4–9.

- >

Dwarf Japanese cedar (*Cryptomeria japonica* 'Elegans Nana') A fat little dumpling of a conifer that thrives in full sun or the dappled light under a deciduous tree. The blue-green foliage takes on a purple cast in winter. Grows to 7 feet high and wide in zones 5–8.

FINISHING TOUCH

- >

Lily (Longiflorum-Asiatic [LA] *Lilium* hybrid) The lily appears to have been mislabeled, so there is no accurate identification for this beautiful variety with melon-colored trumpet-shaped flowers. Lily experts suggest Menorca as a good substitute. Grow these massed in your border for best effect—they will continue to multiply each year. Grows to 5–6 feet tall in zones 3–9.

BERRY FIESTA

SITE **FULL SUN, PARTIAL SUN**   SOIL **AVERAGE TO DRY**   ZONE **7–8**   SEASON **YEAR-ROUND**

You need some serious attitude to stand alongside a bold architectural plant like this New Zealand flax. Fun, colorful foliage from the Fiesta forsythia adds the sunshine touch, while the sheer number of blooms and berries of the St. John's wort can hold their own against the bronze giant. The color connection between the bright variegated forsythia leaves and fuzzy yellow St. John's wort flowers also helps pull this party together.

HOW THE DESIGN GROWS

The show begins in early spring, as a profusion of yellow flowers covers the bare branches of the forsythia, making a colorful splash against the dusky New Zealand flax. Flowers are followed by bold variegated foliage on the forsythia, creating an exciting backdrop to the bejeweled St. John's wort with its large yellow flowers and brilliant red berries that last through fall. The New Zealand flax can hold its own during winter, when its evergreen foliage adds color, structure, and height to the quiet garden. This combination should continue to thrive for many years without the need for pruning.

FOLIAGE FRAMEWORK

- →

New Zealand flax (*Phormium tenax* 'Atropurpureum') Tall bronze blades grow in a fan shape from this evergreen perennial, which is deer resistant and drought tolerant once established. In colder areas this may suffer significant dieback in winter, but pruning will often rejuvenate it. Grows to 5 feet tall and 3 feet wide in zones 7–11.

- →

Fiesta forsythia (*Forsythia ×intermedia* 'Fiesta') An old-fashioned shrub with a twist: variegated yellow-and-green foliage. Like its parents, this cultivar is festooned with golden yellow blooms in early spring before the leaves appear, but its size is more compact. Grows to 2–3 feet tall and 3–4 feet wide in zones 5–8, but late frosts may damage flowers buds in colder areas.

FINISHING TOUCH

- →

Orange Flair St. John's wort (*Hypericum androsaemum* 'Orange Flair') This compact, semi-evergreen mounding shrub is known for its fuzzy yellow flowers that appear in summer and are followed by jewel-like red berries. It is extremely adaptable and will tolerate moist or dry soil and full sun or partial shade. Grows to 2½ feet tall and wide in zones 5–9.

MAKE A WISH

SITE **FULL SUN**   SOIL **AVERAGE**   ZONE **6–7**   SEASON **YEAR-ROUND**

A garden filled with soft mounding shapes like willowleaf pear, pine, and Japanese false holly can be pleasing but predictable, even when the foliage offers interesting colors and textures. Wake things up by adding smoldering orange foxtail lilies that will explode skyward like shooting stars on a summer evening. As the slanting rays of the setting sun touch this scene, the translucent barberry leaves and foxtail lilies glow in the golden light, while the metallic silver foliage beyond twinkles like a constellation of premature stars. What will you wish for?

HOW THE DESIGN GROWS

The Japanese false holly hides the untidy foliage of the foxtail lilies and provides twiggy support for the tall stems. When flowering has ended, the tall spikes will be cut down and the various foliage plants will resume their role as garden stars. The pine and Japanese false holly continue to provide color through the winter. To maintain this vignette, prune the shrubs for size and shape, but leave the bulbs undisturbed and allow them to naturalize.

FOLIAGE FRAMEWORK

----------------------------------➔

Weeping willowleaf pear (*Pyrus salicifolia* 'Pendula') Rather ungainly when young, this small deciduous tree matures into a graceful, rounded weeping form with metallic silver leaves that shimmer in the light. White flowers in spring are followed by limited fruit production, but this is grown for foliage, not food. Prune out upward-growing branches in late winter to maintain a weeping shape. Grows to 15–25 feet tall and 10–15 feet wide in zones 4–7.

----------------------------------➔

Japanese false holly (*Osmanthus heterophyllus* 'Goshiki') This easy-care shrub is deer resistant, drought tolerant once established, and—unlike English holly—does not set seed. Variegated green-and-yellow spiky foliage has new red growth tips in spring. Grows to 10 feet tall and wide in zones 6–9, but you can prune to keep it smaller or grow in a container.

----------------------------------➔

Red carpet barberry (*Berberis thunbergii* f. *atropurpurea* 'Red Carpet') This variety is reported to grow just 12 inches tall and 4 feet wide, but the vignette shows it at least 2–3 feet tall, so clearly that is variable. We can all agree on the beauty of the vibrant foliage, which emerges orange-red, matures to burgundy, and turns scarlet in fall. This is a stiff, spiny shrub, so handle with care when pruning. Hardy in zones 4–8. **CAUTION** Before planting, make sure barberries are not invasive in your area.

continued on next page

Make A Wish continued

Blue Shag pine (*Pinus strobus* 'Blue Shag') Over ten years this soft mounding conifer grows into a dome of long blue-green needles. Lightly shake out the old brown needles from the interior in spring. Prefers full sun and well-drained soil. Grows to 4 feet tall and wide in zones 3–8.

FINISHING TOUCH

Cleopatra foxtail lily (*Eremurus ×isabellinus* 'Cleopatra') These summer-blooming bulbs take several years to really hit their stride, but the wait is well worth it. By the third year, 5-foot spikes of apricot buds open from the base to the tip to reveal fuzzy bottlebrush-type golden flowers. The grass-like basal foliage can appear rather untidy, so obscure it with other plants. Give these spectacular flowers room to naturalize over time, as they look best in large drifts. Prefers full sun and well-drained soil. Grows to 5 feet tall and 2 feet wide in zones 5–8.

LEMON LAYER CAKE

SITE FULL SUN   **SOIL** AVERAGE, WELL-DRAINED   **ZONE** 7   **SEASON** YEAR-ROUND

Dreamy layers of whipped cream and lemon-infused sponge cake with a few chocolate nuggets create a summer dessert worthy of the most elegant dinner party. The key element is the wide-spreading yellow variegated Japanese angelica tree, whose canopy forms a distinct tier under which the smaller perennials and shrubs thrive. Both the iris and moor grass repeat the striped foliage, enhancing the theme, while the tall golden and blue conifers keep the overall texture light and airy. Dark dahlia foliage adds depth and contrast to this leafy picture frame, within which the scattering of flowers are seen. This mouthwatering vignette has it all: premium ingredients, careful mixing, and beautiful presentation.

Lemon Layer Cake continued

HOW THE DESIGN GROWS

With so many evergreen plants, this combination will look good all year. Only the grasses, dahlias, and Peruvian lilies will go dormant in winter. To add color in early spring, a mass planting of Las Vegas daffodils will continue the color scheme with their creamy white petals and yellow cups. In May the iris will have fragrant blue flowers, followed by blooms from the Peruvian lilies and finally the dahlias.

FOLIAGE FRAMEWORK

- →

Golden Lawson's cypress (*Chamaecyparis lawsoniana* 'Lutea') A broadly golden conifer with distinctive yellow tips. Grows to 40–50 feet tall and 12 feet wide in zones 5–7.

- →

Variegated Japanese angelica tree (*Aralia elata* 'Aureovariegata') Tiers of pale yellow-and-white variegated leaves form a distinctive canopy on this large shrub. In late summer and fall panicles of white flowers are held above the foliage. Grows to 15 feet tall and 10 feet wide in zones 4–9.

- →

Variegated purple moor grass (*Molinia caerulea* 'Variegata') Forming a loose mound of green-and-yellow striped blades, this softly textured perennial grass is a great addition to the landscape. In summer, 3-foot purple seed heads shoot skyward, creating a shimmery haze. Grows to 3 feet tall and 2 feet wide in zones 4–9.

- →

Variegated sweet iris (*Iris pallida* 'Argentea Variegata') In May, lightly fragrant blue flowers rise above the foliage, but the bold evergreen blades in blue-green and yellow add color to the garden even when not in bloom. Grows to 2 feet tall in zones 3–9.

Sundance Mexican orange blossom (*Choisya ternata* 'Sundance') To prevent scorching, establish neighboring plants to protect this evergreen shrub from direct afternoon sun. This is an easy-care plant with waxy golden yellow leaves and pungent white flowers in spring, with an occasional repeat bloom in fall. Grows to 5 feet tall and wide in zones 7–10, but you can trim to keep it smaller.

Variegated Himalayan pine (*Pinus wallichiana* 'Zebrina') Long blue needles are banded with gold, the variegation becoming most noticeable in winter. Full sun also helps to bring out the best color. At maturity this conifer can reach 50 feet high, but in the home landscape it more typically grows to 15–20 feet tall and 10 feet wide in zones 5–7.

FINISHING TOUCH

Bishop of York dahlia (*Dahlia* 'Bishop of York') Even if you're not usually a dahlia fan, you'll fall in love with this one for its black foliage and 3-inch-diameter apricot-gold flowers on 3-foot-tall stems. Be sure to bait for slugs in spring. Hardy in zones 7–8, but in colder climates you can lift and store indoors for the winter.

Princess Sara Peruvian lily (*Alstroemeria* 'Princess Sara') As demure as a princess, the pale yellow flowers on this low-growing perennial are blushed with pink and have distinctive maroon speckles that resemble fluttering eyelashes. With their long vase life, Peruvian lilies make exceptional cut flowers. In the garden they do best with some protection from hot sun. Hardy in zones 8–10, possibly colder with winter mulch.

SECRET WEAPON

SITE **FULL SUN, PARTIAL SUN**   SOIL **AVERAGE**   ZONE **6–8**   SEASON **SPRING THROUGH FALL**

Tying together a garden vignette through color is easy when you use repetition as your secret weapon. In this case, the deutzia demands your attention at the front and again in the distance with its glowing chartreuse-golden foliage. The spirea, with similar golden yellow hues and leaf texture, reinforces the idea of the warm tones and takes it to another exciting level with flushes of orange and lime green on the new spring growth. Two ornamental versions of edible plants add some unexpected excitement to this spring vignette. The ornamental onion's spherical blooms dot the scene with bold purple exclamation points, and the ornamental rhubarb's rich pink floral display stands tall and architectural at the back of the border, leading the eye deeper into the setting.

HOW THE DESIGN GROWS

This garden is an explosion of color and textural interest that will inspire the most admiration in spring. When the ornamental onions have peaked and faded from brilliant violet to sandy beige for summer, they make wonderful accents if left in the landscape, their dried seed heads adding artistic presence through fall. To take this into summer with style, try adding blue oat grass (*Helictotrichon sempervirens*) to lend an evergreen element as well as the pale blue that softens gold tones in this garden.

FOLIAGE FRAMEWORK

- >

Chardonnay Pearls deutzia (*Deutzia gracilis* 'Chardonnay Pearls') Showy yellow-green foliage grows on slightly arching branches sporting tiny fragrant, bell-shaped white flowers in spring. In summer, the citrus intensity of the leaves softens to gold for the remainder of the growing season. A great deciduous shrub for small gardens. Does best in full sun to partial shade. Grows to 2–3 feet tall and wide in zones 5–8.

- >

Magic Carpet spirea (*Spiraea japonica* 'Magic Carpet') Celebrate spring with this vibrant, colorful shrub. The new growth glows copper-orange before fading to golden yellow, with abundant spring blooms of bright pink. Fall brings rich russet tones to the foliage for an end-of-season show. Magic Carpet is a compact shrub that fits neatly into small spaces; site in full to partial sun. Grows to 3 feet tall and wide in zones 4–9.

FINISHING TOUCH

- >

Ornamental onion (*Allium* species) This member of the onion family will not make you cry, unless it is tears of joy over its natural resistance to deer and rabbits. Plant this bulb in the fall for spring-flowering glory. The foliage dies back just as the bloom peaks on this tough and drought-tolerant beauty. Attractive to butterflies and bees, the tan autumn seed heads are highly ornamental in the garden if not cut back. Grows to 3–5 feet tall in zones 6–10.

- >

Ornamental rhubarb (*Rheum palmatum* var. *tanguticum*) This cousin to the edible rhubarb grows colossal jagged-edged foliage that brings tons of architectural interest to the landscape and adds deep red-bronze tones to the garden in spring. The summer leaves on this deer- and rabbit-resistant plant mature to deep green with burnished red undersides just as intriguing tall fuchsia-colored bloom spikes rise up. In late summer the red shades on the foliage grow bolder for the summer finale. Prefers full sun to partial shade. Grows to 6 feet tall and 5 feet wide in zones 5–9.

TROPICAL TAPESTRY

SITE **FULL SUN**   SOIL **MOISTURE-RETENTIVE BUT WELL-DRAINED**   ZONE **9–11**   SEASON **YEAR-ROUND**

A feathery haze of fennel foliage meanders through the middle of this sun-drenched border, edged firmly by a bold ribbon of Red Flash caladium, while broad fingers of a deep burgundy cordyline create a backdrop. Weaving informally between these is Hallmark snake flower, a long-blooming perennial whose orange floral spires rise above their chive-like foliage, punctuating the tapestry. The contrast of foliage textures and mingling saturated colors makes this a winning tropical combination.

HOW THE DESIGN GROWS

This combination shouts summer with no apology for its brief turn as a garden star. In fall the caladium and fennel will die down, leaving only the cordyline and evergreen foliage of the snake flower. Caladium does not mind being crowded, so when it becomes dormant you could plant nasturtium or zinnia seeds over the top for a winter color splash.

FOLIAGE FRAMEWORK

- >

Red Flash caladium (*Caladium bicolor* 'Red Flash') Red Flash is known for its oversize vibrant red leaves that have pink freckles and a wide olive green margin. An old favorite for the landscape or containers, this is one of the larger varieties that tolerates both sun and shade. Grows to 2–3 tall and 2 feet wide in zones 9–11.

- >

Common fennel (*Foeniculum vulgare*) Common fennel is more typically grown for culinary use, but its airy foliage also makes it a great addition to the ornamental garden. Although the umbels of yellow flowers are attractive, be aware that fennel can self-seed prolifically. Grows to 6 feet tall and 3 feet wide in zones 4–9 or enjoy as an annual.

- >

Cordyline (*Cordyline australis* 'Purpurea') Like a burgundy palm tree, this evergreen plant rises above its surrounding neighbors. It is fairly drought tolerant but benefits from occasional summer water. Grows to 20–25 feet tall and 6–8 feet wide in zones 8–11, but may benefit from winter protection.

FINISHING TOUCH

- >

Hallmark snake flower (*Bulbine frutescens* 'Hallmark') Evergreen succulent foliage forms a dense mat from which spires of orange flowers emerge over many months. This is drought tolerant once established. Grows to 2 feet tall and spreads by rhizomes in zones 8–11.

PICTURE OF INNOCENCE

SITE **PARTIAL SHADE**   SOIL **AVERAGE, WELL-DRAINED**   ZONE **5–8**   SEASON **YEAR-ROUND**

Resting against a simple picket fence, the oriental lilies scent the air with a heady perfume while their speckled pink, peach, and yellow petals suggest a romantic theme. Rising to meet them, the newly emerged upturned foliage of the andromeda echoes the warm shades of the flowers. Behind these two garden romantics the redbud willow acts as chaperone, bringing a sense of order and providing a support for the tall flowers. Its distinct pale veins link to the soft color in the lilies, offering a subtle connection.

HOW THE DESIGN GROWS

Imagine this scene without the two shrubs. The lily would look beautiful in summer, but otherwise this border would lack interest. Framing the freckled flowers with foliage turns this into an attractive year-round vignette, where every component is even more striking for its association with others. In winter the waxy purple stems and red buds of the willow add color to the landscape, as does the evergreen andromeda.

FOLIAGE FRAMEWORK

- >

Purity andromeda (*Pieris japonica* 'Purity') This shrub stands out from the crowd for its exquisite foliage that opens bronze, transitions to chartreuse, and matures to dark green. Add to that deep red buds and lightly fragrant white spring flowers and you have an exceptional evergreen shrub for a semi-shady spot. Grows to 4 feet tall and wide in zones 5–8.

- >

Redbud willow (*Salix fargesii*) An unusual slow-growing willow, this is notable for its mahogany-colored bark and silky upright catkins that emerge from red buds. The foliage is glossy dark green with distinct veins. This deciduous shrub thrives in moisture-retentive but well-drained soil. Grows to 8 feet tall in zones 5–9.

FINISHING TOUCH

- >

Oriental lily (*Lilium orientale*) This lily was a gift many years ago, and its name is long forgotten. An ideal substitute is the Elusive lily (*Lilium* 'Elusive'), which has very similar coloring and blooms in midsummer. Grows to 4–5 feet tall in zones 5–9, but provide winter mulch in colder areas.

CITRUS SPLASH

SITE FULL SUN OR LIGHT SHADE **SOIL AVERAGE** **ZONE 6–9** **SEASON YEAR-ROUND**

If you like to start the day with a glass of freshly squeezed juice, this fruity cocktail will wake you up in no time. The sharp acidic tang of the succulent chartreuse foliage tempers the sweetness of the zesty orange flowers—you will need no additional ingredients except sunshine. If one of these was diluted it would not work nearly as well; the pairing of highly saturated colors gives it the intense flavor. This combo gets even better with age, as the stonecrop will take on orange tones as the summer comes to an end.

HOW THE DESIGN GROWS

Angelina stonecrop is a versatile and hardworking succulent. As an evergreen ground cover or container plant it makes an easy companion for a wide range of plants. While the twinspur works well for summer, you can continue the same color scheme in winter by planting a backdrop of Midwinter Fire dogwood (*Cornus sanguinea* 'Midwinter Fire'), which would show off its bare stems in shades of gold, orange, and red. In a winter container, dark-leaved spurge (*Euphorbia* species) would be a bold choice with the added bonus of chartreuse flowers in spring. To complete the scene, Princess Irene tulips would make a stunning spring accent in the landscape or a container. This variety has burnt orange blooms with a purple flare at the base and attractive blue-green foliage that marries all the colors together.

FOLIAGE FRAMEWORK

- →

Angelina stonecrop (*Sedum rupestre* 'Angelina')
Drought-tolerant, evergreen, and colorful—this low-growing succulent deserves a spot in every garden. It propagates easily with the smallest piece rooting, so it is an inexpensive way to create an extensive sweep of ground cover. This sedum needs well-drained soil in a sunny spot, but will also take average moisture and partial shade. Grows to 6 inches tall and spreads in zones 6–9.

FINISHING TOUCH

- →

Darla Orange twinspur (*Diascia barberae* 'Darla Orange')
Whether you grow this as an annual or a tender perennial you will love the bold splash of color it adds to the summer garden. Ideal as a ground cover or for edging baskets and containers, this variety is remarkably heat tolerant and is a favorite of hummingbirds. Grows to 12 inches tall and 2 feet wide in zones 8–9 or enjoy as an annual.

FINAL FLOURISH

SITE **PARTIAL SUN, PARTIAL SHADE**   SOIL **AVERAGE**   ZONE **6–8**   SEASON **SPRING THROUGH FALL**

These ornamental onions may be fading in color, but they still add plenty of drama to the garden. With assistance from some artistic metal supports, the large spheres stand tall to contrast with the grid design on the trellis and punctuate the distinct horizontal layers of the tree. Meanwhile, their dusky color and shape mimics the flower buds on the hydrangea, enhancing the shrub's ornamental status early in the season. A skirt of soft golden grasses hides the spent onion leaves and contrasts with the color and texture of adjacent foliage. All these elements work together in part because of their transparency, which allows for interaction without any one feature dominating or hiding another.

HOW THE DESIGN GROWS

The dried onion seed heads will last well into the summer, by which
time the hydrangea will be in full bloom, its flowers offering an
extended display as they dry on the shrub. Winter interest relies on
the skeletal silhouette of the wedding cake tree and trellises. You
could plant Merlin hellebore (*Helleborus ×ballardiae* Gold Collection
Merlin) between the onions to add deep cranberry winter flowers and
low-growing evergreen foliage.

FOLIAGE FRAMEWORK

Wedding cake tree (*Cornus controversa* 'Variegata') With a distinctive
branching pattern that resembles tiers of a wedding cake, this graceful
tree features green-and-white variegated foliage that turns purple in fall
and white summer flowers that set blue-black berries. Prefers full sun but
benefits from some afternoon shade in hotter climates. Grows to 20 feet
tall and wide in zones 4–8.

All Gold Japanese forest grass (*Hakonechloa macra* 'All Gold') This
herbaceous grass needs protection from hot afternoon sun. It forms a
graceful clump of golden yellow foliage that thrives in containers and
shade gardens. Grows to 2 feet tall and wide in zones 4–9.

Sargent's hydrangea (*Hydrangea aspera* subsp. *sargentiana*)
A giant in the hydrangea world, this collector's favorite prefers
afternoon shade. Magnificent fuzzy gray-green leaves support
oversize lacecap-type white-and-purple flowers in summer.
Grows to 10 feet tall and wide in zones 6–9.

FINISHING TOUCH

Giant onion (*Allium giganteum*) A deer-resistant and drought-
tolerant bulb for the garden. Each stalk grows to 3–6 feet tall,
culminating in a globe-shaped purple flower 4 inches in diameter. As
the flowers fade to tan they dry in situ, continuing to add a decorative
touch to the garden for many months. Remove tattered leaves and be
prepared to stake the heavy stems. Prefers partial to full sun and very
well-drained soil. Grows to 3–6 feet tall in zones 6–10; plant in drifts
for the best effect.

SASSITUDE

SITE **FULL SUN**   SOIL **AVERAGE TO DRY**   ZONE **4–8**   SEASON **YEAR-ROUND**

Find your inner wild child with this playful combo. Crayola colors set the scene with a red barberry, blue juniper, and yellow highlights from both the spirea and golden locust tree. Sprinkled throughout and giving the wowza attitude is the flirty Paprika yarrow. Look more closely and notice how the yellow flower stamens repeat the color of the foliage and the fine gold margin on the barberry. Serious spicy sassitude.

HOW THE DESIGN GROWS

This is a brazen display almost all year, with the colorful new barberry and spirea growth in spring and equally bright show in fall. The yarrow blooms in waves throughout the warmer months, each flower aging from scarlet to cream, giving a multicolored effect. The cool blue juniper holds it all together and adds winter color. To maintain this look, thin the yarrow after a few years or it will start to grow into the shrubs.

FOLIAGE FRAMEWORK

- →

Golden Ruby barberry (*Berberis thunbergii* 'Golden Ruby') This dwarf mounding shrub has spring and fall foliage in a medley of fiery orange and deep red, while in summer a narrow gold margin accents the deep burgundy. Rabbit and deer resistant as well as drought tolerant. Grows to 12 inches tall and 2 feet wide in zones 4–8. **CAUTION** Before planting, make sure barberries are not invasive in your area.

- →

Blue Star juniper (*Juniperus squamata* 'Blue Star') An outstanding dwarf conifer with attractive blue foliage, this juniper is drought tolerant once established, and deer and rabbits ignore it. Grows to 2 feet tall and 3–4 feet wide in zones 4–8.

- →

Double Play Gold spirea (*Spiraea japonica* 'Double Play Gold') This spirea is almost as sassy as its floral companion. Copper and gold leaves are topped with hot pink flowers in summer—if the deer don't assist with trimming. The good news is that gardeners have the last laugh: once deadheaded, this shrub continues to push out new coppery foliage. Fall color is soft yellow, an exciting contrast to the barberry. Drought tolerant once established. Grows to 3–4 feet tall and wide in zones 4–9, but you (or the deer) can prune to keep it smaller.

continued on next page

Sassitude continued

Golden locust tree (*Robinia pseudoacacia* 'Frisia') Add sunshine to your garden even on gray days with the golden yellow foliage of this tree. It grows quickly, so even though the branches are brittle and may suffer wind damage, it quickly fills in. Adapts easily to many soil types. Grows to 30–50 feet tall and 20 feet wide in zones 4–9.

FINISHING TOUCH

Paprika yarrow (*Achillea millefolium* 'Paprika') Easy to grow and to love, this drought-tolerant, sun-loving perennial has fern-like gray foliage. Stems carry an abundance of flowers that open vivid red and slowly fade to cream. Grows to 2 feet tall and 3 feet wide or more in zones 3–9.

THE GILDED AGE

SITE **FULL SUN, PARTIAL SUN**   SOIL **AVERAGE**   ZONE **6–8**   SEASON **SPRING THROUGH FALL**

Glittering and golden, this original garden design promotes the use of resplendent foliage as a wonderful base against which flowers in shades of blues and violets can sparkle. The long, pointed leaves of the comfrey create the perfect textural contrast for the ornate foliage of the tansy, while the oval leaves of the billowy smoke bush add another shape in the same color theme but with just a tinge of apricot blush on the new growth. Visual pauses of spring green give the eye a place to rest between all these gold sparkles.

The Gilded Age continued

HOW THE DESIGN GROWS

The flowers in this scene bloom primarily in spring, but the foliage is going to look great from the day it emerges until well into fall before losing its luster. Adding more violet and purple flowers—such as tall garden phlox (*Phlox paniculata* 'Nicky' or 'Purple Kiss') and New England aster (*Symphyotrichum novae-angliae* 'Purple Dome')—for the late summer and early fall show would take this display to the next level. As the smoke bush matures, pruning it each spring will ensure that this fast-growing shrub will not overshadow the rest of these sun-loving plants.

FOLIAGE FRAMEWORK

- →

Axminster Gold Russian comfrey (*Symphytum ×uplandicum* 'Axminster Gold') Making a statement in the garden is easy with this vigorous herbaceous perennial. Broad leaves with a gray-green center sport a showy margin that ranges from yellow to gold. Bell-shaped mauve-pink flowers rise up on tall stems above the rosette of foliage in spring or early summer. Cut back after blooming to encourage the growth of fresh new foliage and more flowers. This deer-resistant plant attracts butterflies and prefers moisture-retentive but well-drained soil in full sun to partial shade. Grows to 4–5 feet tall and wide in zones 4–9.

- →

Golden Spirit smoke bush (*Cotinus coggygria* 'Golden Spirit') A deciduous large-scale shrub or small tree in the landscape with a multistemmed growth habit and glowing golden foliage. Fall's cooler temperatures bring touches of amber and burgundy to the leaves of this fast-growing voluptuous plant. Prefers full sun to partial shade. Grows to 10–12 feet tall and wide in zones 4–8, but you can keep it smaller with judicious pruning.

Isla Gold tansy (*Tanacetum vulgare* 'Isla Gold') The lacy, deer-resistant foliage emerges bright chartreuse in spring and retains the color through fall. Unlike other tansy, this polite version of the herbaceous perennial will not spread by seeding around the garden. Button-like flowers appear in summer, but some gardeners prefer to prune off in favor of the ferny foliage. This easy plant does best in average soil in full sun to partial shade. Grows to 1–3 feet tall in zones 3–8.

FINISHING TOUCH

Ornamental onion (*Allium* species) Part of the onion family, this remarkable spring bulb offers up a royal purple ball of flowers on a tall stalk that features the blooms perfectly above other plants. Deer resistance is a huge benefit for this showy bloom. Attractive to butterflies and bees, the seed heads are highly ornamental in the garden if you do not cut them back. Performs best in full sun. Grows to 3–5 feet tall in zones 6–10.

Mountain bluet (*Centaurea montana*) Two-inch-wide spidery blue cornflowers with violet-red centers appear on this clumping perennial in late spring above narrow gray-green foliage. If you prune after the first flush of bloom, it will often produce another set of flowers in early fall. Makes a wonderfully hardy cut flower. This low-maintenance perennial is drought tolerant in average soils and prefers full sun. Grows to 2 feet tall and wide in zones 3–8.

SUMMER GALAXY

SITE **FULL SUN**   SOIL **AVERAGE**   ZONE **7–8**   SEASON **YEAR-ROUND**

A constellation of starry soft pink flowers is eye-catching enough, but when framed by beautiful foliage it is transformed into a memorable vignette. The fuzzy new white leaves of the rhododendron appear to point upward to the dogwood blooms, while the creamy white-and-green variegated Italian buckthorn repeats the softer tones and adds a finely textured backdrop to show off the bold flowers. The result is a dreamy galaxy of foliage and flowers that you will look forward to every year.

HOW THE DESIGN GROWS

This scene changes with the seasons but always has something exciting to offer. By late summer the ripening dogwood fruit will dangle from the branches like fat red strawberries. Orange and red foliage on the dogwood will be a fall highlight, while the winter garden will rely on the two evergreen shrubs for interest. In spring the rhododendron will bloom with flowers that open pink and mature to white, fading just as the dogwood begins its colorful display once again.

FOLIAGE FRAMEWORK

--➤

Variegated Italian buckthorn (*Rhamnus alaternus* 'Argenteovariegata') This evergreen Mediterranean shrub needs full sun and well-drained soil to flourish and reach its mature size. Each small, rounded gray-green leaf has a distinct creamy white margin that somewhat camouflages the pale spring flowers, although the red berries show up well later in the season. Grows to 8–10 feet tall and 4–10 feet wide in zones 7–9.

--➤

Van Zile rhododendron (*Rhododendron yakushimanum* 'Van Zile') This yak hybrid is both compact and slow growing. The flowers open with pink highlights but quickly mature to pure white. Of special interest to the designer is the felted white indumentum on the new leaves, which lasts throughout the summer. The dogwood tree protects the evergreen rhododendron from the direct afternoon sun. Grows to 4 feet tall and 6 feet wide in zones 5–8.

FINISHING TOUCH

--➤

Satomi kousa dogwood (*Cornus kousa* 'Satomi') Known for its abundant rose-pink flowers in June, this deciduous tree is a popular choice for smaller landscapes. As it matures it exhibits a graceful layered branching pattern that shows off the flowers to perfection. Edible red fruits and rich fall foliage colors add to the ornamental value of this disease-resistant cultivar. Thrives in full sun or partial shade. Grows to 12–15 feet tall and wide in zones 5–8.

PORTABLE PORTRAIT

SITE **FULL SUN**   SOIL **AVERAGE**   ZONE **6–7**   SEASON **YEAR-ROUND**

Here is a great idea to try in your own garden: draw attention to a plant that is having its moment of glory by literally framing it. The weathered patina of an old metal picture frame enhances and highlights the brightly marbled new growth on the Rose Glow barberry. The surrounding blue and green foliage of the blueberry and spruce add cooler notes, further emphasizing the warm barberry colors.

HOW THE DESIGN GROWS

The beauty of this idea is that it is portable. The frame has been welded onto metal tubing legs that you can push into the ground, so you can move it to showcase different plants in other seasons. This particular vignette will continue to get fuller and richer as the blueberry grows to fill the void at the base of the frame. In spring the pink-tinted blueberry flowers will play into the color scheme perfectly, while the summer berries will enhance the blue foliage. As the barberry loses its leaves in fall, the semi-evergreen blueberry foliage turns deep burgundy.

FOLIAGE FRAMEWORK

- >

Rose Glow barberry (*Berberis thunbergii* f. *atropurpurea* 'Rose Glow') This thorny deciduous shrub opens burgundy, but the new growth quickly takes on marbled pink-and-white splashes. For the brightest color, prune in late winter. To achieve the best effect, allow this deer-resistant and drought-tolerant shrub to grow into a natural fountain. Grows to 4 feet tall and wide in zones 4–8. **CAUTION** Before planting, make sure barberries are not invasive in your area.

- >

Dwarf Serbian spruce (*Picea omorika* 'Nana') A perfect accent shrub for the garden, this compact evergreen spruce forms a dense globe-shaped mound. The short blue-green needles have distinct white stripes on the undersides. Grows to 4–8 feet tall and wide in zones 4–7.

- >

Bountiful Blue blueberry (*Vaccinium corymbosum* 'Bountiful Blue') Known for its bright blue foliage, this semi-evergreen shrub produces an abundance of sweet summer berries even without a second variety nearby. Needs acidic soil with regular water. Grows to 3–4 feet tall and wide in zones 6–10.

FINISHING TOUCH

- >

Weathered metal picture frame Hunt thrift stores for something similar, then weld on metal tubing or rebar for legs.

COLOR PLAY

SITE **FULL SUN, PARTIAL SUN** SOIL **AVERAGE** ZONE **5–7** SEASON **SPRING THROUGH FALL**

Timing is everything. The eye moves easily through this scene, captured in late spring, from the vivid pink foliage of the Japanese maple in the background to the translucent tulips at the front of the border, glancing lightly on the new growth of the spirea along the way. Just a few weeks earlier and all those shades of pink would have been closer to crimson; a few weeks later and the tulips would be gone. This ephemeral vignette plays with color to both capture and celebrate the season.

HOW THE DESIGN GROWS

As this scene moves through the color spectrum during the year, each season has its own unique identity. By midsummer, the hot pinks of spring are just a memory, the maple foliage is green, and the tulips are long gone. The spirea assumes greater importance as the soft gold leaves frame clusters of pink flowers that bloom in waves over many weeks. As fall approaches, the maple introduces a fresh palette of orange, gold, and bronze, which the spirea echoes. Only in winter is the scene silent, pausing the cycle of color until spring returns. In many regions you will have to replant the tulips annually, but the maple and spirea will coexist easily for a lifetime.

FOLIAGE FRAMEWORK

- >

Shishio Improved Japanese maple (*Acer palmatum* 'Shishio Improved') A graceful multibranched tree that works equally well as a container plant as it does for the landscape. Crimson foliage in early spring softens to the vivid pink seen here, which lasts until summer, when the leaves turn green. Autumn is equally vibrant as the foliage transitions through orange, yellow, and bronze. Grows to 7–9 feet tall and 6–8 feet wide in zones 5–9.

- >

Magic Carpet spirea (*Spiraea japonica* 'Magic Carpet') Colorful foliage and flowers make this deciduous shrub easy to love. New spring leaves are copper colored, maturing to a soft gold in summer and adding orange-red to the mix in fall. Flat clusters of pink flowers attract bees and butterflies in summer. Grows to 3 feet tall and wide in zones 4–9.

FINISHING TOUCH

- >

Perestroyka tulip (*Tulipa* 'Perestroyka') This is no ordinary pink tulip: the large lily-shaped flowers open scarlet with coral and yellow accents before maturing to salmon pink. Makes excellent cut flowers. Grows to 24–30 inches tall in zones 3–7.

PURPLE PASSION

SITE FULL SUN   **SOIL** DRY   **ZONE** 9–11 OR ANNUALS   **SEASON** YEAR-ROUND

Aim to highlight, rather than overwhelm, the sculptural form of this curvaceous container with rusted ring detail. Plant a soft fountain of purple grass to one side, echoing the color and adding height, while a froth of silver licorice plant caresses the base. The subtle juxtaposition of the glossy pot against the matte leaves shows a true designer touch. This simple foliage picture frame transforms an empty container into an elegant focal point.

HOW THE DESIGN GROWS

For many gardeners both these plants are annuals, making this a spring-through-fall vignette that would require replanting each year. As an alternative, substitute the perennial Silver Brocade wormwood (*Artemisia stelleriana* 'Silver Brocade') for the licorice plant and Shenandoah switch grass (*Panicum virgatum* 'Shenandoah') for the fountain grass—both will return after winter dormancy. The frost-resistant container can stay outside year-round in more temperate climates, where it adds color to the winter landscape.

FOLIAGE FRAMEWORK

- ->

Purple fountain grass (*Pennisetum setaceum* 'Rubrum') Narrow purple blades form a loose fountain from which pink, tan, and purple foxtail like plumes rise in summer. This makes a great container plant or garden accent. Grows to 3–4 feet tall and wide in zones 8–11 or enjoy as an annual.

- ->

Licorice plant (*Helichrysum petiolare*) This vigorous grower has felted silver leaves and makes a wonderful sprawling ground cover for hot, dry gardens. It is rather too robust for containers and hanging baskets, as it will quickly overrun its companions. Grows to 10 inches tall and 3 feet wide or more in zones 9–11 or enjoy as an annual.

FINISHING TOUCH

- ->

Purple container A frost-resistant high-fired ceramic container in rich purple with a speckled blue underglaze. While any glossy purple container would work, the shapely silhouette and iron ring feature make this a perfect candidate for such a simple treatment. This pot is 20 inches tall and wide.

SHADOWS AND SILHOUETTES

SITE **FULL SUN**   SOIL **DRY**   ZONE **9–10**   SEASON **YEAR-ROUND**

This collection of spiky cactus and cactus-like plants would be a jumble of conflicting silhouettes without the solid backdrop of this muted ochre wall. Light transforms this scene into something truly spectacular as the harsh summer sun streams through the overhead canopy, casting long shadows in the desert garden.

HOW THE DESIGN GROWS

Most plants retain color year-round, so this may appear to be a fairly static combination. Yet as the arc of the sun changes, the shadows will soften and elongate, adding a subtle shift of atmosphere and color. The plants still offer seasonal changes, with the ocotillo flowering with tubular scarlet blooms after rainfall, the prickly pear cactus bearing magenta-red flowers in spring, and the agave also projecting tall flowering spikes toward the summer sky.

FOLIAGE FRAMEWORK

- >

Blue myrtle cactus (*Myrtillocactus geometrizans*) Resembling a spiky blue-gray candelabra, this is a slow-growing multibranched cactus. Grows to 25 feet tall and wide in zones 9–10.

- >

Lechuguilla agave (*Agave lechuguilla*) This extremely cold-hardy plant is native to southern Texas and northeastern Mexico. A 10-foot flowering stalk appears from the fleshy basal rosette of mature plants in late summer, after which the parent plant dies but young plants are produced at the base. Grows to 12–18 inches tall and wide in zones 9–10.

- >

Beavertail prickly pear cactus (*Opuntia basilaris*) A spineless, drought-tolerant, clumping cactus that adds color to the desert garden with brilliant magenta-red flowers that appear at the tips in spring. Grows to 6 feet wide in zones 8–10.

- >

Ocotillo (*Fouquieria splendens*) This cactus-like plant has spiny stems that flesh out after a rain (which also brings out long scarlet flowers). It blooms between late spring and early fall, and is a favorite of hummingbirds. When the dry season returns, the foliage drops once again. The cycle repeats during the year. Grows to 30 feet tall and 15 feet wide in zones 8–11.

FINISHING TOUCH

- >

Painted wall No flowers or frills are needed to complete this scene—just a solid canvas on which to project shadows and define silhouettes. This muted paint color works well with the blue-gray tones of the cactus, enhancing but not competing with the plants.

INCREDIBLE EDIBLES

SITE **PARTIAL SUN, PARTIAL SHADE**   SOIL **AVERAGE**   ZONE **ANNUALS**   SEASON **SPRING THROUGH FALL**

These lettuce are too beautiful to be confined to the vegetable garden. With colors ranging from deepest purple to fresh green as well as attractive speckled varieties, these designer salad crops can hold their own on the patio or at the front of a border. Broad flat leaves jostle with tight curly forms and looser wavy ones, creating a bountiful bowl on which to sprinkle edible flowers. Introducing orange and gold blooms to the mix adds fun, flair, and flavor, tempting even the pickiest diners to finish their salads.

HOW THE DESIGN GROWS

All these plants will grow quickly once the sun warms the soil, and you can harvest from spring until fall, especially if you reseed the lettuce at intervals during the season. In high summer, some lettuce types will bolt, at which point the leaves will develop a bitter taste and are best added to the compost pile. These plants are annuals, so the edible display will be over in fall.

FOLIAGE FRAMEWORK

- - - - - - - - - - - - - - - - - - - >

Flashy Trout Back lettuce (*Lactuca sativa* 'Flashy Trout Back') This Austrian heirloom romaine lettuce is splattered with maroon freckles and has a buttery flavor.

- - - - - - - - - - - - - - - - >

Salanova Red Sweet Crisp Frisee (*Lactuca sativa* 'Salanova Red Sweet Crisp Frisee') The frilly deep red leaves are crisp and flavorful.

- - - - - - - - - - - - - - - - - - - >

Cherokee lettuce (*Lactuca sativa* 'Cherokee') A popular dark-leaf variety valued for its bolt resistance and crisp, nutty flavor.

You can grow all lettuce from seed started indoors. Transplant outside when all danger of frost has passed or when you can sow directly into warm soil. Some varieties bolt in high temperatures and others may scorch, so it is ideal to grow them in the shade of taller crops, such as tomatoes or beans. Harvest individual leaves as desired or entire lettuce heads, leaving the root in place (it may regrow). Bait for slugs if necessary, but otherwise these are trouble free.

FINISHING TOUCH

- →

French marigold (*Tagetes patula*) Easy to grow and a
favorite of gardeners for decades; use the edible flowers
to decorate salads and cakes. Anecdotal evidence
suggests that marigolds repel some types of nematodes
and are therefore recommended for planting near tomatoes or other
plants that are prone to such attacks. Grows to 6–10 inches tall;
many named varieties of this annual are available.

- →

Dahlia (*Dahlia* species) Dahlias grown from seed and sold in
bedding packs are typically treated as annuals, their variety name
often unknown. If you want a specific color, wait until they are in
bud to purchase. These flowers are also edible and have a spicy,
tangy flavor that can add some punch as well as
color to a salad bowl. Grows to 10–20 inches tall,
depending on variety.

- →

Nasturtium (*Tropaeolum majus*) Perhaps one of
the best-known annuals, nasturtiums are easy to
grow and a popular addition to hanging baskets or
colorful ground cover. You can direct sow the seed
or start it indoors. Both foliage and flowers are
edible and have a peppery flavor.

UNEXPECTED PRIZE

SITE **PARTIAL SUN, FULL SUN**　SOIL **AVERAGE, MOISTURE-RETENTIVE**　ZONE **7–8**　SEASON **YEAR-ROUND**

Who doesn't love a bargain? This mosaic vase came from a discount store, and the price was further reduced because of some minor damage. In the garden, the unexpected sky blue shards draw the eye and allow the viewer to appreciate the butterflies and sunflower details. Playing off those gold and orange shades, an assortment of foliage plants adds texture and setting. Apricot wallflowers add the finishing touch, evoking a sunny meadow for the butterflies to enjoy.

Unexpected Prize continued

HOW THE DESIGN GROWS

The evergreen laurel and sweet flag foliage ensure interest in this part of the garden year-round, but it will look best between spring and fall, when you can place the vase outdoors. To extend the orange flowers into summer, plant the dwarf orange sneezeweed (*Helenium* 'Short 'n' Sassy') nearby. Prune all the shrubs regularly to maintain this vignette, and thin the sweet flag every three years.

FOLIAGE FRAMEWORK

-- →

Ogon Japanese sweet flag (*Acorus gramineus* 'Ogon') This low-growing evergreen grass does best in partial shade but will also grow in full sun with plenty of moisture, including shallow standing water. The arching fan shape of the variegated gold leaves makes this a winner for containers as well as a ground cover. Grows to 12 inches tall and wide in zones 5–9.

-- →

Otto Luyken English laurel (*Prunus laurocerasus* 'Otto Luyken') Growing in full sun to partial shade, this dwarf form of English laurel is ideal for low hedges and takes pruning well. Glossy evergreen leaves and fragrant spring flowers ensure this looks good year-round. Grows to 3 feet tall and 6 feet wide in zones 6–9, but you can prune to keep it smaller.

-- →

Golden barberry (*Berberis thunbergii* 'Aurea') The foliage of this deciduous shrub is a loose fountain that turns chartreuse in partial shade, as seen here, but is brighter in more light (although it may scorch in full sun). Grows to 5 feet tall and wide in zones 5–8, or you can prune it smaller. **CAUTION** Before planting, make sure barberries are not invasive in your area.

Red leaf barberry (*Berberis thunbergii* f. *atropurpurea*) In full sun this thorny deciduous shrub will be a much deeper shade of burgundy; in this partly shaded setting the overall color is olive green with red highlights. Grows to 5 feet tall and wide in zones 4–8 when unpruned, but you can easily keep it smaller. **CAUTION** Before planting, make sure barberries are not invasive in your area.

Fragrant Star wallflower (*Erysimum* 'Fragrant Star') This variety of wallflower bridges the design gap, offering outstanding variegated foliage and highly fragrant yellow flowers. The blooms are sterile and produced over an extended period of time on a compact, bushy, semi-evergreen shrub. Grows to 2 feet tall and wide in zones 6–9.

FINISHING TOUCH

Mosaic vase Although not suitable for leaving outside during the winter, this delightful vase adds a splash of color and fun to the garden from spring until fall. For special occasions, play up the sunflower motif and add a bouquet of cut flowers.

Apricot Twist wallflower (*Erysimum* 'Apricot Twist') Soft gray-green foliage sets off the purple buds and fragrant apricot-orange blooms. In mild winter areas this evergreen shrub will grow into a compact, mounding shrub, but cutting back by half after flowering will encourage this tidy habit. Does best in well-drained soil and a hot, sunny location. Grows to 2 feet tall and wide in zones 7–9, possibly colder.

NESTING INSTINCTS

SITE **PARTIAL SUN, PARTIAL SHADE**   SOIL **AVERAGE, WELL-DRAINED**   ZONE **6–8**   SEASON **YEAR-ROUND**

Clustered together, these interesting shrubs create a perfect nest for this little bird, which seems ready to take flight. The color connections in this vignette are subtle yet powerful. The thin gold margin on the barberry echoes the prominent golden fir needles, while the color of the unusual bronze rhododendron is repeated in the whimsical rusted metal sculpture. Adding a cool touch to the otherwise rich palette is the Blue Star juniper, whose finely textured foliage completes the scene.

HOW THE DESIGN GROWS

All the shrubs except the barberry are evergreen, so this design provides color all year, yet each season offers subtle changes. In spring the new growth on the fir will be a vibrant gold, creating a dramatic contrast with the bold red shades of the barberry and rhododendron. Lavender-pink rhododendron flowers pack a startling color punch to the mix later in spring. As the barberry foliage matures, a ring of gold appears, fading to taupe by autumn, when the leaves take on bold shades of orange-red.

FOLIAGE FRAMEWORK

- ->

Golden Spreader Nordmann fir (*Abies nordmanniana* 'Golden Spreader') A compact, well-branched, low-mounding conifer that emerges brilliant gold in spring before maturing to yellow. This is an ideal accent shrub in a mixed border. In colder climates, mulch around the root zone may be beneficial. Grows to 4 feet tall and wide in zones 4–8.

- ->

Golden Ruby barberry (*Berberis thunbergii* 'Golden Ruby') This low-maintenance, drought-tolerant, and deer- and rabbit-resistant barberry has all the expected attributes of its relatives. Add to that rich red foliage with a lighter margin and a dwarf, compact habit and this becomes an invaluable addition to even a small garden. Grows to 12 inches tall and 2 feet wide in zones 4–8. **CAUTION** Before planting, make sure barberries are not invasive in your area.

- ->

Blue Star juniper (*Juniperus squamata* 'Blue Star') A favorite conifer for its soft gray-blue color and ability to look at home in a container or the landscape. Grows to 2 feet tall and 3–4 feet wide in zones 4–8.

continued on next page

-->

Ebony Pearl rhododendron (*Rhododendron* 'Ebony Pearl') A truly unique rhododendron with glossy evergreen leaves that glow rich burgundy in spring before maturing to green. In spring, bold lavender-pink flowers add to the display. This rhododendron needs consistent moisture. Grows to 3 feet tall and wide in zones 6–9.

FINISHING TOUCH

-->

Metal bird sculpture Just a few inches tall, this funky rusted sculpture is perfect for adding a whimsical touch to the carefully composed foliage combination, while its bronzed patina emphasizes the unusual foliage of the similarly colored rhododendron.

PRETTY IN PINK

SITE FULL SUN, PARTIAL SUN   **SOIL** POTTING SOIL   **ZONE** 5–8   **SEASON** SPRING THROUGH FALL

As pretty as a frothy pink party dress, this feminine combination will appeal to gardeners who want lots of flowers. The foliage of the two flowering plants contribute little to the design, so it was important to include the assortment of silver, cream, and purple leaves. The oversize silver lamb's ears and a large succulent rosette also help balance the smaller-textured foliage and create a focal point.

Pretty in Pink continued

HOW THE DESIGN GROWS

Although the deutzia, lamb's ears, and purple sedum look good from spring until fall, many of the other plants are treated as annuals, so this is primarily a summer display. Come fall, it is time to dismantle the container: transplant the perennials and deutzia into the garden and set the pot to one side for the winter.

FOLIAGE FRAMEWORK

---------------------------------→

Bella Grigio lamb's ears (*Stachys* 'Bella Grigio') This is the overachiever of lamb's ears, offering foliage that is even softer, more silvery, and more vigorous than our old cottage garden favorite. It grows quickly into large clumps, making a stunning ground cover or container specimen, although you may need to trim it several times in a mixed container to stop it from swallowing its neighbors. It likes full sun or dappled shade and well-drained soil with occasional watering. Grows to 18 inches tall and wide in zones 5–9.

---------------------------------→

Sunburst aeonium (*Aeonium decorum* 'Sunburst') Large rosettes in soft green and creamy yellow stand tall on stout stems. In full sun these take on a pink margin, playing beautifully to the color scheme. Grows to 18 inches tall and wide in zones 9–11, but will stay smaller as a seasonal container plant in cooler climates.

---------------------------------→

Sedum (*Sedum* variety) Although the exact variety of this dusky purple sedum is not known, you can easily find several with a similar habit and color, such as Chocolate Drop and Vera Jameson. All are perennials that are hardy in zones 4–9 or colder.

Fireworks fountain grass (*Pennisetum setaceum* 'Fireworks') While hardy in zones 9–11, cooler-climate gardeners can still enjoy this as a colorful annual grass. The blades are striped hot pink, burgundy, green, and white, the color intensifying during the summer just as the purple tassels appear. Grows to 3 feet tall and 2 feet wide where hardy, but usually smaller as an annual.

Crème Fraiche deutzia (*Deutzia gracilis* 'Crème Fraiche') This is a dwarf deciduous shrub for the landscape or container that blooms with a profusion of white flowers in spring and boasts resistance to deer. The variegated foliage is a clean white and green, although some branches occasionally revert to solid green and must be cut off. Grows to 2 feet tall and wide in zones 5–8.

FINISHING TOUCH

Pink Wonder fan flower (*Scaevola aemula* 'Pink Wonder') An exceptional annual that blooms profusely from spring until fall in full sun or partial shade. The fan-shaped clear pink flowers do not need deadheading, and the plant is drought tolerant and heat resistant. It will meander through and trail from containers and baskets and is hardy only in zones 10–11, so usually enjoyed as an annual.

Bacopa (*Sutera cordata*) This is a favorite for adding to containers with its trailing habit and starry white flowers that bloom all summer in full sun or partial sun. Bacopa is hardy in zones 9–11, but will often overwinter in cooler climates—cut back hard in spring to rejuvenate it or enjoy as an annual.

FOCAL POINT FORMULA

SITE **FULL SUN** SOIL **POTTING SOIL** ZONE **3–7** SEASON **YEAR-ROUND**

How do you add oomph to a mature border? By adding a big, fat pot with bold foliage that stands out from the crowd. The container is planted with the cooling silver tones of cork bark fir and wormwood, which contrast easily with the more traditional green, burgundy, and gold shrubs beyond. Rich orange daisies add a wild blast of color that gives the scene a playful touch, while their silver leaves mingle easily with the other container plants. The subtle connection between the paler fir needles and golden foliage in the border helps move the eye through the space. What could have been a predictable composition is now a powerful focal point.

HOW THE DESIGN GROWS

This rustic brown container will add interest to the garden year-round, as will the featured cork bark fir, which fills the visual gap when the herbaceous wormwood is dormant. Where the African daisy is treated as an annual, you have an opportunity to be creative. Try adding a layer of beach glass in shades of aqua and white to top-dress the soil in winter. Adding a piece of landscape fabric underneath will stop the glass from sinking and prevent perlite from the potting soil from rising to the surface and spoiling the display. Eventually the conifer's girth will leave little room for companion plants, at which point you can add the wormwood to the garden.

FOLIAGE FRAMEWORK

--→

Cork bark fir (*Abies lasiocarpa* 'Glauca Compacta', also sold as *Abies lasiocarpa* var. *arizonica* 'Glauca Compacta') This sturdy dwarf fir has a dense pyramidal habit and is known for its silver-blue needles. In spring the new growth emerges a soft yellow, creating a striking color contrast. Grows to 8 feet tall and 6 feet wide in zones 3–7.

--→

Silver Mound wormwood (*Artemisia schmidtiana* 'Silver Mound') This drought-tolerant perennial forms a soft, fluffy mound of finely dissected silver foliage. To keep it compact, you may need to shear partway through summer, but it will quickly regrow. Deer ignore the aromatic leaves. Thrives in lean, dry soil and full sun. Grows to 2 feet tall and wide in zones 3–8.

FINISHING TOUCH

--→

Pumpkin Pie African daisy (*Arctotis* 'Pumpkin Pie') There is no ignoring this bold orange daisy with its dark chocolate eye. Silvery foliage adds interest even when not in bloom, but you can expect this drought-tolerant hybrid to bloom profusely all season, especially if you remove old flower heads. Grows to 14 inches tall and almost as wide in zones 9–11 or enjoy as an annual.

THE GREEN LIGHT

SITE **SUN, PARTIAL SUN**   SOIL **AVERAGE**   ZONE **5–9**   SEASON **SPRING, FALL**

There is no need for garish hues when you have layer upon layer of lush green trees and shrubs overflowing with texture, as in this creek-side design. The color you do get comes from the frothy white blooms of two voluptuous spirea set wide apart. They lead your eye to the superstar of this composition, the feathery dawn redwood. It rises up in a glow of green light, where its verdant gold-green texture holds court all summer long, impressing even those who longed for gaudiness.

HOW THE DESIGN GROWS

Do you choose the pinnacle of perfection for this design as spring, when the spirea is in full bloom and the redwood is at its ferny soft green best? Or would you prefer this combination in fall, when the spirea is showing off its copper, orange, gold, and even purple colors and the redwood has turned to rich russets and warm golds? It might be a tough choice, but over the winter the structure of both will hold your interest until you decide.

FOLIAGE FRAMEWORK

Gold Rush dawn redwood (*Metasequoia glyptostroboides* 'Gold Rush') Standout golden foliage is the wow factor on this tree, known for its monstrous Redwood Forest cousins. Gold Rush, however, is less imposing and workable for many neighborhood landscapes, and is very slow growing. This unique deciduous conifer prefers partial to full sun and will go from a citrus golden hue to a rich rusty tone before it loses its needles in fall. Grows to 50 feet tall and 20 feet wide in zones 5–10.

FINISHING TOUCH

Bridal wreath spirea (*Spiraea ×vanhouttei*) Long, gracefully arching branches hold the prolific cascading white blooms on this large-scale, low-maintenance shrub. Butterflies and bees love it, and the fall color of the foliage is fantastic. The deep blue-green of spring and summer develops into attractive yellow-orange to purple hues for multiple-season interest. Blooms best in full sun, but also tolerates partial sun well. Grows to 9 feet tall and wide in zones 5–9.

FLAVOR OF THE MONTH

SITE **PARTIAL SUN, PARTIAL SHADE**   SOIL **AVERAGE**   ZONE **6–7**   SEASON **YEAR-ROUND**

Melt-in-your-mouth deliciousness is what we have here. The rich burgundy foliage of the Japanese maple augments the rosy tones of the rhododendron buds and the striking dark red speckles at the throat of each flower. Meanwhile, the conifer adds cooling tones of green and a new texture to the scene, its stiff needles contrasting with the soft maple foliage and leathery rhododendron leaves.

HOW THE DESIGN GROWS

Together these three mounding shrubs offer year-round interest, each plant taking its turn in the limelight. Late spring sees the rhododendron as the winning flavor of the month, the yellow blooms enhanced and framed by its two foliage companions. As the flowers fade the summer view is subtler, but the fresh green growth of the rhododendron shows up well against the burgundy maple and adds a mini taste blast, like peppermint after a rich meal. In autumn the Crimson Queen maple adds some heat to the menu as the leaves turn a vibrant shade of red, while the winter scene is more about structure and the evergreen foliage of the rhododendron and pine.

FOLIAGE FRAMEWORK

- →

Crimson Queen Japanese maple (*Acer palmatum* var. *dissectum* 'Crimson Queen') This popular Japanese maple grows as a soft mound, thriving in full sun to partial shade. The deeply dissected foliage adds rich shades of burgundy to the garden in spring and summer before turning bright scarlet in fall. Grows to 10 feet tall and 13 feet wide in zones 5–8.

- →

Mugo pine (*Pinus mugo*) One of the easiest pines to grow, these compact shrubs are known for their stiff branches densely clothed in 2-inch-long needles. However, left unpruned they can become ungainly. For a smaller garden, select one of the named dwarf cultivars, such as Mops, that does not need pruning. Does best in full to partial sun. Grows to 15 feet tall and 25 feet wide in zones 2–7.

FINISHING TOUCH

- →

Buttered Popcorn rhododendron (*Rhododendron* 'Buttered Popcorn') The rosy buds of this hybrid open to trumpet-shaped yellow flowers, the petal margins suffused with pink while deep burgundy speckles create a distinctive eye. This mound usually blooms in June and prefers protection from afternoon sun. Grows to 4 feet tall and wide in zones 6–8.

EASY BREEZY

SITE **FULL SUN**   SOIL **AVERAGE, WELL-DRAINED**   ZONE **6–9**   SEASON **YEAR-ROUND**

Growing on a high bluff, this combination not only copes with onshore breezes but also looks all the more dreamy for its tousled effect. Billowing fountains of shimmering Mexican feather grass act as buffers and provide gentle support to the slender flower stems of the cupid's dart and flowering tobacco plants, while also creating a translucent meadow-inspired backdrop to showcase each delicate blue-and-white bloom. Originally grown for a garden wedding several years ago, their self-seeding habit has ensured fragrant, romantic memories with which to celebrate each anniversary.

HOW THE DESIGN GROWS

This expansive planting of Mexican feather grass acts as nature's barometer, with movement and color indicating changes in the weather. Interwoven self-seeded clumps of old-fashioned flowers are a summer highlight, bringing color and perfume to the scene as well as rekindling fond memories of when they were first planted. To encourage the blooms' continuance, do not deadhead: when they die back in fall, the grasses will continue to add interest through winter.

FOLIAGE FRAMEWORK

- >

Mexican feather grass (*Stipa tenuissima*, also sold as *Nassella tenuissima*) Thriving in full sun and dry soil, this soft evergreen grass grows as a loose fountain that moves easily in the breeze. Rake the foliage with your fingers to remove tangled seed heads in late summer. Grows to 2½ feet tall and wide in zones 6–10. **CAUTION** This grass can self-seed easily in ideal conditions. Before planting, make sure it is not invasive in your area.

FINISHING TOUCH

- >

Cupid's dart (*Catananche caerulea*) An old-fashioned perennial that still earns its place in today's gardens. Drought-tolerant, deer-resistant, and an enchanting cut flower, it pushes out dozens of periwinkle flowers from silvery capsules all summer long. It often proves to be short lived but tends to self-seed in all the right places to compensate. Prefers full sun and well-drained soil. Grows to 2 feet tall and wide in zones 4–9.

- >

Flowering tobacco plant (*Nicotiana alata*) Releasing their jasmine fragrance in the late afternoon and evening, these pure white flowers are a favorite for the cutting garden. In mild winters the plants may be perennial, regrowing in spring from the root, but they are usually considered annuals. Does best in average soil in full sun or light shade. Grows to 3–4 feet tall and 2–3 feet wide.

WELCOME TO THE PARTY

SITE **SUN, PARTIAL SUN**   SOIL **RICH, WELL-DRAINED**   ZONE **10–11 OR ANNUALS**
SEASON **YEAR-ROUND OR SUMMER ONLY**

This design begs for loud music, dancing, fun food, and happy people. The hot tropical colors of the copperleaf foliage make it clear that this is not an attention-shunning wallflower. This plant is all about being the life and soul of the party as it mingles and leans splashy colored foliage over the low-key but fun-loving revelers. The broad, lush green foliage of the glory bower brings a cool respite from the action while wearing some party-perfect jewelry in the form of electric orange-red bloom clusters that glow brightly even as the lights dim.

HOW THE DESIGN GROWS

Those who live in warm climates get to enjoy this combination at its peak in winter and spring, when the glory bower blooms heaviest (although it will flower sporadically at other times of the year as well). The foliage framework ensures drama even when its floral partner is not in bloom. Cooler-climate gardeners can enjoy this dazzling duo as a summer extravaganza.

FOLIAGE FRAMEWORK

--->

Copperleaf (*Acalypha wilkesiana*) Copperleaf is a popular tropical or tender perennial that provides color throughout the year in a wide range of cultivars. Under ideal, frost-free conditions copperleaf grows as a spreading evergreen shrub with upright branches that originate near the base. This plant loves rich, fast-draining soil and partial shade to partial sun. Grows to 10 feet tall and wide in zones 10–11, but has been known to overwinter in zone 9.

FINISHING TOUCH

--->

Java glory bower (*Clerodendrum speciosissimum*) Glory bowers are grown mostly for their colorful clusters of tubular fragrant flowers that people and butterflies adore. This particular one produces soft, downy leaves and prefers full to partial sun. It is known for being aggressive in its suckering growth habit and needs definite controls to keep it in bounds. Grows to 4–6 feet tall in zones 9–11.

SILVER DUST

SITE **FULL SUN**   SOIL **WELL-DRAINED**   ZONE **3–8**   SEASON **SPRING, SUMMER**

Sweet alyssum is so familiar that gardeners often pass it over for more exciting summer annuals. Yet this simple duo shows what a little foliage bling can do. Paired with the metallic silver wormwood, the old-fashioned white alyssum is transformed from predictable to elegant. Using this low-growing variety of wormwood as a companion creates the perfect balance of textures, foliage, and flowers where taller plants could easily overwhelm the dainty blossom. With bonus points for deer resistance, low maintenance, and sweet honey fragrance, this becomes a scene worthy of any modern garden.

HOW THE DESIGN GROWS

This is an easy combination for summer months, as the alyssum will bloom continuously from spring to fall in cooler climates and all winter in warmer zones. For early spring color, plant white daffodils or crocus around the wormwood. As the wormwood emerges in mid- to late spring, it will hide the dying bulb foliage. A simple backdrop would be best to show off this monochromatic scheme; Baby Blue sawara cypress (*Chamaecyparis pisifera* 'Baby Blue'), with its curled soft foliage in a delightful shade of silver-blue, would be perfect.

FOLIAGE FRAMEWORK

- ->

Silver Mound wormwood (*Artemisia schmidtiana* 'Silver Mound') This herbaceous perennial forms a soft, feathery mound of silver that works beautifully at the front of the border. Although it produces a haze of small yellow flowers in summer, it is often best to sacrifice the blossoms and shear the foliage back in midsummer to keep it tidy. Well-drained soil in full sun is essential for wormwood to thrive. Deer resistant and drought tolerant. Grows to 2 feet tall and wide in zones 3–8.

FINISHING TOUCH

- ->

Sweet alyssum (*Lobularia maritima*) A remarkably versatile annual, growing in most regions either as an annual or a herbaceous perennial and blooming in spring–summer or fall–winter, depending on climate. The plant does not need fertilizer and tolerates drought, although it benefits from occasional watering during hot months. Use it in the landscape to edge a border or add to container gardens as an early filler. Grows to 8–12 inches tall and up to 3 feet wide, depending on variety, in zones 7–11 or enjoy as an annual.

COMBINATIONS FOR SPRING AND SUMMER

Cool Ideas for Shaded Spaces

AQUASCAPES

SITE **PARTIAL SHADE, PARTIAL SUN**   SOIL **AVERAGE**   ZONE **5–8**   SEASON **YEAR-ROUND**

Bronze accents watery shades of aqua and teal in this captivating combination. Steroidal fern fronds and hosta leaves frame a swathe of finely textured bluestar and the smaller leaves of coast leucothoe. The contrast in size and form creates a dynamic layered effect that seems to move with the ebb and flow of an invisible underwater current. This is an unlikely pairing between the shade- and moisture-loving ferns and hostas with bluestar, which requires well-drained soil and prefers full sun. With regular irrigation and dappled shade late in the day, this combination clearly thrives.

HOW THE DESIGN GROWS

By summer the coast leucothoe will be dark green and the flowering interest will switch from the bluestar to the hosta. The scene will shift significantly in autumn as the bluestar, hosta, and fern turn to gold—a startling contrast to the coast leucothoe, which will remain dark green until the following spring. In this easy-care vignette, none of these perennials need dividing.

FOLIAGE FRAMEWORK

- →

Coast leucothoe (*Leucothoe axillaris*) A deer-resistant evergreen shrub with a low, arching habit and layered branches densely clothed in leathery dark green leaves. In spring the new growth is a warm bronze shade that contrasts well with the clusters of white flowers. It prefers partial shade but will grow in more sun if well watered. Grows to 2–4 feet tall and up to 6 feet wide in zones 5–8, but you can prune to keep it smaller.

- →

Blue Angel hosta (*Hosta* 'Blue Angel') This hosta needs room to spread. Deeply quilted blue-green leaves and a mounding habit make this a popular perennial for larger shade gardens. Bait for slugs if they are a problem in your area, but this is more resistant than many. Grows to 3 feet tall and 4 feet wide in zones 3–8.

- →

Royal fern (*Osmunda regalis*) This deciduous fern thrives in moisture-retentive soil and partial or full shade. Tassel-like brown clusters of spores appear at the tips of the fronds. Grows to 3–6 feet tall and 3–4 feet wide in zones 3–9.

FINISHING TOUCH

- →

Halfway to Arkansas bluestar (*Amsonia ciliata* 'Halfway to Arkansas') An easy-care, deer-resistant herbaceous perennial grown primarily for its feathery foliage, which turns gold with purple-brown highlights in fall. The starry pale blue flowers that appear in spring are a bonus for many gardeners. Plant in large groups for the best effect. Needs full sun for best fall color but will take light shade. Grows to 2–3 feet tall and wide in zones 5–9.

UNLIKELY TRIO

SITE **PARTIAL SHADE, PARTIAL SUN**   SOIL **AVERAGE**   ZONE **7**   SEASON **YEAR-ROUND**

Three adept players make up this distinctive musical ensemble, each with a unique color and leaf shape. The dramatic and statuesque Corsican hellebore plays the string bass, its deep, resonant tone balanced by the brighter notes from a golden flute expertly fingered by a finely textured yew. Bridging these two is the virtuoso violin, beautifully played by the weigela, which weaves a rich melody and adds definition and support for its fellow artists. One would not expect these three plants to perform so well together, but if any was missing the music would be incomplete.

HOW THE DESIGN GROWS

The dwarf conifer adds interest to this scene year-round with bright golden needles emerging in spring, maturing to an attractive green. Coinciding with the fresh growth, cup-shaped light green flowers appear on the Corsican hellebore, adding a lighter note to the otherwise dull leaves. The dark foliage of weigela buffers these two evergreens, adding bold pink summer flowers to the otherwise subdued color palette. To maintain this balance of height and texture, prune the weigela after flowering and remove the hellebore flowers before they set seed.

FOLIAGE FRAMEWORK

- ->

Dwarf golden Japanese yew (*Taxus cuspidata* 'Nana Aurescens') This dwarf, compact golden conifer adds year-round color to the garden. Takes both sun and shade, although it performs best with protection from strong afternoon sun. Grows slowly to 3 feet tall and 5 feet wide in zones 4–7, but will benefit from winter mulch around the root zones in colder climates.

- ->

Dark Horse weigela (*Weigela florida* 'Dark Horse') A compact dark-leaved deciduous shrub with tubular pink flowers that hummingbirds love. The best color and flower production occurs in full sun, but it will tolerate light shade. Prune immediately after flowering if needed. Grows to 3 feet tall and wide in zones 4–8.

FINISHING TOUCH

- ->

Corsican hellebore (*Helleborus argutifolius*) An imposing evergreen perennial for the middle of the border with spiny, leathery green leaves and pale green flowers in spring. Corsican hellebore self-seeds readily, so either remove the tired blooms or be prepared to do some judicious thinning. This impressive plant will tolerate sun or partial shade and is adaptable to most soil types, providing they do not become waterlogged. Grows to 3–4 feet tall in zones 7–9; benefits from staking against snow or strong winds.

ALL THE RIGHT NOTES

SITE **PARTIAL SHADE**   SOIL **AVERAGE, MOISTURE-RETENTIVE**   ZONE **5–7**   SEASON **YEAR-ROUND**

You get the groove of cool jazz in the shade when you combine eye-catching hues and patterns. This refined color scheme starts when the barrenwort strikes the perfect chord with red leaf margins balancing the black dissected bugbane foliage. White primrose blooms lighten and brighten this shady composition, while the fresh green leaves of the hellebore help maintain a steady tempo of evergreen foliage in the melody for the year ahead.

HOW THE DESIGN GROWS

When the romantic new growth and small white flowers on the barrenwort appear in spring, it is only the beginning of this ever-changing display of foliage and flower goodness. Spring's abundance is apparent when the primrose blooms turn up the volume and beckon you to take a closer look. As they are fading, the rippled green foliage will remain until it finally wanes in the summer heat. To extend the seasonal drama for summer, add a coleus such as 'Black Prince', which features a dramatic lime margin on a black leaf. In late winter the hellebore proves its value by energetically budding up for a seasonal show of blooms that will last for weeks.

FOLIAGE FRAMEWORK

- >
Cherry Hearts barrenwort (*Epimedium sempervirens* 'Cherry Hearts') With such unique growth in spring you may think this evergreen plant is delicate, but that could not be further from the truth. Each heart-shaped leaf emerges light green with a distinctive bright pink outline and sporting a flurry of spurred pure white flowers on 12- to 15-inch-tall stems, making it an outstanding choice for partial shade. When summer arrives the margin will fade to medium green—unless this plant is in a cool, moist location, in which case the pink tones could remain visible through fall. Grows to 12–15 inches tall and 18 inches wide in zones 5–8.

- >
Pink Spike bugbane (*Actaea simplex* 'Pink Spike', also sold as *Cimicifuga simplex* 'Pink Spike') At home in moist, rich soil and bright shade, this perennial fits into any garden style, from contemporary to country. Dark tufts of delicate foliage erupt skyward with airy stems culminating in pale pink spikes of fragrant flowers from August to October that make a dazzling contrast to the foliage. This three-season plant ends with purple-brown foliage in fall. Grows to 3–6 feet tall and 1–3 feet wide in zones 4–8.

- >
Green Corsican Christmas rose (*Helleborus ×nigercors* 'Green Corsican') Nodding single cup-shaped white flowers are abundant on this late-winter-blooming perennial, which is valued for its deer and rabbit resistance as well as the slightly toothed and leathery evergreen foliage that holds up beautifully in tough garden locations. Prefers partial sun to light shade. Grows to 1–2 feet tall and wide in zones 5–8.

continued on next page

All the Right Notes continued

FINISHING TOUCH

- →

Fuji Snow Japanese woodland primrose (*Primula sieboldii* 'Fuji Snow') Emerging in midspring, this delicate-looking yet surprisingly tough perennial is quite impressive. Light green clumps of wavy, spade-shaped foliage give way to 10-inch-tall stalks of distinctive star-shaped white flower clusters that bloom for weeks in light shade. In moist soil, the leaves may remain, while in dry shade the plant will go dormant for the reminder of the year. Grows to 10 inches high and up to 2 feet wide in zones 4–7.

CASUAL SOPHISTICATION

SITE **PARTIAL SHADE, PARTIAL SUN**   SOIL **MOISTURE-RETENTIVE POTTING SOIL**   ZONE **5–8**
SEASON **YEAR-ROUND**

A sophisticated color scheme in a contemporary metallic black pot transforms this petite design into something special. A swathe of fern-like golden foliage tinged with red adds a touch of unexpected glamour to its humbler companions, while the fresh new growth on the spruce brightens the typically dark green conifer. Simple color echoes between the black pot and bugleweed foliage, as well as the repetition of golden yellow leaves with the central ray of the flowers, create a sense of connection. The modest English daisy adds some childlike fun.

HOW THE DESIGN GROWS

Spikes of royal blue bugleweed flowers will soon lend
more color to this container design, as all three flowering
perennials bloom for several weeks. When the spent
flowers are removed in late spring, you may also need to
trim the bugleweed foliage to keep it in check. The only
limiting factor to long-term enjoyment of this combination is the size of the container, as the plants will outgrow
their allotted space within twelve months. However, you
can transplant each component to the landscape or to a
larger pot and enjoy it for many years.

FOLIAGE FRAMEWORK

Dwarf Alberta spruce (*Picea glauca* 'Conica') Like a
miniature Christmas tree, this very slow-growing evergreen
conifer makes a perfect container specimen or landscape plant.
Thrives in full sun or partial shade. Grows to 6–8 feet tall and
4–5 feet wide in zones 2–8.

Berry Exciting corydalis (*Corydalis* 'Berry Exciting') This colorful
herbaceous perennial will wake up the shade garden with its fern-like
golden foliage. Fragrant lavender flowers bloom in spring, but the plant
is sterile, so self-seeding is not a concern. Use in containers or as a
ground cover, where it will thrive in moisture-retentive soil. Grows to
12 inches high and 18 inches wide in zones 5–8.

- →

Catlin's Giant bugleweed (*Ajuga reptans* 'Catlin's Giant') The dark foliage of this spreading ground cover is reason enough to use it, but the spikes of vivid blue flowers in spring make this garden workhorse especially interesting. An evergreen or semi-evergreen perennial, it thrives in moist soil and partial shade, although it will tolerate sunnier conditions if you water it well. Grows to 8 inches tall in zones 4–8; spreads to form extensive clumps that are easy to control.

FINISHING TOUCH

- →

Galaxy Red English daisy (*Bellis perennis* 'Galaxy Red') A charming old-fashioned perennial for spring color, this compact variety blooms with distinctive semi-double daisy-type flowers in sun or partial shade. Remove spent flowers to extend the bloom period. Grows to 8 inches tall and wide in zones 4–8.

ABSTRACT ART

SITE **PARTIAL SHADE**   SOIL **AVERAGE, MOISTURE-RETENTIVE**   ZONE **4–8**
SEASON **SPRING THROUGH FALL**

With a masterly sweep of a garden artist's brush, this designer uses the abstract foliage of Painter's Palette Virginia knotweed to set the theme, framing the wild splashes and stripes with the bold blue leaves of a hosta. Layered onto this, the crimson flowers of the masterwort appear to leap from the canvas, echoing and highlighting the red tones of the knotweed foliage.

HOW THE DESIGN GROWS

This trio will fill the shade garden with color and texture from spring until fall. The hosta and Virginia knotweed foliage ensure a colorful foundation upon which you can showcase the fall flowers. The red blooms of the masterwort will feature in both spring and fall vignettes, the hosta will add white summer flowers, and in fall the Virginia knotweed will add to the riot of color. A planting of variegated boxwood behind the hosta would add winter interest while repeating the primary colors of the Virginia knotweed. To maintain this balance of foliage and flowers, you may have to prune some self-seeded perennials each spring.

FOLIAGE FRAMEWORK

Painter's Palette Virginia knotweed (*Persicaria virginiana* 'Painter's Palette', also sold as *Tovara virginiana* 'Painter's Palette') A colorful herbaceous perennial for the shade garden. The foliage is splashed irregularly with green and cream, and most leaves have a deep red chevron. Painter's Palette forms a spreading mound of foliage and produces an abundance of unusual red flowers on wiry stems in midsummer. This may spread aggressively by seed and runners in moist soil, so site with care. Grows to 2 feet tall and wide in zones 4–8.

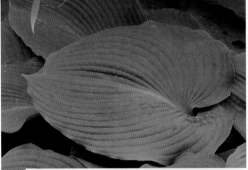

Blue Angel hosta (*Hosta* 'Blue Angel') Heavily textured blue leaves make this hosta a favorite among gardeners, but less so with slugs. Grows to 3 feet tall and 4 feet wide in zones 3–8, with tall spikes of flowers in summer that attract hummingbirds.

FINISHING TOUCH

Ruby Wedding masterwort (*Astrantia major* 'Ruby Wedding') Deep red flowers accented with white blooms in spring and often again in fall. The flowers last an exceptionally long time and are excellent for both cutting and drying. This herbaceous perennial does best in partial shade and moisture-retentive soil. Grows to 2 feet tall and wide in zones 3–9.

TROPICAL STAYCATION

SITE PARTIAL SHADE   **SOIL** AVERAGE   **ZONE** 9–11 OR ANNUALS   **SEASON** SUMMER

Whether you live in Miami or Michigan, you can get the tropical look with houseplants that love going outside for a summer vacation. A red banana sets the scene, adds instant height, and provides additional shade beneath its huge paddle leaves. Exotic crotons introduce new textures and striking crayon-box colors of yellow, red, orange, and green. For an unapologetic look-at-me punch, you cannot do better than the bright red anthurium. And just when you think you have sensory overload, add fragrant angel's trumpet to the mix. This vacation goes on and on.

HOW THE DESIGN GROWS

Live for the moment with this foliage-and-flowers extravaganza. Put aside your winter worries and focus on memories of flamboyant summer colors. Don't worry about deadheading the angel's trumpet, as the seed heads are equally decorative—just grab your sunglasses and enjoy the show. When temperatures begin to dip in fall, you can bring most of these plants indoors.

FOLIAGE FRAMEWORK

------------------------------ →

Red Abyssinian banana (*Ensete ventricosum* 'Maurelii') This outstanding ornamental banana has foliage flushed with burgundy with dark red midribs, with a deeper color in younger leaves and conditions with more light. May suffer some leaf scorch in full sun, so partial sun to partial shade is ideal, and be sure to protect from strong winds. Grows to 10 feet tall and wide in zones 9–11; is twice as big in the tropics.

------------------------------ →

Petra croton (*Codiaeum variegatum* 'Petra') Waxy, vividly variegated foliage with splashes of green, gold, red, and orange make this a colorful choice for the home, summer container, or shade garden. Best grown in partial shade to avoid leaf scorch and maintain vibrancy. Grows to 3 feet tall and wide in zones 10–11 or enjoy as a houseplant or summer annual.

------------------------------ →

Zanzibar croton (*Codiaeum variegatum* 'Zanzibar') A narrow-leaved cultivar of croton that resembles a colorful grass and has a somewhat straggly mounding habit. Fabulous in shade containers and hanging baskets. Grows up to 2 feet tall and wide in zones 10–11 or enjoy as an annual.

continued on next page

Tropical Staycation continued

FINISHING TOUCH

- →

Dakota anthurium (*Anthurium andraeanum* 'Dakota')
Grown for its glossy red flowers (actually a spathe or type of
bract) with distinctive yellow spadix, this popular houseplant is a bold addition to shade gardens and containers in
summer. Grows to 18 inches tall and wide in zones 10–11 or
enjoy as an annual.

- →

Ballerina Purple angel's trumpet (*Datura metel* 'Ballerina
Purple') Releasing their powerful fragrance at night, the ruffled
purple-and-white flowers resemble an elongated trumpet, with
6- to 8-inch-long upward-facing blooms. This compact perennial is
perfect for summer containers and landscapes, and prefers full sun
(in this scene it is placed beyond the shade cast by the banana).
Grows to 3–4 feet tall and wide in zones 9–11 or enjoy as an annual.
CAUTION All parts of this plant are highly toxic, so site with care.

LEMON DROP MARTINI

SITE **PARTIAL SHADE**   SOIL **AVERAGE, MOISTURE-RETENTIVE**   ZONE **6–8**   SEASON **YEAR-ROUND**

Like an expertly blended cocktail, this citrusy mix has the perfect ratio of sweet and sour. The Lunar Glow bergenia was clearly the inspiration, with large leathery leaves in yellow and green. The Japanese forest grass and golden bleeding heart provide additional lemon flavor, balanced by a squeeze of zesty lime hosta, fern, and toad lily. Top it all off with a decorative pink flower or two and you have a designer cocktail that is sure to become a spring favorite.

Lemon Drop Martini continued

HOW THE DESIGN GROWS

Spring through fall offers the most exciting color medley, with both the bleeding heart and bergenia adding pink flowers to the cocktail. In winter the evergreen bergenia will turn burgundy, introducing a new hue into the garden when the perennials are dormant. Underplanting the grass and toad lily with snowdrops would be a lovely way to add contrast to the winter scene, and they would perform well in this partially shady location. As the strappy bulb foliage dies back, the emerging perennials will quickly hide them from view. For ongoing care, you may have to thin out the bergenia occasionally to stop it from overwhelming more delicate plants, but otherwise the perennials should be able to blend easily for many years.

FOLIAGE FRAMEWORK

- →

Dre's Dagger lady fern (*Athyrium filix-femina* 'Dre's Dagger') This dwarf form of the deciduous lady fern has lacy foliage and thrives in moist woodlands in partial or full shade. Grows to 18 inches tall and wide in zones 4–8. Crested lady fern (*A. filix-femina* 'Vernoniae Cristatum') is a reliable performer and may be easier to find.

- →

Hosta (*Hosta* species) While the name of this hosta has been forgotten, any of the taller solid green or green-blue varieties would work well, like Miss American Pie or Krossa Regal. Most hostas prefer moist and semi-shaded conditions, will need baiting for slugs, and are hardy in zones 3–9.

Stripe It Rich variegated Japanese forest grass
(*Hakonechloa macra* 'Stripe it Rich') This herbaceous grass cascades into a soft yellow waterfall, each golden blade lightly striped with white. Grows to 10 inches tall and 20 inches wide in zones 6–9.

Gilt Edge toad lily (*Tricyrtis hirta* 'Gilt Edge') An easy herbaceous perennial for the shade garden. The green leaves are edged with gold, and in midsummer freckled purple flowers appear. Grows to 2 feet tall and 12 inches wide in zones 5–9.

FINISHING TOUCH

Lunar Glow bergenia (*Bergenia* 'Lunar Glow') This evergreen perennial is worth looking for. The new foliage opens creamy yellow, matures to green, and turns burgundy in winter, often resulting in a multicolored effect. Fat spikes of pink flowers appear in spring. Grows to 12 inches tall and 18 inches wide in zones 4–9.

Gold Heart bleeding heart (*Dicentra spectabilis* 'Gold Heart') This herbaceous perennial is a colorful addition to the shade garden, with apricot-pink stems, pure gold leaves, and rose-pink spring flowers. Grows to 2–3 feet tall and wide in zones 3–9.

CONNECT THE DOTS

SITE **PARTIAL SHADE, PARTIAL SUN**   SOIL **AVERAGE**   ZONE **5–8**   SEASON **SPRING THROUGH FALL**

Like a child's dot-to-dot puzzle, the blue star creeper connects every plant along the shaded pathway, from the towering purple smoke bush, bold-leaved hosta, and wispy willow to the tiny ferns. Without this linking thread, the shrubs and perennials could appear as attractive specimens but isolated from one another. But as the tightly woven carpet of blue star creeper meanders between flagstones, the plant collection is united and the journey heightened as visitors are encouraged to stroll leisurely along the path and explore.

HOW THE DESIGN GROWS

From spring until fall this garden path will be a delight of foliage and flowers, unified by the diminutive blue star creeper. In fall the perennials will become dormant and deciduous shrubs will lose their foliage, leaving just the semi-evergreen ground cover to add color during the winter. Interspersing the perennials with some evergreen sweetbox (*Sarcococca ruscifolia*) would add fragrance in January and glossy green leaves year-round.

FOLIAGE FRAMEWORK

- >

Smoke bush (*Cotinus coggygria*) Trained over many years to grow as a single-trunked tree, this is most likely a seedling of Royal Purple. Striking purple foliage will turn scarlet in fall, while smoky flower plumes add an ethereal touch in summer. Prefers full sun to partial shade. Grows to 10–15 feet tall and wide in zones 5–9, but you can prune to keep it smaller.

- >

Gold Standard hosta (*Hosta* 'Gold Standard') Hand-size richly textured leaves and bold variegation make this a popular addition to the shade garden. Leaf centers emerge light green in spring, turning progressively gold throughout the summer. In summer this herbaceous perennial mound produces tall spikes of lavender flowers that attract hummingbirds. Grows to 3 feet tall and wide in zones 3–8.

- >

Dwarf blue arctic willow (*Salix purpurea* 'Nana') Featuring slender blue stems and very narrow blue-green leaves, this deciduous shrub thrives in wet soil. Winter catkins add interest before the new leaves appear. Grows to 5 feet tall in zones 4–8, but is best pruned shorter to keep a compact form.

FINISHING TOUCH

- >

Blue star creeper (*Isotoma fluviatilis*) Preferring moisture-retentive soil and partial sun, this fast-growing ground cover will quickly carpet the ground with a mat of tiny green leaves. It is ideal for edging ponds and pathways. Starry light blue flowers appear in early summer, often with sporadic repeat bloom. This vigorous perennial may be evergreen or semi-evergreen. Grows to 2 inches high in zones 5–9.

PETITE BEAUTY

SITE **PARTIAL SHADE, PARTIAL SUN**   SOIL **AVERAGE**   ZONE **6–9**   SEASON **YEAR-ROUND**

How do you enhance an already beautiful flowering shrub? Frame it with foliage to extend the interest through the year and highlight it when in full bloom. The soft pink stems and new growth on the leucothoe are the ideal shade to echo the hydrangea flowers, while the smaller-leaved azalea emphasizes the shrub's bolder foliage. This is a big-look combination for even small gardens, given that the hydrangea is a compact variety, the azalea is a dwarf ground cover, and the leucothoe is easily pruned for shape and size.

HOW THE DESIGN GROWS

Planted this close together the leucothoe will need regular trimming to allow the hydrangea room to grow, but that is easy to do. As the hydrangea matures it will assert itself between the taller shrub and ground cover. During the winter the leucothoe will turn deep red, followed in spring by white flowers. This is when the azalea will also begin to bloom with its primary flush of orange-red flowers.

FOLIAGE FRAMEWORK

- →

Rainbow leucothoe (*Leucothoe fontanesiana* 'Rainbow') This evergreen arching shrub has waxy leaves splashed with creamy yellow, pink, and green, with deep red added to the mix in winter and creamy flowers in spring. Prefers partial shade to full shade, but can take more sun in moisture-retentive soil. Grows to a 5-foot mound in zones 5–9, but you can prune to keep it smaller.

- →

Flame Creeper azalea (*Rhododendron* 'Flame Creeper') This dwarf evergreen azalea has more of a ground cover habit than most. Red-orange flowers pop up in spring and continue to appear sporadically through summer and fall, set off nicely by the small glossy green leaves. Does best in partial shade and acidic, moisture-retentive soil. Grows to 12 inches tall and 2–3 feet wide in zones 6–9.

FINISHING TOUCH

- →

Cityline Paris hydrangea (*Hydrangea macrophylla* 'Cityline Paris') This petite shrub still packs a lot of color and does not need pruning. Large mophead-type flowers open fuchsia, fade to duskier tones, and finally soften to light green, giving an overall multihued effect to the bush. Use this in a container or as part of a mixed border in the landscape. Prefers partial shade to partial sun. Grows to 3 feet tall and wide in zones 5–9.

SHARING THE SPOTLIGHT

SITE **SHADE, PARTIAL SHADE**   SOIL **AVERAGE**   ZONE **6–8**   SEASON **YEAR-ROUND**

Take one seemingly pedestrian plant like the robust western sword fern, add the star power of black mondo grass and a piece of glass art, and this ensemble of players is automatically elevated in sophistication. The delicate bronze fiddleheads of the fern are worthy of adoration for the geometric details alone, while the nearly black grass garners applause for its stout yet graceful growth and strong color. Electric blue reflective glass highlights each actor to spotlight status for their dynamic individual performances as well as what makes them shine as a trio.

HOW THE DESIGN GROWS

A captivating combination like this one is ready for the paparazzi any time of the year, giving a slightly different look depending on the season. Once the fern has unfurled in spring to reveal tall verdant fronds, it turns to deep green for summer—just as the mondo grass nestled at its base begins to bloom. The mirror-like blue orb is superb for reflecting the perfectly shiny black berries that follow the flowers on the mondo grass in late summer and fall. For winter interest, both the fern and mondo grass are evergreen performers. If you live in a mild climate, leave the glass out to provide enjoyment on cool frosty days.

FOLIAGE FRAMEWORK

– →

Western sword fern (*Polystichum munitum*) Native to the Western United States, this reliable and texturally interesting fern has lush bright green spring growth that turns dark and leathery in summer. To keep it looking tidy, prune off winter-damaged fronds in early spring before new growth appears. This easy plant is suited to shady woodland settings, but once established it will tolerate dry soils under large trees. Grows to 4 feet tall and wide in zones 5–9.

– →

Black mondo grass (*Ophiopogon planiscapus* 'Nigrescens') Dense purple-black tufts of evergreen foliage are low growing and perfect for the front of the border or containers. Bell-shaped lavender flowers turn into glossy black berries in fall. This slow-spreading grass does well in partial to full shade, but tolerates more sun with consistent watering. Grows to 5–6 inches tall and wide in zones 6–10.

FINISHING TOUCH

– →

Gazing balls are frequently placed on pedestals in the garden so they are at an easier height for viewing, but when nestled among the foliage they beckon you to bend down and admire the reflections. The electric blue color of this gazing ball is particularly interesting paired with the striking black mondo grass in lower light.

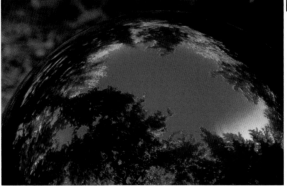

SPRING FEVER

SITE **PARTIAL SHADE, SHADE**   SOIL **AVERAGE, MOISTURE-RETENTIVE**   ZONE **4–8**
SEASON **YEAR-ROUND**

Celebrate spring with some bright, juicy foliage to light up your shade garden. Woven like a patch-work quilt, these plants fuse together effortlessly, yet each leaf shape remains distinct. The color echo between the fiery coral bells and the pink flowers of the bleeding heart with the repetition of golden foliage shows a well-thought-out design with great attention to detail. Introducing an unexpected pop of blue adds the fun factor. This combination of bold color and big textures makes the heart race a little faster—it must be spring fever.

HOW THE DESIGN GROWS

Although this is a combination of perennials, the hellebore and foamy bells are evergreen. Only the bleeding heart and corydalis will die down for the winter; underplanting these with daffodils will bridge that gap in early spring. Fire Alarm heuchera has not been a reliable winter survivor in the Pacific Northwestern United States; Fire Chief promises to be a better option for this climate. Over time the clumps of corydalis, bleeding heart, and hellebore will continue to expand but intermingle easily, without the need for dividing and replanting.

FOLIAGE FRAMEWORK

- →
Fire Alarm coral bells (*Heuchera* 'Fire Alarm') This fiery hybrid will ignite your containers and gardens. The large, smooth leaves transition through shades of deepest mahogany to bright red during the year. The most vivid colors appear in spring, when tall stems of airy white flowers add to the spectacle. Evergreen in milder climates, this showstopper is still worth growing for three-season interest elsewhere. Prefers partial shade. Grows to 14 inches tall and wide in zones 4–9.

- →
Solar Power foamy bells (*Heucherella* 'Solar Power') Bright yellow leaves are splashed with deep red, the perfect marriage of colors for this design. In the north this evergreen perennial does well in full sun, but it prefers afternoon shade in hotter climates. Grows to 12 inches tall and 20 inches wide in zones 4–9.

FINISHING TOUCH

- →
Golden Lotus hellebore (*Helleborus* ×*hybridus* 'Golden Lotus') The evergreen foliage and pale frilled flowers add a soothing note to the combination. Each double flower may be a slightly different shade of yellow; some have a pink picotee edge and back. Like most hellebore the blooms fade to a soft green. Grows to 12 inches tall and 2 feet wide in zones 5–8.

continued on next page

Spring Fever continued

Gold Heart bleeding heart (*Dicentra spectabilis* 'Gold Heart') The fern-like golden foliage of this herbaceous perennial acts as a spotlight in the shade garden. Tall arching stems emerge in spring, from which rows of perfect pink heart-shaped flowers dangle. Bleeding heart will grow in dry shade, but more moisture-retentive soil will encourage healthier and longer-lasting foliage. Grows to 2 feet tall and 3 feet wide in zones 4–8.

China Blue corydalis (*Corydalis* 'China Blue') The blue-toned leaves of this herbaceous perennial highlight the abundant, fragrant light blue flowers that appear in spring and sometimes in fall. Appreciates moisture-retentive soil. Grows to 12 inches tall and 8 inches wide in zones 5–8.

COLOR CAROUSEL

SITE **PARTIAL SHADE, PARTIAL SUN**   SOIL **AVERAGE**   ZONE **6–8**   SEASON **YEAR-ROUND**

A delightful combination for dappled shade, this design will offer an ever-changing display of colorful foliage, flowers, and berries, each season introducing a new blend. The warm burnished bronze coral bells repeats the form and color of the distant cascading maple, while tall spikes of foxglove-like orange flowers punctuate the undulating golden ground cover and echo the vertical lines of the iris. Together they allow for seasonal interest throughout the year.

Color Carousel continued

HOW THE DESIGN GROWS

Spring foliage colors in this woodland range from the bright orange-red maple and purple coral bells to the golden snowberry, highlighted by bright yellow iris blooms. By summer the colors have matured to richer shades that frame the glowing digiplexis flowers, which appear over several months. Fall sees a return to more brilliant crimson, orange, and gold as the deciduous shrubs prepare for their last hurrah, accented with metallic pink berries on the snowberry. Only the coral bells will provide reliable winter foliage interest as the garden waits for the next merry-go-round ride to begin.

FOLIAGE FRAMEWORK

--→

Blade of Sun snowberry (*Symphoricarpos chenaultii* 'Blade of Sun') An outstanding deciduous ground cover for the shade garden with wide-spreading branches that form dense layers of golden foliage. Emerging brilliant yellow, the color fades to chartreuse in summer and in heavier shade, returning to gold in fall when metallic pink berries make the color even more exciting. Grows to 1–2 feet tall and 3 feet wide in zones 4–9, but branches may root as they touch the ground, encouraging an ever-expanding spread.

--→

Mahogany coral bells (*Heuchera* 'Mahogany') Flushed with shades ranging from dark brown to light and changing with the seasons, this foliage will always add a rich luster to combinations. Cream-colored summer flowers add to the display and attract hummingbirds. This evergreen perennial tolerates full sun but does best in partial shade to partial sun. Grows to 8 inches tall and 14 inches wide in zones 4–9.

Orangeola Japanese maple (*Acer palmatum* 'Orangeola')
Noted for its bright orange-red spring growth and fiery colors
in fall, the deeply dissected foliage of this maple forms a
cascading mound and continues to erupt with bright color throughout
the summer. Prefers full sun to partial shade. Grows to 8 feet tall and 7
feet wide in zones 6–9.

Yellow flag iris (*Iris pseudacorus*) Thriving in wetlands, shallow
water, or moisture-retentive soil, this rhizomatous semi-evergreen
perennial blooms with yellow flowers in spring followed by fat glossy
seed capsules. Spreads easily, so you may need to thin annually. Prefers
full sun to partial shade. Grows to 4–6 feet tall in zones 4–8. **CAUTION**
This is classed as a noxious weed in many areas, so consult your local
extension office before planting.

FINISHING TOUCH

Illumination Flame digiplexis (*Digiplexis*
'Illumination Flame') A cross between a foxglove and
its Canary Island cousin, this new introduction has
been causing quite a stir in the gardening world.
Vibrant orange and fuchsia-pink tubular flowers are
sterile, so instead of trying to set seed the plant just
keeps on blooming throughout the summer. Seems to
do best in partial sun to partial shade, but is adaptable
to full sun if you water it well. Grows to 3 feet tall and
2 feet wide in zones 8–10, but you will still want this as
a colorful annual if you live in a cooler climate.

THE NEW BLACK

SITE **SUN, PARTIAL SUN**   SOIL **AVERAGE**   ZONE **5–9**   SEASON **SPRING THROUGH FALL**

Did you hear? Green is the new black—specifically shades of lime or chartreuse because they work so well with everything. In this design, the citrus tones of the Japanese forest grass and lacy golden feverfew are nearly matched in color, although not in texture, and provide a backdrop for the sweet white feverfew daisy flowers. The blue-green foliage of the lady's mantle contributes some contrast and a bit of weight to this fluffy combination.

HOW THE DESIGN GROWS

The emergence of the radiant foliage on the feverfew is a beacon of light in the shade garden right when we need those buoyant and energetic colors to sparkle for spring and summer. As the summer temperatures rise, the lady's mantle sets frothy sprays of chartreuse blossoms. When those blooms fade, the feverfew daisies open for their time in the sun, sparkling from summer through fall.

FOLIAGE FRAMEWORK

- ->

Lady's mantle (*Alchemilla mollis*) Velvety blue-green leaves on this enchanting old-fashioned perennial hold water droplets that sparkle like tiny jewels. Clusters of tiny pale yellow flowers are held above the summer foliage, but shear them off to prevent self-seeding. Happy in full sun to partial shade. Grows to 12 inches tall and 2 feet wide in zones 4–9.

- ->

All Gold Japanese forest grass (*Hakonechloa macra* 'All Gold') A graceful clumping ground cover grass with bold chartreuse color and the appearance of bamboo. This hardy perennial does well in partial shade to partial sun and is ideal in containers or as a color accent in borders. Grows to 2 feet tall and wide in zones 4–9.

FINISHING TOUCH

- ->

Golden feverfew (*Tanacetum parthenium* 'Aureum') Aromatic golden foliage on this herbaceous perennial shines brightest in full sun but also does well in partial shade. In summer, small white daisies add sparkle, but deadhead them if you want to avoid self-seeding. Grows to 2 feet tall and wide in zones 5–9.

THE MAGPIE EFFECT

SITE **SHADE, PARTIAL SHADE**   SOIL **AVERAGE**   ZONE **6–8**   SEASON **YEAR-ROUND**

Transform a shady spot under towering evergreens by incorporating shiny surfaces and pale colors. This glossy ivory urn sits in a spot where tree roots make it challenging to grow many plants. In the more hospitable ground in front of the container are layered foliage plants that either reflect the light (Hart's-tongue fern) or have a bright color (silver Jack Frost Siberian bugloss). A complex tapestry of interesting leaf shapes, colors, and patterns has been woven into a lush design. Just like magpies, we are naturally drawn to shiny objects, and this carefully orchestrated vignette is irresistible.

HOW THE DESIGN GROWS

Most of these plants are herbaceous perennials, so in winter there will be very limited foliage interest around the urn. However, this part of the garden is rarely visited in the colder months, so it can be allowed to rest. A mass planting of Siberian squill (*Scilla siberica*) would be a lovely way to add early spring interest, as the blue or white flowers can naturalize in the shady conditions between the hostas and ferns.

FOLIAGE FRAMEWORK

- ->

Western coltsfoot (*Petasites palmatus*) Not for the faint of heart, this large-leafed shade-loving perennial can quickly become invasive in moist soil. Careful monitoring and a barrier of drain rock maintain the status quo in this garden, but you may wish to substitute Rodger's flower (*Rodgersia aesculifolia*). This plant flowers in spring with leaves that may be 12 inches in diameter. Grows to 2 feet tall and 3 feet wide in zones 6–10.

- ->

Hart's-tongue fern (*Asplenium scolopendrium*) The broad, strap-like fronds are bright green and appear polished to a rich sheen. On the undersides the red-brown spores create a distinctive striped pattern. Prefers shade or partial shade. Grows to 20 inches tall and wide in zones 6–9.

- ->

Jack Frost Siberian bugloss (*Brunnera macrophylla* 'Jack Frost') One of the first perennials to leaf out in spring and one of the last to go dormant, this earns its place in the shade garden. This drought-tolerant, deer-resistant plant has heart-shaped leaves overlaid with an intricate silver netting, and in spring forget-me-not–type flowers add to the display. Grows to 12 inches tall and 18 inches wide in zones 3–8.

continued on next page

Otto Luyken English laurel (*Prunus laurocerasus* 'Otto Luyken') This lowgrowing evergreen shrub has glossy deep green leaves and fragrant white flowers in spring. Prefers full sun to partial shade. Grows to 3 feet high and 6 feet wide in zones 6–9, but you can prune to keep it smaller.

Francee hosta (*Hosta* 'Francee') A compact mound of bold green-and-white variegated leaves adds sparkle to the shade garden. Grows to 2 feet tall and 4 feet wide in zones 4–8.

Frances Williams hosta (*Hosta sieboldiana* 'Frances Williams') Classic heart-shaped leaves with green-and-gold variegation form a large mound. Grows to 2 feet tall and 5 feet wide in zones 3–8.

Jack-in-the-pulpit (*Arisaema* species) The exact identity of this herbaceous woodland bulb is uncertain, but it appears to be Himalayan Jack-in-the-pulpit (*A. consanguineum*), which flowers in June with unusual hooded blooms sometimes followed by orange-red berries. The palmate foliage is attractive from spring until fall. Grows to 3 feet tall and 12 inches wide in zones 5–9.

Japanese painted fern (*Athyrium niponicum* var. *pictum*) A true standout in the woodland garden, the delicate feathery foliage appears to be gilded with silver, while the stem and veins are typically burgundy. Grows to 18 inches tall and wide in zones 4–9.

Solomon's seal (*Polygonatum* ×*hybridum*) Use this perennial to add height to the shade garden. In late spring, dangling pairs of creamy white flowers hang from the arching stems. Drought tolerant and deer resistant. Grows to 4 feet tall and 3 feet wide in zones 3–8.

FINISHING TOUCH

Ivory urn An oversize curvaceous vessel with a high gloss finish makes a statement and distracts the eye from the challenging area behind it, where even weeds struggle to grow.

A PLUM OPPORTUNITY

SITE **PARTIAL SHADE, PARTIAL SUN**   SOIL **AVERAGE**   ZONE **7–8**   SEASON **YEAR-ROUND**

While the evergreen variegated hemlock provides year-round color and structure, the golden leaves of the fuchsia really steal the foliage show and light up this shady border. Sandwiched between the two, the purple flowers of the dwarf daylily introduce a new color, while their yellow throats echo the color of the fuchsia leaves. Completing the scene, the hardy fuchsia produces dangling magenta and purple blooms from midsummer until fall, attracting hummingbirds and linking back to the color of the daylilies. Using golden foliage to brighten shade gardens is a well-known designer trick, but this combination makes the most of an opportunity to incorporate some warm violet tones as well.

HOW THE DESIGN GROWS

With its repeat-blooming habit, the daylily will continue to contribute colorful flowers to this scene until autumn, at which time it typically goes dormant (although in mild winters it can remain evergreen). The fuchsia is deciduous, so only the hemlock will provide reliable color and interest in winter. The addition of a carpet of evergreen black mondo grass (*Ophiopogon planiscapus* 'Nigrescens') would extend this, and would also look especially striking against the fuchsia foliage when it re-emerges in spring.

FOLIAGE FRAMEWORK

- ->

Hardy fuchsia (*Fuchsia genii*) This deciduous shrub makes a bold statement with its golden foliage and pendulous magenta and purple flowers. Protect from hot afternoon sun to prevent leaf scorch and wait until all danger of frost has passed before pruning in spring. Grows to 4 feet tall and wide in zones 7–9.

- ->

Gentsch White Canadian hemlock (*Tsuga canadensis* 'Gentsch White') A special conifer for partial sun to partial shade with a layered, lacy habit and distinctive white tips on the new growth. This evergreen prefers regular watering, especially in summer. Grows to 4 feet tall and wide or more in zones 3–8, but you can prune to keep it more compact, which will also improve the coloring.

FINISHING TOUCH

- ->

Little Grapette daylily (*Hemerocallis* 'Little Grapette') Purple flowers with distinctive golden throats appear throughout the summer on 20-inch-tall stems held high above the grass-like foliage. While naturally blooming in several waves, remove old flowers and stalks to encourage reblooming. This low-maintenance perennial may be evergreen in mild winters and prefers full sun to partial shade. Grows to 18 inches wide in zones 4–10; you can divide easily.

THE BELLS OF SPRING

SITE **PARTIAL SHADE, PARTIAL SUN**   SOIL **AVERAGE**   ZONE **5–8**   SEASON **YEAR-ROUND**

The garden is awake and ready for action. Dangling creamy white flowers and new red-brown foliage on the andromeda hang over heart-shaped barrenwort leaves and blades of moor grass as they push out supple new growth for the year. The unique bronze-and-green veining on the barrenwort foliage surges up to obscure the fading yellow blooms that were the stars of this trio in early spring, while the fluffy grass sends up spiky new growth in complementary buttery tones that unite them all.

HOW THE DESIGN GROWS

Midspring warmth energizes this scene into a new growth frenzy when rust-colored leaves stand out against the warm white of the andromeda flowers, staying for weeks on end while the young leaves of the barrenwort and moor grass show off their new adolescent colors. Quieting down for the warmer months, all but the moor grass turn to rich summer green. Adding the spiky zing of Red Sentinel Japanese astilbe (*Astilbe japonica* 'Red Sentinel') would bring a bold splash of summer color and an extra layer of textural foliage interest.

FOLIAGE FRAMEWORK

- →

Sulphureum barrenwort (*Epimedium versicolor* 'Sulphureum')
Before new heart-shaped foliage emerges with defined bronze markings, lovely spurred yellow flowers top stems reaching 8–12 inches tall. Valued for its evergreen foliage, this ground cover is perfect at the border's edge in partial to full shade, or in woodland areas. Rabbits and deer do not enjoy this menu item. Grows to 12 inches tall and 2 feet wide in zones 5–9.

- →

Variegated purple moor grass (*Molinia caerulea* 'Variegata')
Striped blades of creamy yellow-and-green grass form a soft, arching mound with purple seed heads in summer. In the summer breeze, this grass provides lovely movement in the garden and looks wonderful through the fall before you cut it back for winter. Prefers full or partial sun and average soil. Grows to 3 feet tall and 2 feet wide in zones 4–9.

FINISHING TOUCH

- →

Mountain Fire andromeda (*Pieris japonica* 'Mountain Fire')
The evergreen foliage of this shrub shows off bright red new growth in late winter that fades to mahogany and then chestnut tones just as fragrant chains of bell-shaped creamy white blooms appear in abundance in midspring. In summer, leaves turn leathery deep green and black berries form where flower clusters once hung. Prefers partial shade. Grows to 6–8 feet tall and 8–10 feet wide in zones 5–8.

BLUES WITH A FEELING

SITE SHADE, PARTIAL SHADE   **SOIL** AVERAGE, MOISTURE-RETENTIVE   **ZONE** 5–8
SEASON SUMMER THROUGH FALL

Like the jazzy blues standard recorded in 1953 by Little Walter, "Blues with a Feeling" is the perfect description for this classic hosta-and-hydrangea combo with a rhythm-and-blues twist. The colossal, nearly cerulean blue hosta leaves are the undeniable drumbeat for the looser yet still dazzling harmonica played by the lacecap hydrangea with its wide spectrum of colors. This mix of hues will set just the right tone for sitting back with a New Orleans–style cocktail and listening to the blues.

HOW THE DESIGN GROWS

Early summer warmth encourages the gargantuan blue hosta leaves to spread out in full glory while the hydrangea begins to bud up. As summer gains momentum, the hydrangea blooms begin to show color on the sterile inner flowers as well as the outer petioles. While pale at first, the hue deepens every week to peak in high summer, with soft jewel tones ranging from pink and sapphire to amethyst. Holding these colors for weeks, they begin to fade in autumn to mellow to more classical notes. Fall is the perfect time to add some jazzy white Ice Follies daffodils (*Narcissus* 'Ice Follies') for a long-blooming opening act in spring.

FOLIAGE FRAMEWORK

- ->

Blue Angel hosta (*Hosta* 'Blue Angel') This blue-green hosta is an attention-getter, with ribbed leaves reaching 16 inches across. Thankfully, it is one of the more slug-resistant varieties, as well as a heavy bloomer from spring to early summer, producing bouquets of white flowers that hummingbirds adore. This unique plant tolerates dry shade, although most prefer consistent moisture. Grows to 3 feet tall and 4 feet wide in zones 3–8.

FINISHING TOUCH

- ->

Pink lacecap hydrangea (*Hydrangea macrophylla* var. *normalis*) This is a deceptively hardy large-scale landscape shrub. While the specific cultivar shown here is not known, Blue Wave would work beautifully as an alternative choice to the pink, although the soil pH in your location will affect the final color. Deep and thorough watering at about 1 inch per week will keep it fresh and colorful. Grows to 6 feet tall and wide in zones 5–9.

DOUBLE DUTY

SITE **SHADE, PARTIAL SHADE**   SOIL **WET, MOISTURE-RETENTIVE**   ZONE **7–8**
SEASON **SPRING THROUGH FALL**

There are great foliage plants and there are great flowering plants. There are also some plants that are both, and in this combination two out of the three ingredients provide the foliage framework *and* add the finishing touch with a dazzling seasonal floral display. The large brown leaves of Othello leopard plant add drama to the finer blades of the yellow sedge, while the deep golden daisies echo its color. In the background the muted gray-and-cream variegated leaves of a hardy fuchsia bridge the two leaf textures. Pendulous vivid magenta and purple flowers dangle from the fuchsia branches in summer and fall, adding a fresh blast of color and introducing a delicate flower shape to balance the rather disheveled, gaudy daisies. Even without any flowers this trio works well together, but the blooms enhance the combination and are more beautiful because of the backdrop.

HOW THE DESIGN GROWS

Although both the sedge and fuchsia are semi-evergreen, they can look rather tired by spring. To improve winter interest, plant a cluster of prickly heath (*Pernettya mucronata*) to one side, ideally including one male to every three female plants. These evergreen shrubs have bright winter berries in red, pink, or white. The leopard plant will continue to spread and may eventually need to be divided, while the sedge will just need a quick trim after a hard winter to tidy up the foliage.

FOLIAGE FRAMEWORK

- ->

Bowles' golden sedge (*Carex elata* 'Aurea') This short, mounding fountain of semi-evergreen golden blades adds a bright note to shady areas. The grass-like plant needs moist soil and protection from afternoon sun. Grows to 2 feet tall and wide in zones 5–9.

FINISHING TOUCH

- ->

Othello leopard plant (*Ligularia dentata* 'Othello') If you are willing to battle slugs, this perennial is worth fighting for. Large, leathery leaves emerge purple then mature to brown on top with a purple reverse. Golden daisies appear on thick stalks in summer. This plant needs consistently moist soil in a shaded area. Grows to 2–3 feet tall and 2 feet wide in zones 3–8.

- ->

Variegated Magellan fuchsia (*Fuchsia magellanica* var. *gracilis* 'Variegata') This semi-evergreen arching shrub has attractive variegated foliage in a soft blend of gray-green and cream with pink highlights, veins, and stems. The bright tubular flowers are a favorite of hummingbirds from summer until frost. Ideal conditions are moisture-retentive but not waterlogged soil and morning sun only. In shadier conditions the flower production will be reduced, although the shrub itself will thrive. Do not prune until spring. Grows to 4 feet tall and wide in zones 7–10.

SUNRISE, SUNSET

SITE PARTIAL SHADE, PARTIAL SUN   **SOIL** AVERAGE, WELL-DRAINED   **ZONE** 7–10
SEASON SPRING, SUMMER

The rich, intense colors of a sunrise and sunset captivate our attention in nature just as they do in the garden. This vibrant and aptly named Coral Sunrise coleus is the showy, focal-point foliage that acts as the inspirational element for the other summer annuals, which add even more sparkle. This combination is mainly about bright hues, but the deep green and glossy foliage of the bear's breeches offers a quieter spot for the eye to rest while providing a tropical, architectural element with those oversize leaves contrasting with the smaller plants around it. The rusted metal-and-glass garden art is the final element: it plays right into this color scheme and adds a touch of whimsy.

HOW THE DESIGN GROWS

In high summer all these components come together in a zenith of perfection. The coleus has reached a mature size to bud and bloom, the small-flowering annuals are fluffy and full, and the lustrous bear's breeches are blooming with tall spikes of mauve flowers. This combination will continue to look lively until the truly cold fall weather moves in and the spent annuals are removed for the season. You can also cut back any tired leaves on the bear's breeches at that time.

FOLIAGE FRAMEWORK

- →

Coral Sunrise coleus (*Solenostemon scutellarioides* Wizard Coral Sunrise) Leaves splashed in shades of coral, lime, and olive with fuchsia veins make this an exciting cultivar to play with in the garden. Pinch off the growing tips occasionally to keep it bushy until late summer, then let it bloom for rich purple flowers. Prefers shade to partial shade. Grows to 14 inches tall and wide. Annual.

- →

Bear's breeches (*Acanthus mollis*) An architectural clump-forming perennial known for its foliage and bold cream-and-mauve flower spikes that can stand up above the leaves as much as 3–5 feet high. The glossy dark green leaves can grow to 2 feet long and may be somewhat evergreen in mild climates. Prefers partial sun to partial shade. Grows to 3–5 feet tall and wide in zones 7–10.

FINISHING TOUCH

- →

Volcanic shamrock (*Oxalis vulcanicola* 'Molten Lava') A sassy little plant valuable for foliage and dainty yellow flowers in spring and used in summer for the landscape or containers. In shadier conditions the leaves will be more chartreuse, while in sun you can expect gold with rich orange overtones. Prefers full sun to partial shade. Grows to 6–10 inches tall and 1–12 inches wide in zones 9–11 or enjoy as an annual.

WHIPPED CREAM ON LEMON MOUSSE

SITE **SHADE, PARTIAL SUN**   SOIL **AVERAGE**   ZONE **4–9**   SEASON **SUMMER**

The very idea of dolloping whipped cream on top of an already fabulous dessert full of rich lemon and cream flavors might seem like overkill to some, but others wonder if there is ever really enough of a good thing. Adding the fluffy white astilbe topping to yellow-striped Japanese forest grass is just the thing for those with a sweet tooth. The flowing grass provides exactly the right backdrop to showcase the creamy white vertical flower spikes, giving a perfect contrast in visual texture in this delicately sweet-and-sour mixture.

HOW THE DESIGN GROWS

Summer is when most of us think of tart, pucker-inducing lemon desserts, and it is also the best time for this commingling of flavors. The Japanese forest grass sprouts out and relaxes into its languid flowing form, all laying in one direction. The fern-like astilbe reaches the peak of bloom when we begin to truly get warmth for the growing season in summer. You can almost taste it.

FOLIAGE FRAMEWORK

- →

Golden Japanese forest grass (*Hakonechloa macra* 'Aureola') This is a hardy, low-maintenance, shade-loving deciduous perennial grass that arches gracefully into dense, spreading mounds. It is a favorite for its long gold-and-green-striped leaves, which have a bamboo-like texture. Grows to 12–18 inches tall and 2–3 feet wide in zones 4–9.

FINISHING TOUCH

- →

Visions in White Chinese astilbe (*Astilbe chinensis* 'Visions in White') The ferny bronzegreen foliage of this astilbe is striking in contrast with the multitude of large creamy white flower plumes that float above it for weeks at a time. The combination of foliage and blooms is elegant and refined in full sun as well as full shade. Resistant to rabbits and deer. Grows to 2 feet tall and 18 inches wide in zones 4–9.

TRIPTYCH

SITE **PARTIAL SHADE, SHADE**   SOIL **AVERAGE, MOISTURE-RETENTIVE**   ZONE **4–8**   SEASON **YEAR-ROUND**

When every plant offers exciting foliage as well as seasonal flowers, you know you have a winning combination. The summer scene shown here highlights the bicolor pink flowers of the coral bells framed by a triad of bold, colorful leaves. Hue is also a linking theme. Those pink tones are echoed by the deep burgundy stems of the richly variegated Solomon's seal as well as the dark coral bells foliage, while the mukdenia is beginning to take on its summer blush.

HOW THE DESIGN GROWS

In spring the white flowers of both the Solomon's seal and mukdenia will echo the color of the distinctive creamy white variegated leaves, while the evergreen coral bells add depth. As summer transitions to fall, the mukdenia will turn its namesake crimson while the tall Solomon's seal introduces shades of translucent gold to the scene. In winter only the coral bells will remain, but adding a cluster of Jacob hellebore (*Helleborus niger* Gold Collection Jacob) to one side would add sparkle with their large white flowers and fuzzy yellow stamens. The compact Bella Notte coral bells risks being engulfed by the more vigorous Solomon's Seal and mukdenia, so you may have to thin periodically.

FOLIAGE FRAMEWORK

- ->

Double Stuff variegated Solomon's seal (*Polygonatum* 'Double Stuff') The creamy white leaf margins on this variety are twice the usual size, making Double Stuff really stand out in the shade garden. In spring, bell-shaped white flowers dangle beneath the arching red stems. Grows to 2 feet tall and 18 inches wide in zones 3–8.

- ->

Crimson Fans mukdenia (*Mukdenia* 'Crimson Fans') Green fan-shaped foliage and panicles of white flowers herald spring as this herbaceous ground cover emerges from winter dormancy. As the flowers fade, the foliage takes on red tints that become deeper throughout the summer before turning a brilliant crimson in fall. Grows to 12 inches tall and 2 feet wide in zones 4–9.

FINISHING TOUCH

- ->

Bella Notte coral bells (*Heuchera* 'Bella Notte') This demure coral bells is large enough for the border but will not swallow neighboring plants in a container with overenthusiastic growth. Layers of deep burgundy leaves form a mound. In summer, tall spires of two-tone pink flowers offer a treat for hummingbirds as well as cut flowers for the home. Tolerates heat and humidity. Grows to 9 inches high and 15 inches wide in zones 4–9.

DREAMSICLE

SITE **PARTIAL SHADE**   SOIL **POTTING SOIL**   ZONE **7–9**   SEASON **SUMMER**

Like your favorite frozen summer dessert, this design has tangy flavors of lemon and lime with a sprinkling of bright berries, all served up in a pretty container. This cooling Limelight dracaena and refreshing green-and-white caladium take the sizzle factor out of the shade, while adding just a touch of magenta with a dreamy fuchsia helps to keep things lively. Bold foliage sets off the more delicate flowers in this easy-care combination.

HOW THE DESIGN GROWS

The dracaena is planted for summer indulgence only, but you can take it indoors when temperatures drop in fall and enjoy it as a houseplant. The caladium tuber goes dormant at this time, so you can lift it, allow it to dry, and store it inside for the winter before replanting in spring. In areas where the fuchsia is hardy, you can leave it outside over winter, mulched for protection and pruned to the uppermost buds in spring.

FOLIAGE FRAMEWORK

- →

Caladium (*Caladium bicolor*) Large heart-shaped leaves are paper thin and display beautiful variegation. Cut off older leaves at the base as they fade, and avoid overwatering. Enjoy this plant for summer in filtered morning sun only or in a shaded spot away from direct sun. It makes a beautiful addition to the landscape or containers. Grows to 2 feet tall and wide in zones 10–11 or enjoy as an annual.

- →

Limelight dracaena (*Dracaena deremensis* 'Limelight') Bold, glossy, strap-like chartreuse foliage makes a bright statement in the shade garden or container for summer. When temperatures begin to dip in autumn, plant this up for the home. Grows to 2 feet tall and wide in zones 10–11 or enjoy as an annual.

FINISHING TOUCH

- →

Tom Woods fuchsia (*Fuchsia* 'Tom Woods') This upright-growing fuchsia with creamy sepals and a magenta-purple corolla is a favorite of gardeners and hummingbirds. Protect the crown with mulch in winter. Hardy fuchsias prefer moisture-retentive soil and afternoon shade. Grows to 3 feet tall and wide in zones 7–9; benefits from pruning in spring for shape after danger of further frost has passed.

STAR STRUCK

SITE PARTIAL SHADE   **SOIL** AVERAGE, MOISTURE-RETENTIVE   **ZONE** 3–8
SEASON SPRING THROUGH FALL

Foliage sets the stage for this summer play. You can rely on the large mounding hosta for changing scenery as it transitions from green to gold during the season. The colorful coleus takes the lead for color and drama, getting stronger with each successive show. The starlet is the delicate Lime Green flowering tobacco plant, which dances across the stage, weaving in and out of her fellow actors with grace. When the season comes to a close, only our memories will remain.

HOW THE DESIGN GROWS

This is a no-apologies summer extravaganza, designed to make the most of the seasonal color offered by the coleus and flowering tobacco plant, which are annuals for many gardeners. During this peak the hosta shows off its bold green-and-gold variegated foliage after maturing from the juvenile green. In fall the perennial hosta will die to the ground and enter dormancy for the winter, leaving the garden bare. Heather Bun white cedar (*Chamaecyparis thyoides* 'Heather Bun') would make an interesting four-season companion. This finely textured conifer forms a 3-foot dome that is green in summer and has a purple cast in winter.

FOLIAGE FRAMEWORK

------------------------------->

Beckwith's Gem coleus (*Solenostemon scutellarioides* 'Beckwith's Gem') Considered an heirloom variety, Beckwith's Gem is a strong upright coleus with vivid burgundy-and-pink foliage edged with gold. Coleus need moisture-retentive soil, and this variety prefers protection from hot afternoon sun and benefits from occasional trimming through the summer to maintain a bushy habit. Grows to 20 inches tall and 16 inches wide in zones 10–11 or enjoy as an annual.

------------------------------->

Pineapple Upside Down Cake hosta (*Hosta* 'Pineapple Upside Down Cake') This unusual hosta changes color as it cooks. The long, wavy leaves emerge solid green before the center turns gold to create the variegated look seen here. Hummingbirds are attracted to the 2-foot-tall stalks of lavender flowers in summer. Grows to 18 inches tall and 4 feet wide in zones 3–8.

FINISHING TOUCH

------------------------------->

Lime Green flowering tobacco plant (*Nicotiana alata* 'Lime Green') Bushy plants seem to glow with a profusion of star-shaped chartreuse flowers that slowly fade to a creamy lime. Tobacco plants are deer resistant, make great cut flowers, and attract hummingbirds and butterflies. Prefers rich soil and full sun or partial shade. Grows to 3 feet tall and 2 feet wide in zones 8–10 or enjoy as an annual.

VIVID, VIVACIOUS, AND VIOLET

SITE: **PARTIAL SHADE, PARTIAL SUN**   SOIL **AVERAGE**   ZONE **4–9**   SEASON **YEAR-ROUND**

In the 1960s, high fashion went into a distinctly modern mode of simple color-blocked patterns and shapes. Bold and high-contrast pairings like black and white were the order of the day. This combination is reminiscent of that vivid idea with a simple yet in-your-face carpet of violet blooms on the dramatic black bugleweed foliage. The white variegated daylily brings a vivacious and graphic element with white-and-green stripes that stand out as a horticultural fashion-forward element.

HOW THE DESIGN GROWS

This high-impact mix is most impressive in spring, when the electric violet blooms of bugleweed are charged up with color. This border will still look fabulous when the bugleweed ground cover is not blooming, as it still has semi-evergreen rich black leaves set against the unique daylily foliage. In late summer, this expressive daylily blooms with a bold double orange flower to continue the stylish theme. A wonderfully attractive substitute for the bugleweed is variegated Japanese spurge (*Pachysandra terminalis* 'Silver Edge'). The two white variegated plants together would be classy and chic.

FOLIAGE FRAMEWORK

- →

Variegated double-flowering daylily (*Hemerocallis fulva* 'Kwanso Variegata') This daylily shows off unique white-and-green variegated foliage and a lovely orange double flower blooming in August. This plant is not fussy: as long as it gets at least partial to full sun and average soil, you will not have much else to worry about, except the occasional solid green offshoot that you dig out to keep the beautiful variegation strong. Grows to 2–3 ½ feet tall and wide in zones 3–9.

FINISHING TOUCH

- →

Black Scallop bugleweed (*Ajuga reptans* 'Black Scallop') What do you get when you add black-purple foliage with scalloped edges and dark violet flowers on a matte-forming perennial? A hardy, prolific ground cover that provides a natural weed barrier in sun to partial shade that is striking to look at. Grows to 4–6 inches tall and 12–18 inches wide in zones 4–9 even in heavy, wet soils.

TICKLED PINK

SITE **PARTIAL SHADE, SHADE**   SOIL **POTTING SOIL OR AVERAGE, MOISTURE-RETENTIVE**
ZONE **ANNUALS**   SEASON **SUMMER**

You can pot up this versatile design as a large container combination, site into a shady corner of the garden, or plant as a mixture to make seasonal switch-outs a breeze and allow for the kangaroo paws, which prefer more sun. Pink is the color scheme here, established by the mottled foliage of the Chinese evergreen and highlighted by the exotic urn plant flower and kangaroo paws. Tempering all the sugary sweetness is the acid-green Boston fern, whose fronds also introduce softer, finer textures. This vignette will have you tickled pink all summer.

HOW THE DESIGN GROWS

Be ready for a summer party at a moment's notice and keep a colorful pot of sun-loving kangaroo paws ready to tuck into a shade arrangement for an instant makeover, returning it to a sunnier spot the following day. The remaining plants can stay in the shade garden for the entire summer, where the lush and colorful foliage will provide a low-maintenance display. Come fall, you can bring all of these indoors or simply treat them as annuals.

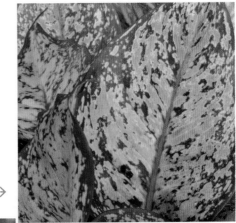

FOLIAGE FRAMEWORK

- →

Lady Valentine Chinese evergreen (*Aglaonema* 'Lady Valentine') A slow-growing tropical houseplant that all gardeners can enjoy outside during the warm summer months. Beautiful speckled foliage in salmon pink and green with distinct green veins make this an eye-catching addition to the shade garden or container. Grows up to 2 feet tall and wide in zones 10–11 or enjoy as an annual.

- →

Boston fern (*Nephrolepis* species) Perhaps the most well known and widely used tropical fern, this is noted for its rich green fronds with almost flat, graceful leaflets. They make lush houseplants, or when temperatures are mild you can enjoy them outside in hanging baskets, on pedestals, in pots, or planted into the landscape. They prefer a rich, moisture-retentive soil and high humidity in full shade to partial sun. Grows to 3 feet tall and wide in zones 10–11 or enjoy as an annual.

FINISHING TOUCH

- →

Urn plant (*Aechmea fasciata*) A bromeliad with arching, leathery leaves that overlap into a rosette, forming a watertight vase or urn that gives rise to its common name. From the center of this vase rises a stalk with its unique spiky pink bloom that can last for several months. Pour water directly into the vase and keep the surrounding soil moist but not wet. You can set this popular houseplant outside in the shade for the summer when temperatures are 70°F or hotter. Grows to 18 inches tall and wide. Annual.

- →

Kangaroo paws (*Anigozanthos* species) Exploding from a grass-like clump of basal foliage, wiry stalks of fuzzy flowers in iridescent colors make a fine summer display. The size of the plant will vary with cultivar, but all grow best in full sun and well-drained soil, thriving both in the landscape and container gardens. Grows to 1–20 feet tall and 1–3 feet wide, depending on cultivar, in zones 9–11 or enjoy as an annual, then overwinter indoors.

LIMITED EDITION

SITE **PARTIAL SHADE**   SOIL **POTTING SOIL**   ZONE **7–9**   SEASON **SPRING THROUGH FALL**

This artistic design offers plenty of flowers but relies on a framework of five-star foliage plants to really make it shine. Attention to detail is evident from the tight color echoes between the purple pot, calla lily, and hosta foliage, while metallic silver accents play off the white flowers and golden leaves connect with yellow blooms. Rather than creating a predictable symmetrical arrangement, try placing the calla to one side and balancing it with the astelia. This adds a sophisticated touch, as does layering one trailing plant over another. Dare to be different.

HOW THE DESIGN GROWS

This design is intended to be taken apart in fall after providing five months of exciting color from both foliage and flowers. Although there are a lot of plants in this pot, they are carefully placed so they do not impede one another. The astelia will easily grow through the loose coral bells foliage and the dichondra will hug the sides of the pot, while the sweet potato vine has a more relaxed trailing habit. The only maintenance required is periodically removing spent flowers and trimming trailing plants when they get too long.

FOLIAGE FRAMEWORK

Leapfrog foamy bells (*Heucherella* 'Leapfrog') Vivid yellow foliage softens to light green as it matures, and each scalloped leaf has deep purple markings. In late spring hummingbirds are attracted to the ivory flowers that appear on tall spikes. Leapfrog makes a tidy mound and tolerates heat and humidity. It does best with morning sun only. Grows to 12 inches tall and wide in zones 4–9.

Sweet Caroline Bronze sweet potato vine (*Ipomoea batatas* 'Sweet Caroline Bronze') Attractive maple-type bronze leaves are purple on the reverse. Plant this annual vine as a ground cover in the landscape or allow it to trail from a container. Grows to just 8 inches high but can trail 5 feet long, so you will need to trim it in shorter pots. Annual.

Silver Shadow astelia (*Astelia* 'Silver Shadow') Bold metallic silver leaves make this evergreen perennial stand out from the crowd. Use in drought-tolerant landscape designs or container plantings. Grows to 2–3 feet tall and 2–4 feet wide in zones 7b–11 or enjoy as an annual before bringing indoors for the winter.

Silver Falls dichondra (*Dichondra argentea* 'Silver Falls') Metallic silver leaves are the hallmark of this popular plant. An evergreen perennial ground cover in warm climates, it is noted for its drought tolerance. However, all gardeners can enjoy it as a trailing container plant, where it will add sparkle to designs in full sun or partial shade. Grows to 2–6 inches tall and 2 feet wide in zones 9–11 or enjoy as an annual.

continued on next page

FINISHING TOUCH

Picasso calla lily (*Zantedeschia* 'Picasso') Even if this never bloomed it would be a beautiful plant for the silver spotted foliage alone. However, the trumpet-shaped creamy white flowers with deep purple throats are truly lovely and appear over many weeks. This dwarf calla lily does not require staking like its larger cousins. Grows to just 2 feet tall and 12 inches wide in zones 9–10 (8 with winter protection) or enjoy as an annual.

Amstel Clara Rieger begonia (*Begonia* ×*hiemalis* 'Amstel Clara') Double white flowers suffused with pink appear all summer, set off by the succulent green foliage. This begonia takes more sun than most but does best with afternoon protection. It has an upright mounding habit. Grows to 12–18 inches in zones 9–11 or enjoy as an annual.

Amstel Blitz Rieger begonia (*Begonia* ×*hiemalis* 'Amstel Blitz') Double yellow flowers and succulent green leaves keep this looking fresh through the summer heat. Grows to 12–18 inches in zones 9–11 or enjoy as an annual.

RUSTIC WITH A TWIST

SITE **PARTIAL SHADE, SHADE**   SOIL **POTTING SOIL**   ZONE **7–9**   SEASON **YEAR-ROUND**

What do you get when you combine bold tropical leaves with woodland perennials in a simple clay pot? A design that is unexpected yet works. The glossy variegated leaves of the tropical-esque fatshedera add height to the design, while the earth tones of the foamy bells pick up on the warm sunset shades that the rustic pot suggests. Dark foliage of purple heart and begonia highlights the rich purple veins of Sweet Tea foamy bells, while the finely textured golden sedge softens the overall composition and adds light. Exploding like tiny orange sparks, the begonia flowers are the perfect finale to this scene.

Rustic with a Twist continued

HOW THE DESIGN GROWS

To keep this design looking its best, you may have to prune the fatshedera and purple heart occasionally to keep them shorter and bushier, balancing the overall proportions. All but the purple heart and begonia are evergreen, so this combination has the potential to remain in the rustic container for some time. However, the pot is not large, so as the fatshedera grows it will become root bound and may need transplanting after the first season. The foamy bells and sedge could certainly remain for many years, and you could also introduce new shade-loving companions, such as the dark-leaved Maroon Beauty strawberry begonia (*Saxifraga stolonifera* 'Maroon Beauty').

FOLIAGE FRAMEWORK

- →
Angyo Star fatshedera (×*Fatshedera lizei* 'Angyo Star') A hybrid between Japanese aralia and English ivy, this evergreen shrub offers the best of both without the problems. The glossy ivy-shaped leaves have a clean creamy variegation that lights up shady areas. Unlike ivy, this does not climb, so you will have to stake the main stem as it grows taller. You can enjoy this versatile shrub as a houseplant, but it is also hardy outdoors in zones 7b–9, where it will grow to 5 feet tall and 18 inches wide.

- →
Sweet Tea foamy bells (*Heucherella* 'Sweet Tea') One of the best foamy bells for shade containers, Sweet Tea forms a bold mound of sunset-colored foliage, each leaf with burgundy veining. Spring tones are typically brighter orange and coral, maturing to deep cinnamon by fall. Spires of creamy white flowers appear throughout the spring and summer. Grows to 20 inches tall and 28 inches wide in zones 4–9.

EverColor Everillo golden sedge (*Carex oshimensis* EverColor 'Everillo') An easy-care evergreen grass for the shade garden and containers, this becomes a loose mounding fountain of gold. Trim away damaged blades after the winter for a tidier appearance. Grows to 20 inches tall and 28 inches wide in zones 5–11.

Purple heart (*Setcreasea pallida* 'Purple Heart') This trailing tender perennial is grown as a ground cover in temperate areas, enjoyed as an indoor plant, or planted as a summer annual in sun or shade containers, where it will meander and trail through companions. Grown primarily for its purple foliage, it also blooms with small lavender flowers. Grows to 12–18 inches tall and 16 inches wide in zones 8–11 or enjoy an annual.

FINISHING TOUCH

Sparks Will Fly begonia (*Begonia* 'Sparks Will Fly') Single orange blooms fade to yellow, packing a serious color punch in the shade garden, but the dark bronze-black leaves really set this begonia apart from the competition. This annual will spill slightly over the edge of containers, but it is not a long trailer and is ideal for shorter pots. Grows to 12 inches tall and wide.

DELICATE DETAILS

SITE **PARTIAL SHADE, PARTIAL SUN**   SOIL **AVERAGE**   ZONE **4–8**   SEASON **YEAR-ROUND**

This combination is well suited for up-close viewing, such as near a path or a low wall where onlookers can appreciate the fine details. The lacy green foliage of the Pacific oakfern weaves easily through the lower tiers of this woodland garden, its soft texture contrasting with the coarse lungwort leaves and the leathery foliage of the Lenten rose. The speckled silver leaves of the lungwort were introduced to break up the carpet of green, and the resulting combination forms a perfect backdrop for the spring flowers in shades of dusky pink, blue, and purple.

HOW THE DESIGN GROWS

The deep plum flowers on the Lenten rose are one of the earliest to appear in spring, and they last for weeks before fading to a soft, muted mauve as the interesting seed heads mature. When the flowering stems are cut back in late spring, this bushy plant will push out new evergreen foliage that holds up beautifully through the year, although you may want to tidy tattered winter leaves just before the new flowers erupt in late winter. Blooms on the lungwort emerge pink and mature to blue, creating a lovely contrast when mixed with the larger flowers on the Lenten rose. The lungwort's interesting foliage remains attractive until fall. The fern's intense green color will stay vibrant through most of the season but can get stressed in excessive heat, so you may need to cut it back in late summer.

FOLIAGE FRAMEWORK

- →

Pacific oakfern (*Gymnocarpium disjunctum*) This charming perennial makes a wonderfully tough ground cover in a garden where it will receive partial to full shade. Creating a bright understory for the larger plants above, this deciduous fern mixes and weaves its lacy foliage with other low-growing shade plants. Trim any distressed foliage in late summer. Grows to 9–15 inches tall and wide in zones 2–8.

FINISHING TOUCH

- →

Lenten rose (*Helleborus ×hybridus* 'Blue Lady') Preferring partial to full shade, this bushy evergreen is a clump-forming perennial. Noted for its glossy, leathery dark green leaves and cup-shaped plum flowers, which bloom at the tips of leafy stems from late winter to midspring. Cut back any tired foliage after winter to reveal the early flowers. Grows to 12–18 inches tall and wide in zones 4–9.

- →

Lungwort (*Pulmonaria*) This unique woodland perennial, which grows in a low clump, is named for the leaves' resemblance to diseased lungs. Bell-shaped flowers that change from pink to blue enhance the display over the long bloom period on splotched, speckled, fuzzy foliage. This adaptable plant can grow in light that ranges from sun to shade depending on the variety and level of soil moisture. Although the name of this particular variety is not known, Mrs. Moon would give a similar look. Grows to 6–12 inches tall and 18 inches wide in zones 3–8.

MIX AND MATCH

SITE SHADE, PARTIAL SHADE   **SOIL** AVERAGE, MOIST   **ZONE** 7–8   **SEASON** SPRING THROUGH FALL

As timeless as the classic twin set of a coordinating sweater and cardigan, this combination has the perfect balance of repetition and uniqueness. Bold hosta leaves separate feathery ferns and fern-like astilbe, while golden oregano and hosta avoid color collision thanks to the ribbon of medium green astilbe foliage that separates them. Adding that finishing touch is a necklace of fluffy pink astilbe flowers that are as pretty when fresh in summer as they are dried in fall.

HOW THE DESIGN GROWS

Early spring sees the slow unfurling of fern fronds behind the bold hosta leaves, which emerge bright chartreuse. The coarse astilbe leaves and softer oregano also add early spring interest. As the season progresses, the hosta leaves turn golden yellow, eventually fading to white, while the fluffy pink flowers of the astilbe introduce a new color in midsummer. All the perennials are herbaceous, so by August this three-season composition will start to fade. The plants will continue to spread, so you may need to divide and thin occasionally to maintain the layered effect. This would be a delightful setting for a mass planting of ephemeral spring bulbs like the dog tooth violet (*Erythronium* 'Pagoda'), whose fringed elfin-cap yellow flowers would suit this woodland setting perfectly.

FOLIAGE FRAMEWORK

- →

Gold Standard hosta (*Hosta* 'Gold Standard') With hand-size (or larger) leaves, this large hosta knows how to make a statement. The golden yellow leaves have an irregular dark green margin with a seersucker-type texture that holds the morning dew like shining jewels. Late summer produces tall spikes of lavender flowers, which hummingbirds favor. Be sure to bait for slugs. Grows to 3 feet tall and wide in zones 3–8.

- →

Golden oregano (*Origanum vulgare* 'Aureum') Although edible, this variety has little flavor and is primarily grown as an ornamental ground cover. The attractive foliage emerges chartreuse before maturing to a softer green. Unlike most herbs, golden oregano needs partial shade rather than full sun. Grows to 12 inches tall and 2 feet wide in zones 7–9, evergreen in milder climates.

- →

Golden male fern (*Dryopteris affinis* (Polydactyla Group) 'Polydactyla Dadds') This easy-care Victorian fern for the shade garden is resistant to deer and rabbits. It is semi-evergreen but benefits from older fronds being cut down in spring. Grows to 3 feet tall and wide in zones 4–8.

FINISHING TOUCH

- →

Visions in Pink Chinese astilbe (*Astilbe chinensis* 'Visions in Pink') Plumes of light pink flowers on this herbaceous perennial accent the blue-green fern-like foliage in summer. Shorter than other species, Visions in Pink is a dense upright form that does not require staking and also tolerates drier soils. Grows to 20–24 inches tall and wide in zones 3–8.

STALWART STANDOUTS

SITE SHADE, PARTIAL SHADE   **SOIL** AVERAGE, MOISTURE-RETENTIVE   **ZONE** 3–8
SEASON SPRING, SUMMER

A woodland garden is a true test of just how tough a plant can be when it has to compete with larger trees and shrubs casting shade and taking up precious room that little roots need to survive. This combination proves that delicate-looking plants can also be resilient. The maidenhair fern fills out along the border in a cool, refreshing river of light green lacy texture that bubbles and froths, allowing the wild sweet William to rise up and bloom in an abundant spring gush of airy lavender blooms and fragrance.

HOW THE DESIGN GROWS

This duo of tenacious perennials peaks in spring, when the five-petaled pale blue wild sweet William is in full glory. When the flowers are done blooming, consider adding an oakleaf hydrangea as a hardy flowering shrub to continue the show for summer. The under-layer of luxurious ferns contrasts with the hydrangea's bold oak leaf–shaped foliage, while fabulously long-lasting blooms and elegant burgundy fall color will carry this woodland mix late into the year with durable elegance.

FOLIAGE FRAMEWORK

Northern maidenhair fern (*Adiantum pedatum*) This herbaceous fern is valued for growing densely in moist, heavy shade conditions, as well as for the airy texture that contrasts so well against broad-leaved plants such as hosta and Siberian bugloss (*Brunnera macro-phylla*). In sites where other plants struggle, such as steep slopes, this creeping fern thrives. If you look closely, the plant has a lot of character, with wiry black stems and sometimes a slight curve to the frond. Grows to 12–18 inches tall in zones 3–8; it will colonize over time, so give it room.

FINISHING TOUCH

Wild sweet William (*Phlox divaricata*) This plant has it all. The flowering woodland perennial's deer resistance, fragrance, star-shaped lavender blooms, and shade tolerance will not disappoint—and hummingbirds and butterflies love it. It is low growing and has the flexibility to be at home in rock gardens, crawl like a ground cover, or work well in naturalized gardens. Grows to 12–15 inches tall and 1–3 feet wide in zones 3–8.

RICH AND ROBUST

SITE **SUN, PARTIAL SUN**   SOIL **POTTING SOIL**   ZONE **4–9**   SEASON **YEAR-ROUND**

This intensely hued and abundantly layered container design is overflowing with ornate foliage patterns that convey the feeling of a baroque tapestry. The rich tones of leaves and blooms weave together subtle and elaborate brocade qualities. The clusters of fuchsia flowers sparkle against unusual creamy variegated leaves that give light to the more deeply toned patterns of the other plants. Yellow-green creeping Jenny vine cascades from underneath the lavish begonia foliage to light up the robust darker colors and textures.

HOW THE DESIGN GROWS

This container has personality that changes with each passing week from spring through fall, but in high summer it hits its max of rich tones and textures from foliage to flower. The coral bells begins to bloom in spring with white flower wands, quickly joined by summer annuals and the fuchsia for bloom power through fall. For most gardeners this will essentially be a summer container, as all but the coral bells are removed at the end of fall.

FOLIAGE FRAMEWORK

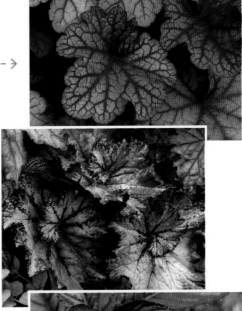

Berry Smoothie coral bells (*Heuchera* 'Berry Smoothie') A year-round winner, this evergreen perennial glows with magenta shades in spring, deepening as the season progresses. The adaptable cultivar will take full sun to full shade, providing the soil does not dry out, and is known for its ability to tolerate heat and humidity. Grows to 18 inches tall and wide in zones 4–9.

Rex begonia (*Begonia rex*) Rex begonia is a fabulous foliage plant for the home or summer garden with many cultivars available, each with unique markings. Use in the shade garden with finely textured ferns or at the edge of a shady container. Each plant forms a tight clump. Be careful not to overwater. Grows to 12 inches tall and wide. Annual.

Persian shield (*Strobilanthes dyerianus*) With its iridescent foliage in shades of purple, green, and silver, this plant is unusual and eye catching. Let it weave in and out of its neighbors for unexpected combinations. Grows to 3 feet tall and 2 feet wide in zones 9–10 or enjoy as an annual.

FINISHING TOUCH

Firecracker fuchsia (*Fuchsia triphylla* 'Firecracker') Clusters of long, tubular orange flowers with pink-orange interiors dangle from the arching branches of this heat-tolerant shrub, while the green-and-cream variegated leaves have glowing rosy veins and undersides. This tender woody perennial prefers sun to partial shade. Grows to 2–3 feet tall and wide in zones 10–11 or enjoy as an annual.

JURASSIC MOMENT

SITE **PARTIAL SHADE, SHADE**   SOIL **AVERAGE, MOISTURE-RETENTIVE**   ZONE **7**   SEASON **YEAR-ROUND**

Bring a tropical look to a temperate garden with these attention-grabbing plants. A big-leaf magnolia forms an overhead canopy, while mountain bamboo acts as a screen to separate this mini-jungle from the sunny garden beyond. Within this dappled enclave, both the moisture-loving darmera and Rodger's flower can reach their full steroidal potential, reminiscent of an ancient forest where dinosaurs might roam. The layering effect of the three bold-leaved plants allows each to have its own distinct space, while the finer-textured leaves of the bamboo add contrast.

HOW THE DESIGN GROWS

The excitement starts to build in spring, as the darmera pushes forth its naked, prehistoric-looking flower stalks. Shortly afterward the rich brown new growth of the Rodger's flower emerges and the dinner plate–size magnolia blossoms open and release their scent. As that spectacle fades, the airy plumes of the Rodger's flower appear, now backed by the bold darmera leaves. In winter only the bamboo foliage remains, and dark green culms provide structure.

FOLIAGE FRAMEWORK

- →

Darmera (*Darmera peltata*) A vigorous herbaceous perennial that needs plenty of room to spread. This shade lover will tolerate more sun if planted in wet soils. Pink and white flowers appear in spring before the leaves. Grows to 3–6 feet tall and 5 feet wide in zones 5–7.

- →

Mountain bamboo (*Thamnocalamus tessellatus*) One of the best clumping bamboos for full sun, this has a strong upright growth habit but does not do well in hot, humid climates. Grows 16 feet tall in zones 7–10; plant within a rhizome barrier to control spread.

- →

Big leaf magnolia (*Magnolia macrophylla*) With leaves that grow up to 3 feet long, this deciduous magnolia will not go unnoticed. In early summer fragrant white blooms appear, each up to 12 inches in diameter, followed by a cone-shaped pod containing large red or scarlet seeds. Prefers moisture-retentive soil in full sun to partial shade. Grows to 40 feet tall and wide in zones 5–9.

FINISHING TOUCH

- →

Red-leaf Rodger's flower (*Rodgersia podophylla* 'Rotlaub') The large jagged foliage of this herbaceous perennial opens bronze and matures to green with overtones of deep red and copper. The heavily textured leaves form a mounding dome, above which plumes of airy white flowers appear in summer. To look its best, this plant needs wet soil and full to partial shade. Grows to 3–4 feet tall and wide in zones 5–9.

PINEAPPLE CRUSH

SITE **PARTIAL SHADE**   SOIL **AVERAGE, WELL-DRAINED**   ZONE **6–7**   SEASON **YEAR-ROUND**

Juicy layers of foliage create a sunny monochromatic framework for the golden daisies. While the Pineapple Upside Down Cake hosta forms a smooth filling against which the flowers can lean, the tall variegated euonymus provides a bold backdrop. The result is a perfect balance between foliage and flowers, yet the hosta is ready to crush and disguise the dormant leaves of the leopard's bane when needed.

HOW THE DESIGN GROWS

The story does not end when this trio is at its peak in spring. As temperatures rise, the leopard's bane will become dormant. The hosta foliage, which will be a wide mound of wavy brilliant yellow, will quickly fill the space. Meanwhile, the evergreen variegated foliage of the euonymus will add height and color even after the hosta dies back in fall. The only necessary maintenance is pruning back the euonymus occasionally to prevent it from crowding the perennials. For additional winter interest, a dwarf mugo pine (*Pinus mugo* 'Pumilio', also sold as *P. Mugo* var. *pumilio*) would repeat the mounding shape of the hosta, while the spiky texture of the needles would introduce a finer texture.

FOLIAGE FRAMEWORK

--→

Silver Queen euonymus (*Euonymus japonicus* 'Silver Queen', also sold as *Euonymus fortunei* 'Silver Queen') A true workhorse in the garden, this evergreen shrub will tolerate poor soils. You can trim it as a hedge or leave it to grow into its natural upright form. The attractive glossy leaves have a bold white margin, making it an ideal candidate to show off darker colors or add a highlight to a mixed border. Grows to 6 feet tall and 3–4 feet wide (untrimmed) in zones 6–9. **CAUTION** All parts of this shrub are toxic if ingested in large quantities.

--→

Pineapple Upside Down Cake hosta (*Hosta* 'Pineapple Upside Down Cake') A unique hosta to add to the shade garden. Long, wavy foliage emerges pure green, then the center turns brilliant gold and leaves develop a narrow green-black margin. (This scene captures it mid-transition.) In summer, lavender flowers held high on 2-foot-tall scapes will attract hummingbirds. Grows to 18 inches tall and 4 feet wide in zones 3–8.

FINISHING TOUCH

--→

Leopard's bane (*Doronicum orientale* 'Magnificum') This golden yellow daisy is a welcome sight in spring, thriving in average or moist soil and sun or partial shade. This perennial may go dormant during the hot summer weather, so add companion plants that will fill the gap. Grows to 2 feet tall and wide in zones 4–7.

STARBURST

SITE **SHADE, PARTIAL SHADE**   SOIL **MOIST**   ZONE **6–9**   SEASON **YEAR-ROUND**

Purchasing garden art is the easy part. Knowing where to put it so you enhance both the art and the garden takes a little more practice, but it is really just observation of the smallest detail. Both the colors and shape of this glass piece provided the design inspiration. The hardy impatiens foliage echoes the star silhouette, a combination made even more striking because of their similarity in size. There is a more subtle connection between the orange striations in the glass and the distinctive veins that culminate in deep rose at each leaf node.

HOW THE DESIGN GROWS

Hardy impatiens is a herbaceous perennial that has attractive foliage from spring until fall with attractive snapdragon-like yellow flowers appearing at the end of summer. The color of these blooms could be enhanced with an adjacent planting of All Gold Japanese forest grass (*Hakonechloa macra* 'All Gold'), while autumn fern (*Dryopteris erythrosora*) would repeat the copper tones of the glass and be an ever-green year-round partner. The glass is frost-proof; you can leave it outdoors year-round in temperate climates, but it is best protected in colder regions.

FOLIAGE FRAMEWORK

- ->

Hardy impatiens (*Impatiens omeiana*) Whorls of pointed dark green leaves are held 18 inches high on dark red stems. Each leaf has a bright yellow vein that helps to make this stand out in shady areas, and in late summer yellow flowers echo this feature. This herbaceous perennial spreads easily from rhizomes to form a ground cover in zones 6–9.

FINISHING TOUCH

- ->

Glass starburst You can place glass art in the garden using rebar or copper tube as a stake. By adjusting the length, you can situate the piece at the perfect height to add artistic detail to a tall shrub or a low ground cover. However, nestling it into the surrounding foliage often strengthens the visual connection. In milder climates you can leave this out year-round, but in colder locales store it in a protected area.

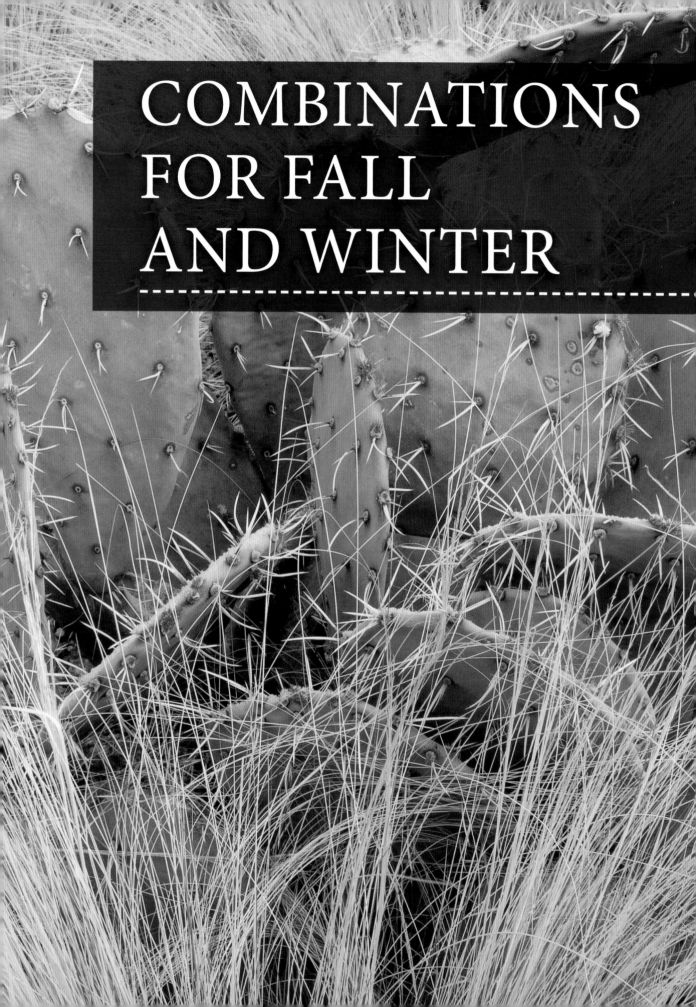

COMBINATIONS
FOR FALL
AND WINTER

Dazzling Displays for Sunny Areas

UNDERSTATED OPULENCE

SITE **PARTIAL SUN, PARTIAL SHADE**   SOIL **AVERAGE, MOISTURE-RETENTIVE**   ZONE **6–8**
SEASON **YEAR-ROUND**

A ribbon of black mondo grass weaves between all the elements in this sophisticated design, pulling together individual threads to make a striking winter vignette. Bright yellow stems, softer yellow flowers, a yellow-green conifer, and golden succulent needles are unified, although their physical spacing allows them to remain distinct. Each component introduces a new texture, but the composition remains understated thanks to its restrained color scheme.

HOW THE DESIGN GROWS

This garden was clearly designed for winter interest. Once the dogwood and spike winterhazel are clothed in their green leaves, the effect will be muted, with only the stonecrop and Japanese cedar adding golden highlights to the black carpet. Monitor the scene carefully to maintain the balance of colors and textures, and thin the yellow twig dogwood regularly to prevent it from developing into a dense thicket.

FOLIAGE FRAMEWORK

- →

Sekkan-sugi Japanese cedar (*Cryptomeria japonica* 'Sekkan-sugi')
The dense, finely textured foliage of this conifer remains bright green for most of the year, with new creamy yellow growth in spring. Unlike many golden conifers, this tolerates full sun well but also takes partial shade. Grows to 30 feet tall and 10 feet wide in zones 6–9.

- →

Black mondo grass (*Ophiopogon planiscapus* 'Nigrescens') Dramatic strappy black foliage forms an evergreen carpet in sun or shade, although protection from hot afternoon summer sun is desirable. Lavender summer flowers mature to black berries in fall. Black mondo grass is drought tolerant but grows equally well in moisture-retentive soil. Grows to 5–6 inches tall and wide in zones 6–10.

- →

Angelina stonecrop (*Sedum rupestre* 'Angelina')
This easy-care, drought-tolerant succulent thrives in full sun or partial shade, but is brighter in more light. As temperatures drop the foliage turns orange. Use at the edge of containers or as a ground cover. Grows to 6 inches tall and spreads in zones 6–9.

continued on next page

Understated Opulence continued

FINISHING TOUCH

- →

Spike winterhazel (*Corylopsis spicata*) For much of the year this is an unexceptional deciduous shrub, but in winter it becomes a star. Clusters of fragrant yellow flowers dangle from bare branches in profusion at a time when much of the landscape is still dormant. This spreading multistemmed shrub prefers moistureretentive soil and afternoon shade. Grows to 4–8 feet tall and 6–8 feet wide in zones 5–8.

- →

Yellow twig dogwood (*Cornus sericea* 'Flaviramea') Tolerating clay soils and wet conditions, this deciduous suckering shrub brings beauty to tough areas of the garden but may be too vigorous for small areas. Prune out one third of the stems each spring, as the best color is always on the youngest canes. Foliage color is medium green in summer and yellow in fall. Prefers full sun to partial shade. Grows to 5–6 feet tall and wide in zones 3–8; spreads aggressively.

BERRIES, BLADES, AND BRANCHES

SITE **FULL SUN, PARTIAL SUN**   SOIL **AVERAGE**   ZONE **6–8**   SEASON **YEAR-ROUND**

This is an attractive, low-maintenance, deer-resistant combination for a transitional border that separates the ornamental garden from the more naturalistic plantings beyond. In this fall scene the clusters of red berries highlight the exposed scarlet branches of the vine maple, while the loose form of the variegated maiden grass shimmers in the sunshine. The silk tassels of the grass also have a pink hue, echoing the warm tones of the berries and branches. Foliage is both the framework and the glue that binds all the elements together, with berries, seed heads, and stems adding accents throughout the year.

Berries, Blades, and Branches continued

HOW THE DESIGN GROWS

The pleated bright green leaves of the vine maple slowly unfurl in spring as tiny dark red-and-yellow flowers mature into two winged scarlet seedpods. As spring gives way to summer and the maple leaves mature to medium green, the grass quickly gains height while clusters of white flowers adorn the lax stems of the cotoneaster. By fall these flowers have developed into red berries and the grass has thrown up tall flower spikes with silky tassels. The dried, bleached grasses often remain intact for the winter, rustling in the breeze or transforming into frozen sculptures. This winter vignette will simply get larger as it ages, the grass clump growing wider while both the vine maple and shrub gain height and width.

FOLIAGE FRAMEWORK

- >

Vine maple (*Acer circinatum*) A native of the Pacific Northwestern United States, this small tree is equally at home in the landscape and in the forest. Scarlet seedpods in spring contrast with the light green leaves that slowly mature to a medium hue. In early autumn the foliage turns shades of orange and gold, and as the leaves fall to the ground the young red branches are revealed. Grows to 12 feet tall and wide in zones 6–9; larger in the natural environment.

- >

Variegated maiden grass (*Miscanthus sinensis* 'Variegatus') A tall, arching grass with green-and-white variegated blades that sparkle in the sun. In late summer pink tassels appear, which slowly fade to cream. Like all maiden grasses this variety does best in full sun or light shade and well-drained soil. Wait until spring to cut it down to 12 inches. Grows to 6 feet tall and 5 feet wide in zones 5–9.

FINISHING TOUCH

- →

Parney's cotoneaster (*Cotoneaster parneyi*, also sold as *Cotoneaster lacteus*) This large evergreen shrub grows to a loose fountain. Dark green leaves are silvery on the undersides, and white summer flowers mature to clusters of red berries that persist well into winter. Drought tolerant, and most deer leave it alone. Grows to 8–10 feet tall and wide in zones 6–8. **CAUTION** In areas where this is invasive, toyon (*Heteromeles arbutifolia*) would be a suitable alternative.

A WARM EMBRACE

SITE **FULL SUN**   SOIL **AVERAGE AND POTTING SOIL**   ZONE **5–8**   SEASON **YEAR-ROUND**

The lacy foliage of this Japanese maple flirts with the masculine glossy black pot, tickling the smooth stones as the gentle breeze blows. A ruffle of colorful heather surrounds the container, embracing it with a delicate touch while mounding shrubs behind add color and visual strength. The contrast of colors and finely textured foliage with the bold container creates a memorable, beautifully executed vignette.

HOW THE DESIGN GROWS

Every season offers something new. The fall scene shown here will be even more vibrant as the maple turns deep orange and the barberry transitions to crimson. The blaze continues throughout winter as the heather becomes deep red, a standout against the dark container. In spring the fresh new maple growth contrasts with the purple barberry, while the heather offers sunny shades of yellow, accented in summer with pink flowers. This is a low-maintenance, deer-resistant combination. The maple would benefit from being transplanted to a larger container in three years or so, but otherwise the scene will age gracefully.

FOLIAGE FRAMEWORK

Japanese maple (*Acer palmatum* var. *dissectum*) The cultivar in this combination is unknown, but it is very similar in habit and color to Viridis. The lacy green foliage cascades to form an elegant dome. Fall color transitions through gold to orange with crimson highlights. Grows to 8 feet high and 12 feet wide in zones 5–8.

Crimson Pygmy barberry (*Berberis thunbergii* var. *atropurpurea* 'Crimson Pygmy') A tough, mounding deciduous shrub with rich purple foliage and red berries. Barberries are drought tolerant once established. Grows to 3 feet tall and wide in zones 4–9. **CAUTION** Before planting, make sure barberries are not invasive in your area.

Magic Carpet spirea (*Spiraea japonica* 'Magic Carpet') A wonderful colorful shrub with bright red new foliage that matures to gold and finally turns deep scarlet in fall. Add pink flowers in summer, and this deciduous shrub is a head-turner. Grows to 3 feet tall and wide in zones 4–9.

FINISHING TOUCH

Firefly heather (*Calluna vulgaris* 'Firefly') This is one of the most exciting heathers for the garden, with foliage that transitions through gold to green, orange, and deep red. The pink flowers are almost too much. Grows to 18 inches high and 3 feet wide in zones 5–8.

DINOSAUR SOUP

SITE **FULL SUN, PARTIAL SUN**   SOIL **POTTING SOIL**   ZONE **6–8**   SEASON **YEAR-ROUND**

Like a good pot of minestrone soup, these ingredients are blended to perfection. The dark green leaves of the dinosaur kale add a rich, nutty flavor, balanced by the fresh green fern and bright curly leucothoe. Ginger is the spice of choice, provided by the small mounding Rheingold arborvitae and a dwarf coral bells, whose foliage and flowers both contribute exceptional seasoning. Sometimes the best recipes are born from using whatever is at hand, and this unexpected splash of magenta certainly adds the final flavor boost. Simmered slowly over low heat, this is the perfect soup for a chilly fall day.

HOW THE DESIGN GROWS

Most plants in this container are not only evergreen but actually change color. The coral bells transitions through shades of gold and brown, with an abundance of pale ginger flowers in summer and fall. Rheingold arborvitae is a golden conifer that takes on orange tints in winter. Meanwhile, the leucothoe turns red and the fern becomes copper as temperatures dip. For spring interest, the emerging foliage of the Japanese false holly is rose-pink. Only the kale is a seasonal component and will need replacing in spring, perhaps with Krossa Regal hosta (*Hosta* 'Krossa Regal') if you site it in partial sun. This upright-growing hosta is a similar color to the kale, with lightly quilted foliage. In more sun, you could substitute a young Wissel's Saguaro false cypress (*Chamaecyparis lawsoniana* 'Wissel's Saguaro'), which is also deep blue-green and has interesting texture.

FOLIAGE FRAMEWORK

- ->

Dinosaur kale (*Brassica oleracea* 'Lacinato') Edible dark blue-green leaves have an earthy, nutty flavor and a bumpy texture in sun, partial sun, and partial shade. Grows to 2–3 feet tall and wide. Annual.

- ->

Rheingold arborvitae (*Thuja occidentalis* 'Rheingold') Fan-shaped golden foliage turns orange in winter. Grows to 3–5 feet tall and wide in zones 4–8.

- ->

Curly Red leucothoe (*Leucothoe axillaris* 'Curly Red') Twisted, thick, leathery leaves transition through summer green to scarlet in fall and purple in winter. This deer-resistant shrub is best in partial shade, but in fall and winter will take full sun. Grows to 18 inches tall and wide in zones 6–8.

- ->

Japanese false holly (*Osmanthus heterophyllus* 'Goshiki') Low-maintenance, drought-tolerant, deer-resistant, and colorful—just a few of the reasons you need to try this evergreen shrub with spiky leaves speckled green and creamy yellow with rosy new growth in spring. Does well in sun, partial sun, and partial shade. Grows to 4–6 feet tall and wide in zones 6–9, but you can prune to keep it smaller.

continued on next page

Dinosaur Soup continued

Autumn fern (*Dryopteris erythrosora*)
This evergreen fern prefers partial sun
or partial shade and moisture-retentive
soil. New fronds are often copper
colored, with a more pronounced hue in
late summer and fall. Trim back any
damaged fronds in spring. Grows to 3
feet tall and wide in zones 5–9.

FINISHING TOUCH

Blondie coral bells (*Heuchera*
'Blondie') An exceptional variety that
tolerates full sun or full shade and
blooms prolifically in summer and fall.
It keeps a tidy, compact shape with
mounding foliage. Grows to 5 inches
high and 8 inches wide in zones 4–9.

Pansy (*Viola* species) Of no particular parentage, this little
pansy found its way into the design simply because it was
available. Deadhead old flowers to prevent seed formation and
encourage more blooms. Annual.

GOLDEN MOMENTS

SITE **FULL SUN**   SOIL **AVERAGE**   ZONE **5–8**   SEASON **YEAR-ROUND**

Repetition of color and form are the two key ingredients here. The rusted metal agave mimics the upright habit of the golden yucca, and the tall leader of the golden pine in the foreground strengthens this feature. Repeating the gold but adding width is the Golden Spreader fir, which also serves to pull back the eye by adding a distinct boundary to the frame. To the right, a prostrate Blue Star juniper cools all the excitement and grounds the vignette while connecting visually to the green stripes of the yucca. Finally, the rich brown artwork is the perfect counterpoint to all these bright notes, adding a simple earthy touch.

HOW THE DESIGN GROWS

All these elements are evergreen, but only the Chief Joseph lodgepole pine turns gold in winter, so this combination definitely looks best in the colder months—although the story does not end there. As winter gives way to spring, the pine will slowly return to green while the new growth on the fir seizes its moment in the golden spotlight. By summer—as the fir softens to yellow—the yucca will bloom, adding fragrance and flowers to this four-season medley. Throughout it all, the blue needles of Blue Star juniper will help temper the golden moments and the metal agave will thrive. Appropriate spacing at planting time will ensure that this scene can mature unhindered.

FOLIAGE FRAMEWORK

- →

Chief Joseph lodgepole pine (*Pinus contorta* var. *latifolia* 'Chief Joseph') In summer you would never know that this ordinary-looking green pine was anything special. Yet seemingly overnight in November it is transformed into vivid gold, becoming ever more brazen as the temperatures drop. Be sure to place this where you can enjoy it from the comfort of your favorite armchair. Grows to 8–12 feet tall and 4–6 feet wide in zones 5–9.

- →

Golden Sword yucca (*Yucca flaccida* 'Golden Sword', also sold as *Yucca filamentosa* 'Golden Sword') This evergreen shrub forms dramatic clumps of broad striped green-and-gold foliage, and in summer bears a 6-foot-tall spike of fragrant white flowers. Grows to 2 feet tall and 3–4 feet wide in zones 4–9; in colder climates you may have to trim after a harsh winter.

232 COMBINATIONS FOR FALL AND WINTER

Golden Spreader Nordmann fir (*Abies nordmanniana* 'Golden Spreader') This slow-growing conifer shrub forms a squat pyramidal mound and makes a beautiful year-round accent in the garden, transitioning from brilliant gold in spring to yellow in summer and fall. Winter color may be a little more chartreuse. Grows to 4 feet tall and wide in zones 4–8.

Blue Star juniper (*Juniperus squamata* 'Blue Star') A low-growing blue-gray juniper with short, stiff branches and spiky needles. This is a low-maintenance dwarf conifer to include in containers or the landscape. Grows to 2 feet tall and 3–4 feet wide in zones 4–8.

FINISHING TOUCH

Metal sculpture Made from rusted metal, this agave will come through a hard freeze without any problem (unlike its living counterpart). Looks perfect in a pot surrounded by a semi-evergreen sedum.

ICE CREAM SANDWICH

SITE **FULL SUN**   SOIL **AVERAGE**   ZONE **7–8**   SEASON **YEAR-ROUND**

Ice cream is delicious at any time of year, but these double scoop–size hydrangea cones are a special mouthwatering treat in winter. Nicely wedged between the satisfyingly solid Irish yew and the lighter Siberian bear grass, this winter dessert promises a series of flavor explosions to appease the toughest critic. Three different shapes and textures are layered together in an enticing recipe that will have seasonal variations yet will always be satisfying.

HOW THE DESIGN GROWS

This trio changes personality with each season. In spring new foliage will emerge on the hydrangea, the soft oval leaves contrasting nicely with small textured conifer needles and the broad grass-like blades of the evergreens. Hydrangea flowers will start to develop in early summer, eventually erupting in huge creamy white cones that turn to shades of pink in fall. When the Siberian bear grass matures, it will also produce a tall spike of white flowers. Although the hydrangea leaves quickly succumb to frost, the skeletonized Limelight flowers persist well into winter. The design will mature with minimal maintenance, but be sure to prune the hydrangea canes in late winter to approximately 12 inches tall. This will form a twiggy support structure for the new growth on which the flowers will appear.

FOLIAGE FRAMEWORK

- →

Siberian bear grass (*Nolina* 'La Siberica') A remarkable evergreen perennial that forms a symmetrical fountain of 2-inch broad blades, eventually growing a trunk 6 feet or taller. When mature this grass-like green clump is topped with a 4- to 5-foot spike bearing white flowers. Prefers full sun and well-drained soil. Once established, it is deer resistant and drought tolerant. Hardy in zones 7–10.

- →

Irish yew (*Taxus baccata* 'Fastigiata') Tolerating sun or shade, drought or regular watering, this is a useful conifer to include in any garden design. Its erect habit and reliable evergreen needles add color and structure year-round, while this variety also offers red winter berries. Grows slowly to 20 feet tall and 3–4 feet wide in zones 6–9; takes pruning well. **CAUTION** All parts of this plant are poisonous, so site with care.

FINISHING TOUCH

- →

Limelight hydrangea (*Hydrangea paniculata* 'Limelight') Definitely not your grandma's hydrangea, Limelight screams for attention, but in a very elegant way. Oversize cone-shaped creamy white flowers transition to dusky pink and burgundy before drying tan as the weather cools. For monster-size blooms, thin the canes; the resulting larger panicles weight down the branches to create a loose fountain. Grows to 6–8 feet tall and wide in zones 3–8.

A POINT IN TIME

SITE **FULL SUN**   SOIL **POTTING SOIL**   ZONE **5–7**   SEASON **YEAR-ROUND**

This is one of those container combinations where you cannot go wrong. Every plant is evergreen, yet each one changes during the seasons, so no matter when you view it there is always something new happening. Two reliable conifers, bold yellow Forever Goldie and the attractive two-tone Ellwood's Empire, form the backdrop. Bringing together these two colors is the spiky variegated foliage of Japanese false holly. Two winter-blooming heathers add the color punch: the golden foliage of Anouk is as pleasing as the blooms, and Svenja is beloved for its brilliant magenta-red vertical spikes of flowers.

HOW THE DESIGN GROWS

All four seasons offer a fresh perspective. Shown here in fall, the vibrant heather will continue to bloom for many months, while the golden conifer takes on orange tints in winter. As spring rolls around, the Japanese false holly will push out new rose-colored growth that the surrounding plants set off perfectly. This is a tightly packed container, so by the second or third year you may have to transplant some plants into the garden to allow others more room.

FOLIAGE FRAMEWORK

Ellwood's Empire false cypress (*Chamae-cyparis lawsoniana* 'Ellwood's Empire') The soft, feather-like foliage of this conifer is a delicate blue-green tipped with gold, resulting in an attractive two-tone effect. This slow-growing columnar conifer is ideal for containers. Grows to 4 feet tall and 16 inches wide in zones 5–9.

Forever Goldie golden arborvitae (*Thuja plicata* 'Forever Goldie') Soft, fluffy yellow foliage is the hallmark of this outstanding conifer; it may be bright yellow in full sun or more chartreuse if shaded. In winter the tips turn orange, making a lovely highlight in containers or the landscape. Grows to 15–20 feet tall and 3 feet wide in zones 3–7.

Japanese false holly (*Osmanthus heterophyllus* 'Goshiki') This is a deer-resistant evergreen shrub with holly-like variegated green-and-yellow foliage. Drought resistant when established. Grows to 10 feet tall and wide in zones 6–9, but you can prune to keep it smaller or grow in a container.

continued on next page

FINISHING TOUCH

- →

Svenja heather (*Calluna vulgaris* 'Svenja') Bud bloomer
heathers are unique in that they are sterile and remain in
colorful bud form for many months, unlike the more typical
heathers that quickly set seed and lose color. Svenja has
especially vibrant magenta-red flowers. Grows to 2 feet tall
and wide in zones 5–8.

- →

Anouk heather (*Calluna vulgaris* 'Anouk') This
evergreen perennial has white flowers, but it is the
upright form and golden foliage that make it a
welcome addition to containers. Grows to 18
inches tall and wide in zones 5–8.

RAINLESS, ROCKY, AND RESTFUL

SITE **FULL SUN**   SOIL **AVERAGE, WELL-DRAINED**   ZONE **8–9**   SEASON **YEAR-ROUND**

Whether you live in a hot climate or simply want to save water in the landscape, this design—based on evergreen plants from New Zealand—may be just the solution. The subdued color scheme is visually soothing and easy on the wallet with water savings. The large scale of the cordyline and hefty boulders make a wonderful duo that visually weights this light-colored composition to the ground, while grasses such as the reddish leatherleaf sedge and icy green Frosted Curls sedge soften the edges of the rocks. The shimmering astelia and chalk blue foliage of the hebe in the foreground offer additional color to the rhythm of this arrangement.

Rainless, Rocky, and Restful continued

HOW THE DESIGN GROWS

In midwinter, this garden scene is quiet yet still appealing. You will need to perform minimal grooming to make this combination shine for the remainder of the year. In summer, the hebe will bask in the heat and produce spikes of white flowers that open from lovely red buds. If you want a little more color in this garden, add a ground cover such Elfin thyme (*Thymus praecox* 'Elfin'), whose dusky amethyst blooms will provide a carpet of color at the feet of these sturdy plants.

FOLIAGE FRAMEWORK

- ->

Cordyline (*Cordyline australis*) A popular evergreen plant for its exotic, palm-like appearance. This slow grower drops its lower leaves over time to reveal a narrow trunk. Gardeners often use young plants in bedding and container displays. The hottest, driest garden location is ideal for this sun-loving plant, but it will also handle some light shade. Well-drained soil is key to overwintering, as cordyline can die all the way to the ground in a harsh or wet season. However, it tends to spring back up from the hardy roots and rebound to full size within a few years. Grows to more than 10 feet tall and 3 feet wide in zones 8–11; may get much taller in mild climates.

- ->

Leatherleaf sedge (*Carex buchananii*) This evergreen rusty red sedge is a terrific curly-tipped companion for many plants in garden designs where you may want a soft-mounding element. Deer resistant, drought tolerant, and well suited to being a container plant as well as a specimen in the landscape. This New Zealand native does best in fast-draining soil in full sun to partial shade. Grows to 3 feet tall and wide in zones 6–9.

Frosted Curls sedge (*Carex comans* 'Frosted Curls')
The fine texture of this slender-bladed grass is known
for its curly tips and frosty blue color with lighter green
to almost white tips, although it can take on tinges of
bronze in more sun. One of the more compact sedges,
this particular cultivar will tolerate drier conditions in
well-drained soil. Prefers full sun to partial shade.
Grows up to 12 inches tall and wide in zones 7–10.

Sussex Carpet hebe (*Hebe albicans* 'Sussex Carpet') This
sun-loving, low-growing, spreading form of hebe stays quite
compact. It forms a dense, bushy, evergreen shrub with white
flowers in summer that are highly attractive to pollinators.
Blue-gray foliage is perfect in a sun-drenched landscape, where
cooler color is welcome. This makes an interesting ground cover
shrub to snuggle up to boulders. Grows to 8–12 inches tall and
16–36 inches wide in zones 8–10.

Silver Shadow astelia (*Astelia* 'Silver Shadow')
Recurved metallic silver leaves make this unique
clumping grass-like perennial shine. This
drought-tolerant New Zealand native with a broad
blade makes an excellent counterpoint to plants
with finer textures. It appreciates well-drained soil
in partial sun, although it will take full sun with
occasional watering. This plant is considered an
evergreen in mild climates, and in cooler areas it
may die down fully in winter and come back from
the roots. Grows to 2–3 feet tall and 2–4 feet wide
in zones 7b–11 or enjoy as an annual before
bringing indoors for the winter.

FINISHING TOUCH

Boulders are the perfect finishing detail in a drought-tolerant landscape
like this one. They also serve a particular function other than simply
adding scale and dimension to a setting; they also add a source of warmth
from which these heat-loving plants can draw, which is important for
survival in cooler climates. The addition of sharp gravel as a ground cover is
a simple way of tying the stone element down low, drawing the eye around
the composition as well as providing moisture-saving mulch. If you want to
get creative, you could also use crushed seashells.

SCENTSATIONAL

SITE FULL SUN   SOIL AVERAGE TO DRY, WELL-DRAINED   ZONE 9–11   SEASON YEAR-ROUND

Garlands of pale yellow acacia flowers drape over the spiky century plant, the tiny powder-puff blooms perfuming the late winter garden. Adding a spicy edge to the floral sweetness is the aromatic myrtle foliage, whose soft colors repeat the tones found in its companions. Contrasting small leaves and miniature flowers with bold, waxy foliage keep to a simple color palette of soft gray and yellow and create a wholly feminine composition.

HOW THE DESIGN GROWS

This evergreen trio promises foliage, flowers, and fragrance for many years. In summer the myrtle will add its sweetly perfumed flowers to the mix, the seeds maturing to blue-black berries that will show up well against the lighter colors. At some point the long-lived variegated century plant will bloom, heralding the end of its life and shifting the balance of this composition while the younger plantlets mature.

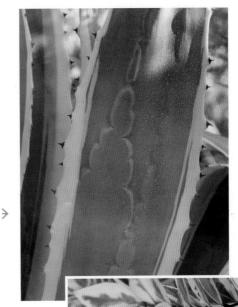

FOLIAGE FRAMEWORK

- ->

Variegated century plant (*Agave americana* 'Variegata', also sold as *Agave americana* var. *marginata*) Attractive blue-gray and creamy yellow variegated succulent foliage grows in rosettes. Tall flowering stalks on mature plants attract hummingbirds, but after blooming the parent plant dies. Beware of sharp spines and situate away from paths. Grows to 5–6 feet tall and wide in zones 8–11.

- ->

Variegated myrtle (*Myrtus communis* 'Variegata') Luminous creamy white-and-green variegated leaves make this myrtle a favorite for the garden. The evergreen foliage has a spicy fragrance when crushed, while the summer flowers add a sweet perfume. This dense shrub takes shearing well and makes a useful privacy screen. Prefers full sun and needs moderate water. Grows to 8–10 feet tall and wide in zones 9–11.

FINISHING TOUCH

- ->

Knife acacia (*Acacia cultriformis*) This small multitrunked evergreen tree has unusual triangular gray-green leaves, while its clusters of fuzzy yellow flowers perfume the air in late winter and early spring. Drought tolerant, deer resistant, and not fussy about soil except that it must drain well. Grows to 15 feet tall and wide in zones 9–11.

WINTER WHITES

SITE PARTIAL SUN   **SOIL AVERAGE, WELL-DRAINED**   **ZONE 6–8**   **SEASON YEAR-ROUND**

Nestled between mossy boulders, this unassuming combination captivates our attention by virtue of its simplicity. While the pale yellow native primrose is commonly found in English woodlands, this pure white form is less familiar. Caressed and semi-veiled by the whisper-soft Mexican feather grass, the single blooms add sparkle to the late winter garden. Unlike its gaudy cousins in their kaleidoscope of colors, this primrose looks perfectly at home with simple grasses. Such effortless beauty is a reminder that sometimes less is more.

HOW THE DESIGN GROWS

Although the primrose blooms for only a few months, its basal foliage rosette is often evergreen, creating year-round interest. The grass and primrose will coexist indefinitely, although you can divide and thin both. To add summer color, introduce Profusion Mexican daisy (*Erigeron karvinskianus* 'Profusion'): the pink-and-white daisies and simple gray-green carpet of foliage tie in easily to the theme of this charming vignette.

FOLIAGE FRAMEWORK

- →

Mexican feather grass (*Stipa tenuissima*, also sold as *Nassella tenuissima*) This evergreen, deer-resistant, drought-tolerant grass is a wonderful low-maintenance addition to the naturalistic garden. To thrive it needs well-drained soil, and it prefers a hot, sunny spot but will also do well in partial sun. Run your fingers or a rake through the foliage in late summer to remove tangled seed heads. Grows to 2½ feet tall and wide in zones 6–10. **CAUTION** This grass can self-seed easily in ideal conditions. Before planting, make sure it is not invasive in your area.

FINISHING TOUCH

- →

White English primrose (*Primula vulgaris* 'Alba') This European native is typically evergreen with a basal rosette of medium green foliage. The fragrant white flowers have a distinct yellow eye and appear in late winter and early spring. You can divide the mature clumps in spring to share with friends. This perennial thrives in dappled woodland shade or in settings where you can protect it from hot afternoon sun. Grows to 8–10 inches high and 18 inches wide in zones 4–8.

BEJEWELED

SITE **PARTIAL SUN, PARTIAL SHADE**   SOIL **MOISTURE-RETENTIVE**   ZONE **7**   SEASON **YEAR-ROUND**

This artisan collection sparkles with shades of red set in a distinctive framework of gold. From the vivid dogwood stems to the smoky sweetspire foliage and tiny clusters of crimson flowers nestled within the isu tree, red foliage is clearly the linking theme, yet each of these layers showcases a unique texture. The glowing golden Japanese cedar in the background sets off all the flowers, foliage, and bare stems. Any one of these elements would add beauty to the garden, but the artistry comes from achieving the perfect balance between each component.

HOW THE DESIGN GROWS

The ultimate season for this combination is winter, when the bold stems of the red twig dogwood are exposed. In spring the new green foliage will obscure them, coinciding with the leafing out of the Virginia sweetspire and the new creamy yellow growth on the Japanese cedar. By early summer fragrant white flowers will cover the sweetspire. Autumn brings deep yellow shades to the dogwood and rich red to the sweetspire. You will have to thin out both of these suckering shrubs periodically to avoid overcrowding, but otherwise this is an easy-care design.

FOLIAGE FRAMEWORK

- →

Sekkan-sugi Japanese cedar (*Cryptomeria japonica* 'Sekkan-sugi') The soft golden foliage of this conifer is tipped with creamy yellow in spring and early summer, creating a sun-kissed effect. It adapts well to full sun or partial shade. Grows to 30 feet tall and 10 feet wide in zones 6–9.

- →

Henry's Garnet Virginia sweetspire (*Itea virginica* 'Henry's Garnet') If you need a large suckering shrub that can handle tough conditions, consider this beauty. Racemes of fragrant white flowers in early summer and red fall foliage that can persist through mild winters are just two highlights. It is deer tolerant and low maintenance, thrives in wet soil, and prefers full sun or full shade. Grows to 3–4 feet tall and 4–6 feet wide in zones 5–9.

- →

Isu tree (*Distylium myricoides*) The evergreen foliage of this witch hazel relative grows in distinct arching layers. In late winter and early spring, tiny red flowers appear nestled within the evergreen blue-green leaves. Prefers partial sun or partial shade. Grows to 3–4 feet tall and 6–8 feet wide in zones 7–9.

FINISHING TOUCH

- →

Red twig dogwood (*Cornus alba* 'Sibirica') Vivid red stems are the hallmark of this deciduous suckering shrub. To maintain the dramatic color, cut back one third of the stems each spring, as the brightest color will always be on the youngest growth. The medium green foliage turns yellow in fall. Thrives in clay soils, is ideal for rain gardens, and does well in full sun to partial shade. Grows to 4–7 feet tall and spreads vigorously in zones 3–7.

CABBAGE QUEEN

SITE **PARTIAL SUN** SOIL **POTTING SOIL** ZONE **6–7** SEASON **YEAR-ROUND**

Mixing a native ground cover and a specialty conifer with a funky ornamental kale may sound risky, but it works. The purple and pink tones of the ruffled coral bells and holly-like Oregon grape accent the color echo between the heather and conifer. This foliage backdrop sets the stage for the star of the container to take the spotlight—the diva-like ornamental kale with its three lavender and green roses. Clearly this is no place for a mere princess.

HOW THE DESIGN GROWS

Although this container was designed to celebrate fall, all the plants except the ornamental kale are evergreen and offer the potential for year-round interest. This coral bells hybrid needs afternoon shade during the summer, however, so in spring replace it with a sun-tolerant variety, such as Peach Flambé. You could substitute one of the rose-like succulents, such as Perle von Nurnberg echeveria (*Echeveria* 'Perle von Nurnberg'), for the annual kale. These would offer comparable bold texture, rosette shape, and color.

FOLIAGE FRAMEWORK

------------------------------ >

Forever Goldie golden arborvitae (*Thuja plicata* 'Forever Goldie') A soft columnar conifer that is vibrant yellow in full sun and chartreuse in partial sun, and takes on orange tints in winter. Grows to 15–20 feet tall and 3 feet wide in zones 3–7.

------------------------------ >

Cascade Oregon grape (*Mahonia nervosa*) This evergreen suckering ground cover is native to the Pacific Northwestern United States. The large, spiky green leaves can turn purple in full sun, but this tough plant is equally happy in deep shade. Yellow flowers appear in May, followed by grape-like edible blue fruit in fall. Grows to 12 inches tall and 4 feet wide in zones 6–9.

------------------------------ >

Carnival Peach Parfait coral bells (*Heuchera* 'Carnival Peach Parfait') This tidy mound is one of the more heat-tolerant coral bells, but it still needs protection from hot afternoon sun. The large, ruffled peach leaves are overlaid with silver, while the undersides are a distinct bright purple. Grows to 12 inches tall and 12 inches wide in zones 4–9.

continued on next page

Cabbage Queen continued

FINISHING TOUCH

- ->

Pink Crane ornamental kale (*Brassica oleracea* 'Pink Crane') A fun designer cabbage that resembles a rose. Lavender-pink inner leaves transition to medium green, the compact head held upright on strong stalks. Grows to 4 feet tall with 4- to 6-inch heads. Cool-season annual.

- ->

Anouk heather (*Calluna vulgaris* 'Anouk') Grown primarily for its golden foliage, this heather also has white flowers that last for several months. Grows to 18 inches tall and wide in zones 5–8.

FALL SYMPHONY

SITE **FULL SUN**   SOIL **AVERAGE, WELL DRAINED**   ZONE **5–7**   SEASON **YEAR-ROUND**

The slender Persian ironwood tree oversees this seasonal performance. The spirea plays a soothing melody, supported by rippling chords from the grasses, while the pine adds bold trumpet blasts. No orchestra is complete without the percussion section, and the drumstick-like seed heads of the faded black-eyed Susan punctuate the rhythm with a series of staccato beats. Together they compose an unforgettable fall symphony.

Fall Symphony continued

HOW THE DESIGN GROWS

Each season introduces a new movement. In winter the skeletal Ruby Vase Persian ironwood will display thread-like red flowers on bare branches, adding color beyond the rich green pine needles and straw-like grasses. Silky white candles project from the pine branches in spring, coinciding with the emergence of new copper-colored spirea leaves and purple-edged ironwood foliage. Summer continues to be colorful, with clusters of pink flowers on the spirea, the leaves of which have turned a softer yellow. This is when the black-eyed Susan really shines: the golden daisy flowers add sunshine to the late summer and early fall border. Autumn is perhaps the most exciting sonata, as the leaves on Ruby Vase turn orange, gold, red, and purple and the switch grass becomes a warm haze of orange and burgundy. To maintain a perfect rhythm, you will need to thin the flowers every few years, but the clumps are easy to dig up.

FOLIAGE FRAMEWORK

- ->

Ruby Vase Persian ironwood (*Parrotia persica* 'Ruby Vase') Interesting bark, winter flowers, multitoned foliage, and stunning fall color—this slender tree fits into even small gardens and gives a lot in return. Grows to 30 feet tall and 12 feet wide in zones 5–7.

- ->

Thunderhead Japanese black pine (*Pinus thunbergii* 'Thunderhead') A compact, sculptural conifer with long deep green needles and silky white candles in spring. Grows to 10 feet tall and 15 feet wide in zones 5–10.

Shenandoah switch grass (*Panicum virgatum* 'Shenandoah') Vertical green blades tipped with burgundy produce attractive seed heads in fall that last well into winter. Grows to 4 feet tall and 2 feet wide in zones 4–9.

Double Play Gold spirea (*Spiraea japonica* 'Double Play Gold') This low-maintenance deciduous shrub offers colorful foliage as well as flowers. Drought tolerant and mostly deer resistant (they may nibble the flowers, but rarely do damage). Grows to 3–4 feet tall and wide in zones 4–9, but you can prune to keep it smaller.

FINISHING TOUCH

Seed head of black-eyed Susan (*Rudbeckia fulgida* var. *sullivantii* 'Goldsturm') Although known for its golden yellow daisy flowers, this herbaceous perennial has interesting seed heads, which the birds enjoy throughout fall and winter (don't cut down the stems too soon). Grows to 3 feet tall and 3 feet wide in zones 5–7.

MIXED-UP MOSAIC

SITE **PARTIAL SUN, FULL SUN** SOIL **MOIST, WELL-DRAINING** ZONE **5–7**
SEASON **SPRING THROUGH FALL**

Individual tiles may not be especially inspiring, but when you combine them in interesting ways, the results can be intriguing. This mosaic of soft striped Japanese forest grass paired with stiff, polka dot–like rock cotoneaster with tiny rounded leaves and scarlet berries makes fascinating artwork. This imaginative design shows that allowing plants to snuggle up tight can sometimes make for the best, yet most unexpected, pairings. The three-way gold, green, and red color mix is another alluring element in this composite, particularly in autumn when the berries are bright and bold.

HOW THE DESIGN GROWS

Late summer and fall are the most captivating times for this combination, when the Japanese forest grass is flowering with fluttery seed heads and the rock cotoneaster shows off a feast of berries on which birds can gorge. The rigid branches hang on to the lustrous deep green leaves and even turn a rich purple tone before dropping off for winter. As the forest grass ages it will benefit from dividing every 4–5 years to have the fullest and strongest growth and color, while the sprawling ground cover of cotoneaster will provide a dense thicket in which birds can hide and nest. The plant needs only occasional pruning for shape as long as it has plenty of room to spread out.

FOLIAGE FRAMEWORK

- →

Golden Japanese forest grass (*Hakonechloa macra* 'Aureola') This herbaceous grass forms the most beautiful cascading waterfall of buttery yellow blades, each with a green central stripe. It works well in Asian, woodland, or contemporary designs as well as in containers. Blooming in fall with fluffy soft tan seed heads, this wonderfully hardy perennial is known to take on pink tinges of color from the cold fall weather before going fully dormant. Spreads out slowly to a clump. Grows to 12–18 inches tall and 2–3 feet wide in zones 4–9.

FINISHING TOUCH

- →

Rock cotoneaster (*Cotoneaster horizontalis* 'Perpusillus') A slow-growing, spreading deciduous shrub that thrives in partial shade to full sun and features tiny glossy green leaves and small pink flowers in spring that mature to red berries in fall. The tight fishbone-patterned growth habit is an attractive texture in the garden. A wonderful shrub for erosion control and rabbit resistance, this plant will also be quite drought tolerant once established. Grows to 12–18 inches tall and 5–8 feet wide in zones 4–7.

SWIMMING WITH SUCCULENTS

SITE **FULL SUN**   SOÍL **DRY, WELL-DRAINED**   ZONE **9–11**   SEASON **YEAR-ROUND**

Shades of aqua and coral set the theme for this aquarium-like succulent landscape. Bold green-and-blue agave foliage reaches upward, resembling seaweed moving gently in the underwater current, while coral-like sticks on fire and the blooms of a coral aloe glow amid the cooler tones. Adding drama to the watery scene is the glossy black rose, its succulent rosettes topped with fat clusters of starry yellow flowers.

HOW THE DESIGN GROWS

Late winter and early spring are the most floriferous seasons for this design, but all the foliage is evergreen, so it will never be dull. As the agaves mature and bloom, the parent plant will die but new plantlets will appear at the base to replace them. Over time larger specimens may crowd out less robust succulents, so you may have to do some thinning, but otherwise this is a low-maintenance, water-wise combination.

FOLIAGE FRAMEWORK

- →

Swan's neck agave (*Agave attenuata*) This unusual agave gets its name from the long, curved flowering stem that appears on mature plants. The basal rosette of succulent foliage is a lovely green and prefers full to partial sun. Grows to 2–3 feet tall and wide in zones 9–11.

- →

Century plant (*Agave americana*) Succulent ice blue foliage grows in rosettes. Each blade has a spiny tip and thorns, so handle with care. Mature plants throw up a spectacular 15- to 30-foot flowering spike. Afterward the plant will die, but there will be plenty of offsets at the base for the future. Grows to 6–8 feet tall and wide in zones 8–11.

FINISHING TOUCH

- →

Black rose (*Aeonium* 'Zwartkop') Glossy black rosettes are topped with cones of yellow flowers in late winter. Prefers full to partial sun. Grows to 3 feet tall and 2 feet wide in zones 9–11 or enjoy as an annual.

continued on next page

Sticks on fire (*Euphorbia tirucalli* 'Rosea') This colorful succulent will always make a statement. Its pencil-like leafless branches are brightest in winter when grown in full sun, the red tones fading to yellow in summer. Wear gloves, as the sap is a skin irritant. Grows to 4–8 feet tall and 3–5 feet wide in zones 9–11.

Coral aloe (*Aloe striata*) The attractive broad succulent foliage is typically gray-green, but in more sun it will have blue undertones. Flat clusters of coral flowers are held high on fat stalks and add lots of color in late winter and early spring. Grows to 1–2 feet tall and 2–3 feet wide in zones 9–11.

SCULPTURES AND SKELETONS

SITE **FULL SUN**   SOIL **AVERAGE**   ZONE **6–7**   SEASON **YEAR-ROUND**

Conifers are the workhorses of the winter garden, and each of the three shown here has a unique sculptural quality and distinctive color. They provide visual strength amid the stark, frost-covered branches of neighboring trees and shrubs. Yet as the ice crystals sparkle in the watery sunshine, it is clear that the winter skeletons also enhance the evergreen foliage, their ghostly tracery emphasizing the shades of blue, green, and gold in a way that broadleaf evergreen shrubs could not.

HOW THE DESIGN GROWS

This border may change character with the seasons, but it is always photo-worthy. Spring will see the emergence of colorful new foliage, including the golden leaves of the locust tree and copper-colored spirea featured here, but there are also shades of burgundy and green within the vignette. Pink spirea flowers in summer and an array of fall colors will prevent this scene from ever becoming dull. Other than an optional trimming of the spirea for shape, no special maintenance is needed.

FOLIAGE FRAMEWORK

- →

Forever Goldie golden arborvitae (*Thuja plicata* 'Forever Goldie') This soft golden teddy bear of the conifer world shines year-round, with its color transitioning from bright yellow in spring to orange-tinted gold in winter. Shadier conditions result in more chartreuse tones. Prefers full sun but also grows in partial shade. Grows to 15–20 feet tall and 3 feet wide in zones 3–7.

- →

Wissel's Saguaro false cypress (*Chamaecyparis lawsoniana* 'Wissel's Saguaro') This rich blue-green conifer has quite the personality thanks to its cactus-like arms, which seem to reach out for a hug. Ideal for narrow spaces or a vertical accent. Grows to 10 feet high and 2 feet wide in zones 6–8.

Blue Star juniper (*Juniperus squamata* 'Blue Star') This low-growing conifer is the perfect color to include in a container or landscape design. Stiff dusky blue needles grow densely to form a spreading mound. Grows to 2 feet tall and 3–4 feet wide in zones 4–8.

FINISHING TOUCH

Golden locust tree (*Robinia pseudoacacia* 'Frisia') Usually praised for its luminous golden foliage, this winter scene shows the value of its elegant branching silhouette and pale bark. Grows to 30–50 feet tall and 20 feet wide in zones 4–9.

Double Play Gold spirea (*Spiraea japonica* 'Double Play Gold') Grown for its colorful foliage and summer flowers, the skeletal branches and dried flower heads on this deciduous shrub provide twiggy mounding structure that adds interest to the front of the border even in winter. Grows to 3–4 feet tall and wide in zones 4–9, but you can prune to keep it smaller.

MISE EN PLACE

SITE **FULL SUN, PARTIAL SUN**   SOIL **AVERAGE AND POTTING SOIL**   ZONE **6–8**   SEASON **YEAR-ROUND**

Mise en place is a French culinary term meaning "putting in place," a phrase that totally suits this combination. The bright red container complements this Japanese black pine so perfectly in scale and color, adding order to a very casual setting of native plants in this bed. The structure of the stiff green pine needles is an excellent contrast to the mounded broad leaf salal, while the ultra-red dwarf cranberry bush branches echo the spiky pine in a true winter drama. Simple ingredients yield amazing flavors in this dish.

HOW THE DESIGN GROWS

Although this low-maintenance mixture is going to look great through the year, these ingredients are at the peak of ripeness in winter. The Japanese black pine is a star performer year-round, and a standout against the rich green broadleaves of the salal on a gray winter day. The dwarf cranberry bush drops its foliage in fall to show its zesty shades of red, orange, and coral branches that stand up to anything winter weather throws at it. Planting white daffodil bulbs such as *Narcissus* 'Thalia' under the edges of the salal and dwarf cranberry bush would take this combination to the next level in early spring as they peek through those branches with hardy cold-weather blooms.

FOLIAGE FRAMEWORK

- >

Thunderhead Japanese black pine (*Pinus thunbergii* 'Thunderhead') Whether you use this architectural pine in a formal Asian-style garden or a soft casual landscape for the irregular growth pattern, it is a flexible and interesting shrub for its new silver-white growth tips in spring or deep green needles in winter. In partial to full sun this will be a tough and drought-tolerant plant once established. Grows to 10 feet tall and 15 feet wide in zones 5–10.

- >

Salal (*Gaultheria shallon*) This leather-leaved cousin of the heather family is a wonderful native plant to North America, and the foliage is a favorite of floral designers. It blooms in spring with delicate pink-and-white flowers that attract hummingbirds and later turn to edible berries that hikers and bears adore. This evergreen prefers partial shade but also does well in brighter sunlight, where it will stay shorter and more compact. Grows to 3–5 feet tall and wide in zones 6–10.

- >

Dwarf European cranberry bush (*Viburnum opulus* 'Nanum') The lovely maple-like dark green foliage of this incredibly hardy and compact shrub does not bloom and berry like its larger cousins, but it is no less of a garden hotshot for the colorful red branching it shows off in winter. This tough little shrub needs little to no pruning, and pests and diseases do not bother it. Prefers full sun to partial shade. Grows to 2 feet tall and 3 feet wide in zones 3–8.

continued on next page

Mise en Place continued

FINISHING TOUCH

- →

Bright red pot Adding the bright red container directly
into this casual bed creates a focal point, but also master-
fully adds to the drama of the winter color palette. Had this
container been any other color, it might serve as a distrac-
tion rather than pull the combination together. We eat with
our eyes first, so "putting in place" is very fitting here.

LOVABLE ROGUE

SITE FULL SUN, PARTIAL SHADE   **SOIL** POTTING SOIL   **ZONE** 8   **SEASON** YEAR-ROUND

Scallywag holly is the mischief-maker of this combo, threatening to poke those who come too close. However, this dwarf holly is not all that sharp. Its dark burgundy foliage adds high contrast to the yellow tones found in the hebe while echoing its subtle purple tints. Velvety Fire Alarm coral bells and rose-colored berries raise the temperature, while Blue Star juniper cools it down. Finally, the soft and most definitely not prickly Rheingold arborvitae will glow amber as soon as colder weather arrives, adding another layer of color.

Lovable Rogue continued

HOW THE DESIGN GROWS

You can enjoy the fun year-round thanks to the evergreen holly, conifers, coral bells, and ivy. When seasonal accents are spent, you could fill the gaps with pinecones for the winter and add fresh color in spring. Or take the design apart, transplanting some shrubs into other containers or the garden, allowing those that remain more room to grow.

FOLIAGE FRAMEWORK

Scallywag holly (*Ilex ×meserveae* 'Scallywag') A relatively new introduction, this dwarf holly is sure to become a favorite. The glossy dark green foliage takes on deep burgundy tones in winter, making it a striking addition to containers or the landscape, and it has drool-worthy black stems. Grows to 4 feet tall and 3 feet wide in zones 5–9.

Fire Alarm coral bells (*Heuchera* 'Fire Alarm') This perennial leafy mound really seeks attention. Moving through spring shades of vibrant red-orange to more subtle dusky tones in fall, it has something to offer in every season. Best in a protected area during colder months, or select the variety Fire Chief for similar color but greater cold tolerance. Grows to 14 inches tall and wide in zones 4–9.

Variegated hebe (*Hebe* 'Variegata') Variegated foliage is invaluable in design, and this compact shrub also offers purple blooms in summer for those who need their flower fix. Grows to 2–3 feet tall and wide in zones 8–9 or enjoy as an annual.

Blue Star juniper (*Juniperus squamata* 'Blue Star') This blue foliage is effective in so many color schemes. Young junipers are wonderful additions to the front of containers, where they will mound gently over the edge. You can enjoy this slow-growing plant for several seasons. Grows to 2 feet tall and 3–4 feet wide in zones 4–8.

Rheingold arborvitae (*Thuja occidentalis* 'Rheingold') A tufty mounding conifer in a unique shade of copper, this underused evergreen adds great color and texture to the landscape or containers. Grows to 3–5 feet tall and wide in zones 4–8.

Variegated ivy (*Hedera helix*) If you are going to use ivy, restrict it to a container, trim the length as necessary, and root prune in fall to prevent it from taking over. This is a great plant for adding a little sparkle to containers. Unrestrained this rampant vine can climb or trail more than 90 feet long and 20 feet wide in zones 6–10.

FINISHING TOUCH

Hypearls Olivia St. John's wort (*Hypericum* 'Hypearls Olivia') Berries are a wonderful addition to any container combination, and this is a stellar deciduous shrub for fall designs. Yellow flowers are followed by bullet-shaped rosy fruit that remain for several months, and blue-green leaves are the perfect foil. Trim in late winter. Grows to 3 feet tall and wide in zones 5–8.

A VERTICAL TWIST

SITE **FULL SUN**   SOIL **AVERAGE**   ZONE **6–8**   SEASON **YEAR-ROUND**

Like a beaded curtain, Helmond Pillar barberry creates a semi-transparent screen through which you can glimpse the distant garden, while glossy scarlet berries stud its thorny stems. Layered in front of this vertical silhouette is the twisted form of a Black Dragon Japanese cedar, which offers contrast in color, texture, and shape. This simple combination is most appealing when cast in the soft light of a winter sun, each unique profile highlighted while the berries glisten in the background.

HOW THE DESIGN GROWS

In spring purple leaves will emerge on the barberry along with small yellow flowers. This will coincide with the bright green new growth on the conifer. By summer the needles of the Japanese cedar will turn almost black, a somber companion to the dark purple-burgundy barberry. The mood is lightened in autumn, as the deciduous shrub transforms into a bold red pillar, the berries revealed once the leaves have fallen. This duo will mature slowly without maintenance or pruning. A suitable third companion might be a ground cover of evergreen black mondo grass (*Ophiopogon planiscapus* 'Nigrescens') or, for something brighter, a golden hinoki cypress such as Fernspray Gold (*Chamaecyparis obtusa* 'Fernspray Gold').

FOLIAGE FRAMEWORK

- >

Black Dragon Japanese cedar (*Cryptomeria japonica* 'Black Dragon') Black Dragon grows slowly, developing into a contorted sculptural pyramid as it matures. The dense branches are clothed in short needles that open light green before turning very dark. This Japanese cedar thrives in full sun or light, dappled shade, requires additional water only when the weather is exceptionally dry, and does well in average, well-drained soil. Grows to 10 feet tall and 8–10 feet wide in zones 6–9.

FINISHING TOUCH

- >

Helmond Pillar barberry (*Berberis thunbergii* 'Helmond Pillar') This columnar deciduous shrub lends itself well to flanking entrances, narrow spaces, and containers, and is a stunning vertical accent in the broader landscape. The dark purple foliage turns red in fall to reveal scarlet berries. This thorny shrub is low maintenance, drought tolerant, and deer resistant and will grow equally well in full sun or partial shade, although the best color develops in sun. Grows to 6 feet tall and 3 feet wide in zones 4–8. **CAUTION** Before planting, make sure barberries are not invasive in your area.

THE TICKLISH PORCUPINE

SITE **FULL SUN**   SOIL **DRY**   ZONE **7–10**   SEASON **YEAR-ROUND**

Like a favorite children's picture book, this scene holds your attention. The counterpoint of whisper-soft grasses caressing the large, fleshy paddles of the spiky cactus is unexpected enough, but the real surprise lies in the way the bleached Mexican feather grass echoes the color of those stiff spines, drawing attention to a detail that would otherwise be overlooked. The muted color scheme also keeps the emphasis on the extreme contrast in textures. Two unusual companions that live together happily ever after.

HOW THE DESIGN GROWS

Spring will be the most colorful season for this duo, as the cactus explodes with brightly colored flowers followed by edible red fruit. The new grass growth at this time of year is medium green, but the mature clumps reveal mostly bleached white stems. More subdued shades of khaki and tan persist for the remainder of the year on both plants. This water-wise, deer-resistant combination can withstand extreme heat and drought while also contributing structure and texture to the landscape for year-round interest. This design requires no special ongoing care other than occasionally tidying the grasses to remove tangled seed heads.

FOLIAGE FRAMEWORK

- ->

Mexican feather grass (*Stipa tenuissima*, also sold as *Nassella tenuissima*) A soft evergreen grass that thrives in hot, dry conditions and grows to a loose fountain that moves gently in the slightest breeze. Rake the foliage with your fingers in late summer to remove tangled seed heads, or trim it for a tidier appearance. Grows to 2½ feet tall and wide in zones 6–10. **CAUTION** This grass can self-seed easily in ideal conditions. Before planting, make sure it is not invasive in your area.

FINISHING TOUCH

- - - - - - - - - - - - - - - - - - - ->

Prickly pear cactus (*Opuntia engelmannii*) This segmented cactus is made up of large oval stem pads that are studded with wicked curved spines. In spring the dull green succulent is transformed when 3-inch-wide cup-shaped blooms appear in shades of red, orange, and yellow, followed by fat edible red fruit. Grows to 5 feet tall and wide in zones 7–10, possibly colder in protected areas.

FIRE AND ICE

SITE FULL SUN, PARTIAL SUN   **SOIL** AVERAGE, WELL-DRAINED   **ZONE** 8–9   **SEASON** YEAR-ROUND

The stiff branches of the low-growing heather poke skyward, the burnt orange leaves resembling tiny flickering flames that threaten to melt the icicle-like tassels of the silk tassel tree. The ultimate yin-yang of hot and cold work together without the damaging consequences of either. This balance, together with the interplay between the sweeping horizontal plane of heather foliage and the distinct vertical lines of the pendulous catkins, results in a dramatic winter scene.

HOW THE DESIGN GROWS

As the winter white catkins fade, the heather will continue to add color as its finely textured foliage softens to a golden glow, still contrasting well with the backdrop of dark green broadleaf foliage. By midsummer the heather is changing color yet again, adding orange to its foliage color palette together with a flush of lavender-pink flowers. Both shrubs will continue to grow without encroaching on the other, the silk tassel tree adding height while the low-growing heather forms a carpet at its base. Adding a tall Sekkan-sugi Japanese cedar (*Cryptomeria japonica* 'Sekkan-sugi') to the side of this duo would introduce a new texture and add sparkle to the dark green foliage as well as a color echo with the heather in spring.

FOLIAGE FRAMEWORK

- >

Robert Chapman heather (*Calluna vulgaris* 'Robert Chapman') Golden spring foliage slowly transitions to orange in summer before turning fiery red in winter. Lavender-pink flowers appear in midsummer, adding yet another layer of color to this four-season evergreen shrub. Heathers are deer resistant and drought tolerant once established, and thrive in acidic soil and full or partial sun. Grows to 2 feet tall and 30 inches wide in zones 5–9.

FINISHING TOUCH

- >

Carl English silk tassel tree (*Garrya ×issaquahensis* 'Carl English') Make a statement in your garden with this deer-resistant evergreen shrub. Glossy leaves are attractive year-round, but the winter display of long pale catkins is the real talking point. Prefers full sun to partial shade. Grows to 8–9 feet tall and wide in zones 8–9; with protection from extreme winter winds it may tolerate colder conditions.

SERENDIPITY

SITE **FULL SUN**   SOIL **AVERAGE, WELL-DRAINED**   ZONE **4–8**   SEASON **YEAR-ROUND**

Sometimes it pays to be a lazy gardener. This sea holly and blue spruce were likely planted together for a summer display, when the metallic blue bracts of the sea holly would echo the dusky blue spruce needles. But the papery, often overlooked seed head draws attention not to the needles but rather to the caramel-colored stems and nodules of the conifer. Serendipity can be an inspiring designer.

HOW THE DESIGN GROWS

When the seed heads finally crumble in spring, new blue stems will rise up above the rosettes of spiky foliage and open into teasel-esque blue flowers, each of which has a star-like collar. A mature clump of sea holly will continue to send up flowering stems throughout the summer, but you can enhance this combination in spring with a mass planting of wind flower (*Anemone blanda*) in shades of blue or white. The spruce remains a constant color companion throughout the year.

FOLIAGE FRAMEWORK

Dwarf Colorado blue spruce (*Picea pungens* 'Montgomery') This slow-growing conifer forms a dense mound that grows best in full sun but will also take partial shade, and needs moisture-retentive but well-drained soil. The dusky blue needles keep their color year-round. Colorado blue spruce is susceptible to spruce mites in some areas, which result in speckling or bronzing of needles. The most common treatment involves horticultural oils, but they can cause loss of the blue. Ask a local nursery professional for advice. Grows to 3–4 feet tall and 3 feet wide in zones 2–8.

FINISHING TOUCH

Sapphire Blue sea holly (*Eryngium* 'Sapphire Blue') One of the bluest sea hollies, this makes a colorful statement in any hot, dry garden. It has the best color in full sun and will be less likely to flop in poor soil, but a few well-placed twigs can give it a discreet support if necessary. This makes a fun addition to floral arrangements. It is a favorite of bees and butterflies, but deer and rabbits ignore it. Grows to 30 inches tall and 18 inches wide in zones 4–8.

TRAFFIC ALERT

SITE **FULL SUN, PARTIAL SUN**   SOIL **AVERAGE, MOISTURE-RETENTIVE**   ZONE **7–8**
SEASON **YEAR-ROUND**

When cars screech to a halt and neighbors stop to stare, you know the design works. In this case, the combination is as much about placement as the plants themselves. When the sun hits these aptly named Midwinter Fire dogwood twigs, the display is breathtaking, especially when framed by rich green foliage. The broad leathery leaves of the viburnum have short red stems reminiscent of small glowing embers hidden within. Contrasting in texture and form, the weeping blue atlas cedar bridges the two tiers with its draping branches.

HOW THE DESIGN GROWS

This is one of those special combinations that needs careful planning. Be sure to select an area you can see from indoors, and place the dogwood so the low-angled winter sun can stream through from behind at some point in the day. In spring, green leaves will hide the dogwood stems, and the viburnum will bloom with flat clusters of white flowers followed by blue berries. The anticipation builds in fall as the dogwood foliage turns a soft yellow, which is the prelude to another fiery show. You will need to prune both the dogwood and the viburnum to stop one from overtaking the other.

FOLIAGE FRAMEWORK

--→

Weeping blue atlas cedar (*Cedrus atlantica* 'Glauca Pendula') Whorls of short blue-green needles cover the pendulous branches of this dramatic evergreen conifer. You can train it with a tall vertical trunk and allow the branches to cascade to the ground, or keep it lower so the weeping branchlets give the impression of a richly textured curtain. Grows to 15–25 feet tall and wide in zones 6–9.

--→

David's viburnum (*Viburnum davidii*) Familiarity can cause us to overlook this evergreen shrub, which is a reliable performer in the garden. Deeply veined leathery leaves are held on short red stems, forming a low cushion. Clusters of white spring flowers give way to metallic blue berries if there is a pollinator nearby. Deer resistant and drought tolerant once established. Grows to 4 feet tall and wide in zones 7–9; spreads with age.

FINISHING TOUCH

--→

Midwinter Fire dogwood (*Cornus sanguinea* 'Midwinter Fire') Medium green leaves clothe this deciduous shrub in spring and summer, fading to yellow in fall. When the leaves are gone, the real beauty is revealed. The twiggy branches are a vibrant blend of red, orange, and gold, especially beautiful when backlit by the sun. For the best color, cut back one third of the oldest branches each spring. Grows to 4–5 feet tall and wide in zones 5–8.

BALANCE

SITE **FULL SUN, PARTIAL SUN, PARTIAL SHADE** SOIL **AVERAGE** ZONE **6–9** SEASON **YEAR-ROUND**

An asymmetrical planting of Green Groove and big-leaved bamboo establishes the frame into which the traditional stone lantern is set. This piece closes the triangle, balancing the whole. This Asian-inspired vignette blends seamlessly into the wider landscape, but is also complete in itself. Each component of this understated yet carefully planned scene enhances the other, creating a sense of quiet order—the embodiment of Japanese garden design.

HOW THE DESIGN GROWS

Seen here on a bleak January day, this scene does not lack for interest thanks to the evergreen bamboo foliage and bright canes. From spring until fall a planting of golden Japanese forest grass (*Hakonechloa macra* 'Aureola') would add a waterfall of soft yellow to the base of the lantern. The blades on this grass are striped with green, echoing the Green Groove bamboo in the background, while the style and color palette blend perfectly with the surroundings. Both bamboo will need careful management over time: thin out the culms as they become overly congested to ensure the rhizome barrier remains intact.

FOLIAGE FRAMEWORK

- →

Green Groove bamboo (*Phyllostachys* 'Green Groove') This bamboo is not meant for small spaces. Corral it carefully with a rhizome barrier, as it will quickly grow into a dense thicket. The 2-inch-thick canes typically have a zigzag habit and are golden yellow with a noticeable green stripe. This bamboo needs regular water and will grow in full sun or partial shade. Grows to 30 feet tall and spreads indefinitely in zones 6–10.

- →

Big-leaved bamboo (*Indocalamus tessellatus*) A dwarf form with the longest leaves of any bamboo in cultivation, each one growing up to 2 feet long and 4 inches wide. This spreading bamboo needs containing within a rhizome barrier, and its growth is noticeably denser in full sun. Grows to 8 feet tall and spreads indefinitely in zones 6–9, but you can keep it shorter and even shear it to the ground.

FINISHING TOUCH

- →

Stone lantern Rather than a more ornate pagoda-style lantern, this simple form accents the surrounding garden without being overly stylized. The homeowner felt it was a little short, especially when the perennial grasses emerge, so added a flat boulder at its base for additional height.

EMERALD ISLE

SITE FULL SUN **SOIL** AVERAGE **ZONE** 7–9 **SEASON** YEAR-ROUND

Emerald green is a classic color that speaks to the heart of garden design inspiration because of its inherent freshness and vitality—and the constant reminder of nature's renewal. When shades of green are layered, you feel like you can reach out and brush the feathery soft texture of the golden Japanese cedar with your fingertips and rub the stiff, shiny leaves of the California lilac. The contrast of the weeping brown sedge adds fluidity and movement, while the warm brown tone elevates the cool greens to an even more intense resonance.

HOW THE DESIGN GROWS

This hardy, elegant combination looks excellent year-round with little maintenance, and it shines all the more in the winter landscape, when gray tones tend to dominate. The golden Japanese cedar is a small tree that is wonderful for creating a lush privacy screen, but also brings color excitement in spring with new growth in green and gold. When summer arrives, the California lilac will burst into bloom with masses of deep blue flowers that blanket the entire shrub, giving this scene a light sapphire jewel to pair with the emeralds.

This simple border has few maintenance needs. Divide the sedge every three to five years to keep it looking full and abundant, and keep the California lilac's sprawling habit in check with a quick annual shaping.

FOLIAGE FRAMEWORK

----------------------------------→

Golden Japanese cedar (*Cryptomeria japonica* 'Elegans Aurea') Unlike other Japanese cedars, this cultivar holds the light green tones through winter and does not turn the more typical bronze. This showy but smaller scale tree is excellent for many landscape uses. Grows to 10–12 feet tall and 6 feet wide in zones 6–9.

----------------------------------→

Weeping brown sedge (*Carex flagellifera* 'Bronze') When this New Zealand native is young, its fine-textured red-bronze leaves are quite upright, but as the plant matures the foliage begins to arch and weep over toward the ground. Evergreen in mild climates, this low-maintenance grass has a lot of personality. It will tend to be redder in less sunlight and browner in brighter locations. Does best in full sun to partial shade. Grows to 18–20 inches high and 24–30 inches wide in zones 6–10.

FINISHING TOUCH

----------------------------------→

Victoria California lilac (*Ceanothus thyrsiflorus* 'Victoria') This evergreen shrub is wonderful in so many landscape applications, from a terrific tall hedge to a drought-tolerant focal point. Prune this fast-growing plant after the summer bloom so next year's flowers have plenty of time to develop. Prefers full sun and good drainage. Grows to 9 feet tall and 10–12 feet wide in zones 7–10.

PUMPKIN SPICE LATTE

SITE **FULL SUN, PARTIAL SHADE**   SOIL **POTTING SOIL**   ZONE **8–9**   SEASON **YEAR-ROUND**

Put an extra log on the fire with Little Flames leucothoe, settle into a comfy chair, and sip a warm pumpkin latte with just a hint of chile pepper added for spice. The toasty shades of caramel from the coral bells, mirror plant, grass, and ornamental millet are paired with the dark espresso container in a seasonal combination that is just the right blend of sweetness and spice.

HOW THE DESIGN GROWS

While this container offers autumnal highlights, you can enjoy many evergreen elements year-round and make quick substitutions for seasonal accents. In winter you will need to replace the colorful but annual Jester ornamental millet and stems of chile peppers; a few curly willow twigs would be a fast, inexpensive filler. The mirror plant is hardy only in milder climates, so be prepared to replace it—perhaps with autumn fern (*Dryopteris erythrosora*), which offers orange-suffused evergreen fronds.

FOLIAGE FRAMEWORK

Jester ornamental millet (*Pennisetum glaucum* 'Jester') This fun annual changes color every day. Emerging chartreuse with subtle burgundy details, it slowly turns a deep burgundy with green highlights—a harlequin balance that varies depending on light levels. Purple flower spikes in late summer complete the scene. Grows to 3–4 feet tall and 12 inches wide. Annual.

Little Flames leucothoe (*Leucothoe axillaris* 'Little Flames', also sold as *Leucothoe fontanesiana* 'Little Flames') An exciting new introduction, this dwarf evergreen shrub has flame-shaped glossy green leaves that turn peach, orange, and finally red as temperatures drop. This deer-resistant, low-maintenance plant does well in both sun and partial shade. Grows to less than 2 feet tall and wide in zones 7–9, possibly colder.

Belinda's Find sedge (*Uncinia rubra* 'Belinda's Find') This evergreen tufted grass in variegated brown and deep red prefers sun or partial shade. Grows to 12 inches tall and 15 inches wide in zones 8–10.

Caramel coral bells (*Heuchera* 'Caramel') Shades of apricot, peach, and gold with a magenta reverse make this an attractive hybrid to design with, especially as the colors shift throughout the year. Tolerates heat and humidity. Grows to 12 inches tall and 18 inches wide in zones 4–9.

continued on next page

Pumpkin Spice Latte continued

- →
Whipcord hebe (*Hebe ochracea* 'James Stirling')
Resembling a conifer more than a hebe, this unusual
evergreen shrub makes a great addition to containers with
its striking orange-green foliage and tiny
white flowers in spring. Grows to 10 inches
tall and 16 inches wide in zones 7–10.

- - - - - - - - - - - - - - - - - - - →
Tequila Sunrise mirror plant (*Coprosma
repens* 'Tequila Sunrise') An exceptional
evergreen shrub in mild climates with glossy
foliage in shades of green, gold, and orange
that intensify in fall. You can shear this plant
to shape. Grows to 5 feet in zones 9–10 or
enjoy as an annual.

FINISHING TOUCH

- - - - - - - - - - - - - - - - - →
Chile pepper A miniature pumpkin
and cut stems of colorful peppers
found at a grocery store add a fun
finishing touch to this fall mélange.

GOLDEN THREADS

SITE **FULL SUN**   SOIL **AVERAGE, WELL-DRAINED**   ZONE **7**   SEASON **YEAR-ROUND**

Broad sweeps of color weave through this large border with layers of trees, shrubs, and perennials all playing their part to create a hazy medley into which the flowers blend. The rich purple smoke bush and flowering plum tree enhance golden foliage from the feathery bluestar, conifer, and locust tree. Floral accents echo these colors, with the tall verbena punctuating the lower level and filtering our view of the golden black-eyed Susan. Restraint in color palette combined with adventurous textures is the hallmark of this misty autumnal vignette.

Golden Threads continued

HOW THE DESIGN GROWS

With the conifer providing year-round color, this scene will always have something to offer. Trees and shrubs add winter silhouettes, but the main drama begins in spring and continues until late fall, when the last of the leaves tumble to the ground. Planting large clusters of yellow daffodils among the Arkansas bluestar will fill the early season gap. To maintain this tapestry, thin out the vigorous black-eyed Susan every few years and allow the tall verbena to set seed, as parent plants may die in a severe winter. Annual spring pruning of the smoke bush will keep it more compact and result in larger foliage, a key to the success of this drought-tolerant, deer-resistant border.

FOLIAGE FRAMEWORK

- →

Arkansas bluestar (*Amsonia hubrichtii*) Early spring flowers are blue, but this is all about the feathery green foliage, which turns golden orange in fall. This perennial takes a few years to establish but is well worth the wait. Grows to 2 feet tall and wide in zones 5–8.

- →

Golden locust tree (*Robinia pseudoacacia* 'Frisia') A fast-growing tree that glows even on gray days. Tolerates many soil types but may sucker in some gardens. Grows to 30–50 feet tall and 20 feet wide in zones 4–9.

- →

Forever Goldie golden arborvitae (*Thuja plicata* 'Forever Goldie') An outstanding columnar fluffy conifer that is vibrant yellow in full sun or chartreuse in partial sun. Grows to 15–20 feet tall and 3 feet wide in zones 3–7.

Thundercloud plum (*Prunus cerasifera* 'Thundercloud') Although it has small pink flowers in spring, this plum tree is typically grown for its dark purple leaves, which persist through fall. Grows to 25 feet tall and 20 feet wide in zones 5–8.

Grace smoke bush (*Cotinus* 'Grace') An outstanding variety with large blue-toned purple foliage that turns red in fall. Prune hard in spring for larger leaves and to reduce height, although this will sacrifice the flowers. Grows to 10 feet tall and 8 feet wide (unpruned) in zones 5–9.

FINISHING TOUCH

Black-eyed Susan (*Rudbeckia fulgida* var. *sullivantii* 'Goldsturm') A well-known perennial that is easy to grow. Golden yellow daisies in late summer and early fall are followed by black seed heads for the birds to enjoy. Grows to 2 feet tall and spreads easily in zones 3–9.

Tall verbena (*Verbena bonariensis*) This perennial self-seeds easily, so if the parent plant dies in winter or your area is a little colder, don't worry—chances are you will still have some next spring. The clusters of lavender flowers on top of sturdy stems are a favorite of bees, butterflies, and hummingbirds. Grows to 4 feet tall and 3 feet wide in zones 7–11.

SOUP FOR THE SOUL

SITE **FULL SUN**   SOIL **AVERAGE**   ZONE **8**   SEASON **YEAR-ROUND**

When the skies are gray and the ground is winter white, you may have to look to material goods for bold color, and this bright pot delivers. Like a steaming bowl of tomato soup that revives the body and spirit, the welcome jolt of saturated orange provides warmth to the winter garden. Its solid form stands out against the finer textures of surrounding shrubs and grasses, while the rich orange enhances the bright red berries and frost-etched foliage of the wintergreen. In the foreground, the arching Feelin' Blue deodar cedar provides a visual connection between the foliage in the pot and the garden. This recipe is sure to become a favorite.

HOW THE DESIGN GROWS

When the frost finally thaws, the surrounding shrubs will slowly come to life, bringing more foliage and flowers to the scene. As spring transitions to summer, you will have to transplant the wintergreen into a shadier location, making way for a few summer annuals under the grass in the container. The grass inflorescences are purple, so some lavender trailing verbena would be an easy choice. For more sparkle, try Lemon Slice million bells (*Calibrachoa* 'Lemon Slice').

FOLIAGE FRAMEWORK

- →

New Zealand wind grass (*Anemanthele lessoniana*, also sold as *Stipa lessoniana* and *Stipa arundinacea*) An evergreen or semi-evergreen grass with arching dark green blades that take on a distinct orange tone in fall and winter. Late summer inflorescences are an attractive purple. Even in colder areas the bleached foliage can add winter interest, as seen in this design. Grows to a 3-foot-tall and 4-foot-wide in zones 8–10; you can divide if necessary.

- →

Feelin' Blue deodar cedar (*Cedrus deodara* 'Feelin' Blue') You can grow this striking blue conifer as a wide ground cover or train it as a short standard. The stiff, spiky needles are evergreen. Grows to 2–4 feet tall and 6 feet wide in zones 7–9, possibly colder; taller if grown as a standard.

- →

Wintergreen (*Gaultheria procumbens*) A reliable evergreen ground cover that spreads easily by rhizomes. In summer bell-shaped white flowers appear, followed by bright red winter berries. Use as a year-round ground cover in the shade garden or as a colorful winter accent in sunnier spots, as pictured. Grows to 4 inches tall and 12 feet wide in zones 3–8.

FINISHING TOUCH

- →

Orange pot Big, bold, and beautiful: this frost-resistant ceramic container does not need any ornamentation to look good, and its classic shape allows for easy seasonal replanting.

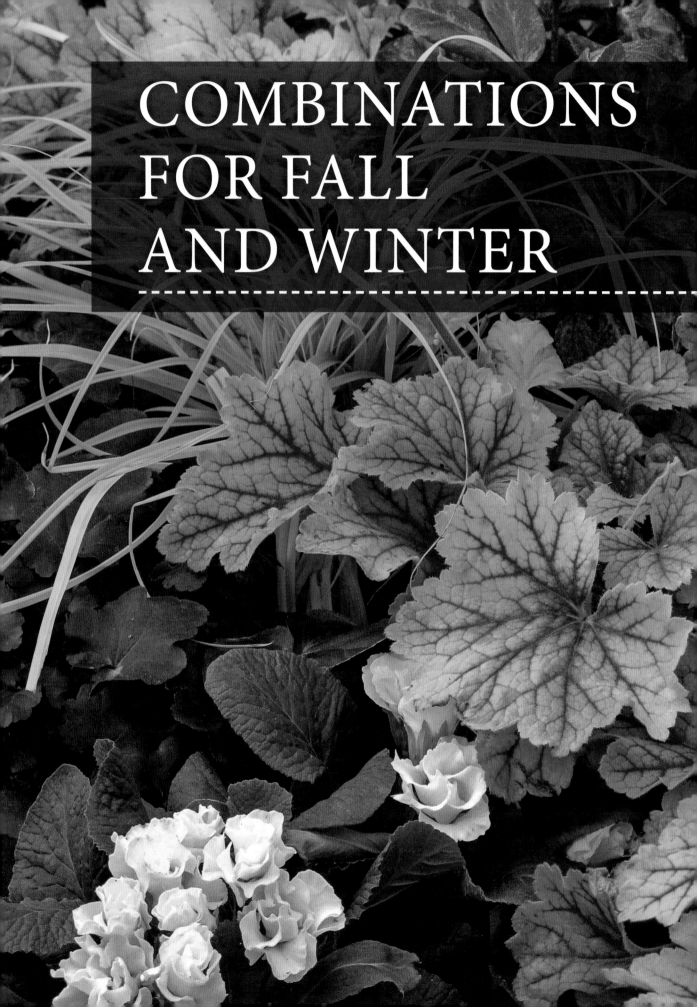

COMBINATIONS
FOR FALL
AND WINTER

Inspired Designs for Shady Locations

WINTER SPARKLERS

SITE **PARTIAL SHADE**   SOIL **AVERAGE**   ZONE **6–9**   SEASON **YEAR-ROUND**

If this book was the scratch-and-sniff variety, you would swoon over the intense, spicy perfume of the witch hazel. These thread-like golden flowers add much-needed sparkle to the winter garden and are best viewed against an uncluttered background, so the large heart-shaped barrenwort leaves are ideal. This foliage creates a dense carpet beneath the deciduous shrub, forcing the focus upward into the gnarled lichen-encrusted branches of the witch hazel. This simple combination is more about structure than overstuffed exuberance, encouraging visitors to linger and enjoy the fragrance of winter.

HOW THE DESIGN GROWS

Winter Beauty witch hazel is guaranteed to entice you outdoors on the dreariest winter day with its intoxicating scent and vivid flowers. Just as they begin to fade, the barrenwort takes its turn in the spotlight, pushing yellow flowers above the cushion of leaves on wiry stems, each little bloom resembling a bishop's hat. In midspring the emerging heart-shaped leaves steal the show with their mosaic of red veins overlaying the green. Summer is the quietest month, but in autumn the green leaves of the witch hazel light up the garden with shades of copper, orange, and gold. You do not have to divide the barrenwort to maintain vigor, so this scene will not change much in the future.

FOLIAGE FRAMEWORK

- →

Barrenwort (*Epimedium ×perralchicum*) This fast-growing ground cover copes with dry shade, poor soil, and deer, rewarding the gardener with an abundance of hat-like yellow flowers in early spring. Dense heart-shaped foliage opens green with burgundy markings before maturing to medium green. It is usually evergreen, although clipping away older leaves in spring gives a tidier appearance. This plant is easy to remove and not invasive. Grows to 16 inches tall and spreads easily in zones 5–9.

FINISHING TOUCH

- →

Winter Beauty witch hazel (*Hamamelis ×intermedia* 'Winter Beauty') Winter Beauty has the largest flowers of all the witch hazels, each spidery deep golden petal exploding from a dark red eye produced in abundance along the bare branches. The heady fragrance is a winter treat, so be sure to plant this where you can enjoy it. Does best in full sun or light shade. Grows to 12 feet tall and wide in zones 6–9.

PURE INDULGENCE

SITE **PARTIAL SHADE**   SOIL **AVERAGE**   ZONE **6–9**   SEASON **YEAR-ROUND**

Forget the calories: add a generous swirl of sour cream to your coffee cake with these luxuriant hellebores. Their large pale blooms have a soft pink blush and deep red stems, both of which echo the warm tones of the Cappuccino sedge. A hint of pale green is blended into the creamy flowers, which highlights the foliage of the draping Naylor's Blue Leyland cypress and dusky blue-gray leaves of the hellebore. The complex flavors of this indulgent breakfast will linger on the taste buds and in the mind, but not on the waistline.

HOW THE DESIGN GROWS

Every plant in this combination is evergreen so it will never fail to impress, but the most colorful months are from late December to March, when the hellebore is in full bloom. To expand the color theme, a variegated Goshiki Japanese false holly shrub (*Osmanthus heterophyllus* 'Goshiki') would provide spiky evergreen leaves splashed with creamy yellow and rosy new growth in spring. As the conifer grows, remove the lower limbs to allow the hellebores room to spread and the clumps of grasses to mature.

FOLIAGE FRAMEWORK

- ->

Naylor's Blue Leyland cypress (*Cupressocyparis ×leylandii* 'Naylor's Blue') This fast-growing evergreen conifer has dusky blue foliage held in flattened sprays. You can grow it as a hedge and it takes well to shearing, but its striking color also sets it apart as a specimen in the landscape. Drought tolerant and deer resistant, and prefers full sun but will adapt to partial shade. Grows to 30–40 feet tall and 10–15 feet wide in zones 6–9.

- ->

Cappuccino New Zealand hair sedge (*Carex tenuiculmis* 'Cappuccino') Warm shades of coffee predominate, with autumnal tints of copper and orange in colder months, making this evergreen sedge a fabulous contender for winter combinations in containers and the landscape. Needs well-drained soil and prefers full sun or partial shade. Grows to 12 inches tall and wide in zones 6–9.

FINISHING TOUCH

- ->

Monte Cristo hellebore (*Helleborus ×ericsmithii* Gold Collection Monte Cristo) Monte Cristo is a great selection if you are looking for a compact hellebore that blooms profusely for several months. The large flowers are soft cream suffused with dusky pink and are held high on stout red stems that contrast beautifully with the blue-gray leaves. This deer-resistant evergreen perennial does best in moisture-retentive soil and partial shade. Grows to 12 inches tall and up to 2 feet wide in zones 5–9.

A QUEEN AND HER COURT

SITE **PARTIAL SUN, PARTIAL SHADE**   SOIL **AVERAGE**   ZONE **4–9**   SEASON **YEAR-ROUND**

The queen of this combination is the gilded Electra coral bells, which reigns in bold style. One of the showiest of her adoring supporters is the strappy golden sedge, which gives textural contrast to the broad, ruffled leaves of the aristocratic coral bells. This regal mix gets a spark of freshness and light from the pure white primrose that blooms with wavy soft petals. Obsidian coral bells is the perfect contrast for gold and white, its dark foliage grounding the whole scene and adding unexpected color.

HOW THE DESIGN GROWS

White flowers are most welcome on winter days, especially when they bloom together for many weeks, as this primrose and hellebore do. Add in the finer sedge and bold coral bells and a dreary garden is transformed into an elegant, long-lasting vignette. As the weather warms, the coral bells will bloom through most of spring and summer with airy wands of white flowers. Adding hosta and ferns to the mix would extend the interest and add drama to the summer shade garden.

This low-maintenance combination of perennials needs dividing in spring every three to five years, which results in more plants to enjoy in the garden over time. Pinch off faded primrose blooms to promote more growth, and remove old foliage as needed.

FOLIAGE FRAMEWORK

- ->

Electra coral bells (*Heuchera* 'Electra') The dramatic red veins on the ruffled golden foliage give this plant year-round interest. While the leaf color changes through the seasons from yellow to chartreuse to a warm tan, the red remains eye-catching throughout. This adaptable cultivar shines in full to partial shade and blooms with showy clusters of airy white flowers. Grows to 8 inches tall and 14 inches wide in zones 4–9.

- ->

EverColor Everillo golden sedge (*Carex oshimensis* EverColor 'Everillo') This elegant, weeping evergreen clump of neon golden foliage is a dynamic way to light up areas of the garden that need an energy boost. Morning sun and afternoon shade give this grass the best golden color. Best suited to partial to full shade. Grows to 12 inches tall and 2 feet wide in zones 5–9.

- ->

Obsidian coral bells (*Heuchera* 'Obsidian') The rounded almost-black foliage of this compact coral bells is dramatic when contrasted with other bold colors. It blooms in a compact mound with panicles of airy white flowers on wiry stems rising nearly 2 feet high above the foliage. Prefers partial sun to partial shade. Grows to 8–10 inches tall and 16 inches wide in zones 4–9.

FINISHING TOUCH

- ->

Sweetheart primrose (*Primula ×polyantha* 'Sweetheart') This ruffled Sweetheart variety is particularly romantic in late winter as Valentine's Day approaches. This long-blooming, rabbit-resistant annual may be perennial in mild climates. Prefers partial to full shade. Grows to 6 inches tall and up to 12 inches wide in zones 3–8.

HANKY PANKY IN THE SHADE

SITE **PARTIAL SHADE**   SOIL **MOISTURE-RETENTIVE**   ZONE **6–8**   SEASON **YEAR-ROUND**

Be warned: this garden has some rather shady characters. The arrowhead-shaped bright green leaves of the arum display striking white veins that catch the light. This is always an advantage in the shade garden, but in some areas this plant can become invasive. Adding height to the design are branches of the evergreen Rubinetta skimmia: the leathery deep green foliage adds color and depth to the scene while also supporting clusters of flower buds. Sandwiched between these two, the dusky rose flowers of a hellebore jostle for space, their sultry color echoing the skimmia. The blooms may be the stars of the winter season, but without these foliage partners the show would be lackluster.

HOW THE DESIGN GROWS

As temperatures slowly begin to rise in spring, the unusual hooded flowers of the Italian arum will appear just as the hellebore blooms fade to light green and the last of the fragrant skimmia buds open. The scene shifts significantly, as the bright orange berries of the arum ripen on fat stalks while the foliage becomes dormant. From summer until fall the combination offers a solid green backdrop for more colorful plants, so this would be a good time to introduce some sparkle with Blade of Sun snowberry (*Symphoricarpos chenaultii* 'Blade of Sun'). This low-maintenance deciduous shrub has small golden leaves that remain vivid gold all season. Metallic pink berries in fall add an extra color punch on this low-growing carpet. Other than occasionally trimming the skimmia to maintain shape, this combination needs no special care if the arum stays in bounds.

FOLIAGE FRAMEWORK

- >

Italian arum (*Arum italicum*) Arrowhead-shaped, distinctly veined leaves appear in fall and are evergreen in milder climates. In spring an unusual hooded light green flower appears. After blooming the foliage goes dormant and the outer spathe disappears and leaves the central thick spadix, which develops into bright orange berries. This is a fascinating perennial for shaded and semi-shaded locations. Grows to 12–18 inches tall and wide in zones 5–9. **CAUTION** Before planting, make sure it is not invasive in your area.

- >

Rubinetta skimmia (*Skimmia japonica* 'Rubinetta') This male skimmia cultivar has glossy evergreen deep green foliage and fat clusters of deep red flower buds that open to fragrant pink-white flowers in late winter or early spring. It is a suitable pollinator for the berry-bearing female skimmia. This shade-loving shrub grows to 3–4 feet tall and wide in zones 6–9.

FINISHING TOUCH

- >

Hellebore hybrid (*Helleborus* hybrid) Hellebores are notoriously promiscuous, quickly cross-pollinating to produce generations of uncertain parentage, as is the case with this beauty. Anna's Red hellebore (*Helleborus* 'Anna's Red') is as an ideal candidate for re-creating this combination: its flower color and height are almost identical, but it is sterile so there is no risk of it misbehaving. It also has the most beautiful mottled foliage. Grows to 15 inches tall and 2 feet wide in zones 5–8.

CLASSICS ABLAZE

SITE **PARTIAL SHADE**   SOIL **AVERAGE, MOISTURE-RETENTIVE**   ZONE **6–7**   SEASON **YEAR-ROUND**

This garden celebrates fall with a smoldering display of orange, gold, and red foliage from Japanese maples, Japanese stewartia, and a hybrid magnolia. Yet this lavish scene is all the more dramatic within the classic green framework of clipped boxwood and conifers. The finishing touch is a symmetrical grouping of terra-cotta pots, which are weathered and mossy with age. These warm tones connect to the fiery foliage, while their formality in shape and style serves to temper the looser structure of the garden beyond.

HOW THE DESIGN GROWS

Japanese maples are known for their dazzling fall show, but many are equally exciting in spring. Together with the stewartia flowers in summer and starry magnolia blossoms in spring, these trees have much to offer. Winter is also attractive thanks to the boxwood topiaries, conifers, and salmon-and-cream patterned bark of the stewartia. This scene gets even better with age. The trees are all spaced to allow for their mature size; their layers of color and texture promise many more years of beauty. The boxwood requires trimming twice a year to maintain its form; replace it when it outgrows the containers.

FOLIAGE FRAMEWORK

--→

Low Glow Japanese red pine (*Pinus densiflora* 'Low Glow') A dense, low-mounding conifer with twisted bright green needles. Grows to 3 feet high and 5 feet wide in zones 4–7.

--→

Confucius hinoki cypress (*Chamaecyparis obtusa* 'Confucius') This is a dwarf form of the popular conifer. The foliage has golden highlights on the tips that contrast with the interior medium green, giving a two-tone effect. Grows to 8–10 feet tall and 6–8 feet wide in zones 5–8.

--→

Mikawa yatsubusa Japanese maple (*Acer palmatum* 'Mikawa yatsubusa') A dwarf variety with green foliage that turns orange and burgundy in late fall. Grows to 4–5 feet tall and 3–4 feet wide in zones 5–9.

continued on next page

Japanese stewartia (*Stewartia pseudocamellia*) A perfect tree for smaller spaces with decorative bark, cup-shaped white flowers, and flaming orange-and-red fall foliage. Grows to 25 feet tall and 12 feet wide in zones 5–8.

Kasagi yama Japanese maple (*Acer palmatum* 'Kasagi yama') A low-spreading variety with red summer foliage that turns orange-red in fall. Grows to 5 feet tall and 6 feet wide in zones 5–9.

Tsukushi gata Japanese maple (*Acer palmatum* 'Tsukushi gata') Deep burgundy foliage emerges in spring with prominent yellow veins, and the fall color on this rounded form varies from orange to scarlet. Grows to 12 feet tall and wide in zones 6–9.

Iijima sunago Japanese maple (*Acer palmatum* 'Iijima sunago') Emerging leaves are orange-red, maturing to rich purple with yellow veins. In summer tiny green spots on the surface resemble grains of sand, giving rise to the name that means "sand sprinkled." Fall brings a dramatic display of intense red and orange shades. Grows to 30 feet tall and 15–20 feet wide in zones 5–9.

Gold Star magnolia (*Magnolia* 'Gold Star')
Star-shaped creamy yellow flowers open in spring
before the leaves emerge. Young foliage is bronze,
maturing to green and then turning gold in fall.
Magnolias are shallow rooted and dislike being
transplanted, so find the perfect spot in the garden
and leave it alone. Grows slowly to 20–30 feet tall
and 15–20 feet wide in zones 5–9.

Fireglow Japanese maple (*Acer palmatum*
'Fireglow') A vigorous red-leaved Japanese maple
that retains its color even in full sun. This has
become a popular, smaller alternative to Bloodgood.
Grows to 12–15 feet tall and wide in zones 5–9.

FINISHING TOUCH

Terra-cotta pots with boxwood Weathered
terra-cotta containers provide the perfect accent, and
a simple clipped boxwood (*Buxus sempervirens*) is
ideal for filling them. To transform newer pots, brush
the surface with a blend of buttermilk and moss and
set in a shady location, spraying occasionally with
water. Be sure to protect terra-cotta in winter if you
live in a cold climate.

A WOODLAND ROMANCE

SITE **PARTIAL SHADE**   SOIL **MOISTURE-RETENTIVE, WELL-DRAINED**   ZONE **7–8**   SEASON **YEAR-ROUND**

Soothing shades of blue and green set a serene tone. Add clusters of heart-shaped white flowers and the mood turns romantic. Rosettes of soft, succulent-like foliage snuggle up to the fern-like leaves of the bleeding heart, and both perennials tempt us to reach out and caress them. Overhead a chandelier of dangling flowers from the willow-leaf spiketail completes the scene. This may be a short-term romance, but it is beautiful while it lasts.

HOW THE DESIGN GROWS

Spring is the peak season for this woodland design, when the bleeding heart and willow-leaf spiketail are in bloom. By summer the bleeding heart foliage may turn yellow and go dormant if the soil is dry, and when the shrub loses its leaves in autumn only the dainty ground cover will remain. Rather than interrupt this delicately balanced composition, add some larger shrubs to the sides to create a frame. A variegated boxwood (*Buxus sempervirens* 'Variegata') would work well, adding year-round structure without dominating the combination. This scene will largely stay the same over the years, the perennials mingling easily under the slow-growing shrub.

FOLIAGE FRAMEWORK

- ->

Toothed saxifrage (*Saxifraga ×geum* 'Dentata') Succulent green spoons, each with a distinctive toothed margin, overlap in dense rosettes to form an evergreen carpet. In spring, tiny white flowers are held high like a froth of fairy wands. Spreads easily in lightly shaded gardens and rich soil. Grows to 8 inches tall in zones 5–8.

- ->

Willow-leaf spiketail (*Stachyurus salicifolia*) Willow-like leaves hang from the graceful arching branches of this deciduous shrub. In late winter and very early spring, strings of unusual pale yellow flowers appear, dangling in clusters like glamorous pendant earrings. Does well in full sun or partial shade and moisture-retentive, well-drained soil. This is a fairly new introduction, but purportedly grows to 6–8 feet tall and wide in zones 7–9, possibly colder.

FINISHING TOUCH

- ->

Langtrees bleeding heart (*Dicentra formosa* 'Langtrees') Ferny blue-gray leaves and a vigorous yet compact habit set this selection apart. In spring this herbaceous perennial blooms with heart-shaped white flowers that dangle from 12-inch-tall stems. It does best in light or dappled shade but will go dormant in summer unless the soil remains moist. Grows to 12 inches high and 18 inches wide in zones 4–9.

FUSS-FREE DRAMA

SITE **PARTIAL SHADE**   SOIL **AVERAGE**   ZONE **5–8**   SEASON **YEAR-ROUND**

High impact but low maintenance—isn't that the sort of garden we all want? These three surprisingly tough plants bring an exciting carousel of foliage and flowers to the shade garden. Leathery leaves mingle with softer forms and rich red foliage jousts with splashes, spots, and stripes. Completing the scene is a carpet of magenta flowers resembling spinning pinwheels, a delicate companion to these robust partners. Surviving neglect and ignored by deer, this may be the hardest-working combo in your garden.

HOW THE DESIGN GROWS

There is never a dull moment with this design. Bold magenta flowers from the bergenia and dangling white blooms of the leucothoe add to the drama in spring, just as the leaves of both evergreen shrubs lose some of the deepest red shades and gain more green, resulting in an exciting kaleidoscope of color. By summer the cyclamen becomes dormant, reappearing in fall to create a silver carpet before flowering begins in winter. Without annual trimming the leucothoe and bergenia will quickly overgrow the cyclamen. A simple solution would be to space the evergreens further apart and plant multiple clusters of cyclamen in the foreground, creating a mass of color without the risk of being smothered.

FOLIAGE FRAMEWORK

Bressingham Ruby heart-leaved bergenia (*Bergenia cordifolia* 'Bressingham Ruby') Tolerant of deer, rabbits, salt-laden air, poor soil, neglect, and dry shade, this evergreen perennial is worth getting to know. The large, glossy, leathery leaves are green in spring and summer but turn a rich burnished burgundy during colder weather. Hyacinth-like hot pink flowers are held high on fat stalks in spring just as the foliage colors are in transition, creating an interesting multihued effect. Tidy up old leaves as needed and protect against vine weevils if they are a problem in your garden. Divide clumps every 3 to 4 years. Grows to 14 inches tall and spreads easily in zones 4–9.

Rainbow leucothoe (*Leucothoe fontanesiana* 'Rainbow') Like bergenia, this evergreen shrub will thrive in tough situations where other plants would give up or be eaten. In spring the waxy leaves are splashed and streaked with creamy yellow and green, but they are at their most colorful in winter, when dark red and purple are added to the mix. In spring, drooping clusters of fragrant bell-shaped white flowers add another layer of interest. This arching mound prefers partial shade but can take full sun if soil is moisture-retentive. Grows to a 5-foot mound in zones 5–9, but you can prune to keep it smaller.

FINISHING TOUCH

Silver Leaf cyclamen (*Cyclamen coum* 'Silver Leaf') In fall, just as much of the perennial garden is sliding into dormancy, this diminutive beauty emerges. The round silver leaves are edged with green and spread easily to form colonies in the shade garden that the deer rarely nibble. In late winter the pinwheel flowers emerge on 4-inch stems in shades of white, pink, or magenta. In winter they need rich moisture-retentive soil, but require drier conditions in summer when they become dormant. Grows to 4 inches tall and 12 inches wide in zones 4–8.

A WINTER ROMANCE

SITE **PARTIAL SHADE**   SOIL **MOISTURE-RETENTIVE**   ZONE **4–7**   SEASON **YEAR-ROUND**

This cheery little pot will always make you smile with its easy-care evergreens that do not mind winter. Vivid golden conifers and a cascading golden creeping Jenny bring sunshine to the grayest months, while dusky purple bugleweed foliage and heather blooms add a hint of romance. The blue-toned foliage of the dwarf juniper and grass-like rush echo the bold blue pot and complete the charming scene.

HOW THE DESIGN GROWS

The heather will continue blooming for several months, but just as it wanes the bugleweed will add spikes of blue flowers in spring, so this design has a lot to offer from September through May. However, although all these plants are evergreen, they will not have sufficient room to grow indefinitely in this small container. Take apart the design in spring by transferring these plants into the garden and creating something new for the next season.

FOLIAGE FRAMEWORK

Forever Goldie golden arborvitae (*Thuja plicata* 'Forever Goldie') Enjoy this golden conifer in a pot while young, then transplant it into the garden. Although best in full sun, in partial shade the color will be more chartreuse. In winter the foliage will take on an orange cast. Grows to 15–20 feet tall and 3 feet wide in zones 3–7.

Blue Star juniper (*Juniperus squamata* 'Blue Star') This fuss-free dwarf conifer works well in containers or the land-scape. The dense, spiky blue-gray needles blend with any color scheme. Prefers full sun but will also grow well in light shade. Grows to 2 feet tall and 3–4 feet wide in zones 4–8.

Golden creeping Jenny (*Lysimachia nummularia* 'Aurea') In the landscape this will quickly form a carpet of chartreuse leaves bearing buttercup-type golden flowers in late spring. If you use it as a trailing accent in shade containers, you can contain its enthusiasm. This semi-evergreen perennial needs moist soil. Grows to 2 inches high and spreads 20 inches or more in zones 3–8.

Burgundy Glow bugleweed (*Ajuga reptans* 'Burgundy Glow') An excellent evergreen perennial for the shade garden or container, with attractive mottled foliage in shades of burgundy, green, and cream. In spring 5-inch-tall blue flower spikes stud the carpet. This variety is less vigorous than its darker-leaved cousins. Bugleweed needs moist soil. Grows to 5 inches high and 12 inches wide in zones 4–9.

continued on next page

Blue Dart rush (*Juncus tenuis* 'Blue Dart') This compact blue-toned rush adapts to standing water and thrives in full or partial sun. Its upright habit makes it well suited to containers and baskets, but you could also use it as a water plant. Grows to 16 inches tall and 10 inches wide in zones 4–9.

Mirjam arborvitae (*Thuja occidentalis* 'Mirjam') Forms a perfect golden sphere in spring and summer, turning orange and bronze-green in winter. It is low maintenance and needs no pruning to maintain its shape. Arborvitae can tolerate moist soil but not standing water and will grow in full sun or partial shade. Grows to 2 feet tall and wide in zones 3–7.

FINISHING TOUCH

Renate heather (*Calluna vulgaris* 'Renate') Renate is one of the new heathers with an exceptionally long bloom time. It has an upright habit with dark green leaves and purple flowers. Needs acidic, well-drained but moisture-retentive soil and will thrive in full sun or partial shade. Grows to 2 feet tall and wide in zones 4–8.

RING OF FIRE

SITE **PARTIAL SHADE** SOIL **AVERAGE, MOISTURE-RETENTIVE** ZONE **7–8** SEASON **YEAR-ROUND**

Like flickering flames, the red and orange foliage of Japanese maples combines with a golden-leaved fuchsia to create a fiery window through which you can view the more distant smoky purple and bronze tones. As a backdrop for all these hot colors, the soft green hydrangea leaves provide a welcome reprieve before they also turn mellow gold. To complete the scene, the dangling magenta and purple flowers of the fuchsia pull the vivid color of the Red Spider Japanese maple and dusky barberry into the foreground.

Ring of Fire continued

HOW THE DESIGN GROWS

When the last leaf has fallen, you can fully appreciate the peeling red-brown bark of the Chinese stewartia, which looks especially striking against winter snow. The new foliage of all the maples and barberry signals spring, with the emerging leaves taking on the freshest colors. Summer flowers on the hydrangea, fuchsia, and stewartia add the final layers to this foliage-rich scene. As the trees mature, some judicious thinning of the branches will ensure that the fuchsia will continue to thrive and keep its bright golden foliage. Over time the barberry and hydrangea may begin to compete for space, so move the barberry or prune back the hydrangea.

FOLIAGE FRAMEWORK

- ->

Beni shigitatsu sawa Japanese maple (*Acer palmatum* 'Beni shigitatsu sawa') This attractive foliage opens cream with a pink hue and green veins, giving it an overall ghostly appearance. The color fades to a rose-flushed green for summer before turning shades of crimson and orange in fall. Grows to 8–12 feet tall and wide in zones 5–8.

- ->

Red Spider Japanese maple (*Acer palmatum* 'Red Spider', also sold as *Acer palmatum* 'Beni-kumo-no-su') This slow-growing dwarf tree is noted for its ultra-fine leaves that emerge red, fade to bronze, and turn a brilliant scarlet in fall. Red Spider develops the best colors in full sun, but will do equally well in partial shade. Grows to 6 feet tall and 3 feet wide in zones 5–8.

- ->

Chinese stewartia (*Stewartia sinensis*) Beautiful peeling bark, fragrant summer blooms, and stunning fall color—this small tree has it all. Grows to 25 feet tall and 15 feet wide in zones 6–9.

Orange Rocket barberry (*Berberis thunbergii* 'Orange Rocket') Noted for its upright growth and ruby color that turns orange in fall, this is a deer-resistant, drought-tolerant, low-maintenance variety. Grows to 4 feet tall and 2–3 feet wide in zones 4–9. **CAUTION** Before planting, make sure barberries are not invasive in your area.

Sharp's Pygmy Japanese maple (*Acer palmatum* 'Sharp's Pygmy') One of the most attractive dwarf green maples, with dense foliage that turns bronze and then red in fall. Grows to 3–4 feet tall and wide in zones 6–9.

Rotdrossel lace leaf hydrangea (*Hydrangea macrophylla* 'Rotdrossel') A compact, bushy deciduous shrub with large flower heads that color dark red to purple, depending on soil pH. Grows to 3–4 feet tall and wide in zones 6–9.

FINISHING TOUCH

Hardy fuchsia (*Fuchsia genii*) The bold golden foliage is dazzling enough, but combined with the dangling hot pink and purple flowers this deciduous shrub is a showstopper as well as a hummingbird favorite. Grows to 4 feet tall and wide in zones 7–9.

ALMOST NATIVE

SITE **PARTIAL SHADE**   SOIL **AVERAGE**   ZONE **5–9**   SEASON **YEAR-ROUND**

Many gardeners try to eradicate the Western sword fern from their gardens, but in a naturalistic setting or a woodland shade garden there is merit in working with what you have and finding a way to enhance it. In its native setting these ferns coexist with vine maples, so using this colorful Pacific Fire variety is the perfect solution. The bright red stems add height as well as color and a finer texture into this simple scene, but the fern still looks perfectly at home.

HOW THE DESIGN GROWS

Winter is the showcase season for this unassuming combination, the bare branches of the vine maple contrasting with the old fern fronds. In spring new fern fiddleheads will slowly unfurl, just as the foliage on the vine maple is emerging. By summer the ferns will be full size and the maple leaves will be a soft blend of greens before turning yellow in fall. To build on this combination, add the native creeping Oregon grape (*Mahonia repens*), whose evergreen holly-like leaves take on a purple cast while yellow flowers turn to blue-black berries. As the maple slowly reaches maturity, only the younger branches will continue to display the bright color, but the increased height and width will give it a more established presence as it rises above a thick carpet of self-seeding ferns.

FOLIAGE FRAMEWORK

- >

Western sword fern (*Polystichum munitum*) A coarse semi-evergreen fern native to the western United States. The long, glossy dark green fronds are leathery to the touch and deeply dissected. This fern thrives in shaded woodlands, even in the dry soil under towering conifers. Before the new growth appears in spring, clip off older winter-damaged fronds for a tidier appearance. Grows to 4 feet tall and wide in zones 5–9.

FINISHING TOUCH

- >

Pacific Fire vine maple (*Acer circinatum* 'Pacific Fire') A stunning variety noted for its vivid red stems that are especially vibrant on the new growth of younger trees. As the trees mature, these colors become more muted but are still attractive. Spring foliage is a soft light green, turning more yellow in shade or orange in full sun, while the fall color is soft yellow. Prefers full sun or partial shade. Grows to 18 feet tall and 12 feet wide in zones 5–9.

COOL COLA

SITE **PARTIAL SHADE**   SOIL **MOISTURE-RETENTIVE**   ZONE **6–8**   SEASON **YEAR-ROUND**

Refreshing white hellebore blooms create a bubbly sparkle of contrast for the auburn foliage of the coral bells in this winter design. Whether you choose to create this combination in a container or as a cold-season focal point in the garden, you will find that the unique slender leaves of bear's foot hellebore provide the perfect texture and red color echo that ties together these fizzy old-fashioned soda fountain flavors.

HOW THE DESIGN GROWS

This medley begins in winter, when the color of the coral bells shows off rich bronze tones that take on red tints in spring and a profusion of red-pink flowers from summer through fall. The long-blooming Josef Lemper white hellebore paired with the larger and more structural Wester Flisk hellebore adds just the perfect touch of green blooms for late winter. Trim off any unsightly foliage as the hellebores and coral bells begin to grow. In late spring, remove spent blooms to help tidy the group for summer. The coral bells does well when divided occasionally in early spring.

FOLIAGE FRAMEWORK

- →

Cherry Cola coral bells (*Heuchera* 'Cherry Cola') The red-brown of this coral bells is a showoff during the colder months. In spring and summer it morphs into a red tone, a vibrant backdrop for the long-flowering display of fluffy bright red blooms that appear in late spring and last well into fall. Evergreen in milder climates, this compact superstar is worth growing for year-round seasonal interest. Prefers full sun to partial shade. Grows to 6 inches tall and 14 inches wide in zones 4–9.

- →

Wester Flisk hellebore (*Helleborus foetidus* 'Wester Flisk') The charming red-tinted stems and leaf stalks of this slender-leaved hellebore are a welcome color treat in winter, when not much else is in bloom. In spring it sports green blooms on tall stems that rise above the unique foliage. Deer resistance is a bonus. Prefers full sun to partial shade. Grows to 2 feet tall and 3 feet wide in zones 6–9.

FINISHING TOUCH

- →

Josef Lemper hellebore (*Helleborus niger* 'Josef Lemper') This compact hellebore is a garden workhorse, blooming for weeks. It makes a great indoor seasonal alternative to the poinsettia, and you can transplant it outside in spring. Deep green foliage supports bouquets of pure white blooms in winter in partial to full shade. Grows to 15–18 inches tall and 21 inches wide in zones 4–8.

FRILLS AND FRONDS

SITE **PARTIAL SHADE**   SOIL **AVERAGE**   ZONE **6–8**   SEASON **YEAR-ROUND**

Bold and frilly, these spidery blooms may appear inconsequential, but their sweet perfume lingers in the cold January air, enticing the winter-weary gardener to leave the fireside. Balancing the finely textured flowers is an underplanting of native western sword ferns, with long broad fronds that clearly define the silhouette of the sunny yellow flowers.

HOW THE DESIGN GROWS

Although this duo offers something of interest in every season, it shines brightest in winter, when the witch hazel brings color and fragrance to the garden. The spring and summer foliage of the deciduous shrub is medium green, turning bolder shades of orange and gold in fall. This vignette will change little over the years except for the continued proliferation of ferns. For dramatic four-season color, combine these with the evergreen Gilt Edge silverberry (*Elaeagnus ×ebbingei* 'Gilt Edge'). This shrub adds gold-and-green variegated foliage to highlight the winter blooms while brightening the garden year-round.

FOLIAGE FRAMEWORK

- →

Western sword fern (*Polystichum munitum*) Often overlooked in favor of more delicate ferns, the native western sword fern may be coarse, but it is also tough, semi-evergreen, and tolerant of dry shade. It survives despite hungry deer, inquisitive rabbits, and romping dogs. As the new growth emerges in spring, remove older fronds to maintain a tidier look. Grows to 4 feet tall and wide in zones 5–9.

FINISHING TOUCH

- →

Goldcrest witch hazel (*Hamamelis mollis* 'Goldcrest') Each sweetly scented sunny yellow flower is tinged with maroon at the base. These thread-like blooms are clearly visible on the bare winter branches. Spring and summer foliage is green, with warm shades of copper, orange, and gold dominating in fall. Grows to 10–15 feet tall and wide in zones 6–8.

CONTEMPORARY HOLIDAY

SITE FULL SHADE, FULL SUN   **SOIL** POTTING SOIL   **ZONE** ALL   **SEASON** WINTER

This welcoming winter design is a modern option for a front-entry container during the holidays, when planting choices are slim and creativity is abundant. The strong horizontal lines of the siding contrast beautifully with the eye-catching vertical lines of this statuesque pot. Using locally sourced cut pieces such as noble fir, stems laden with vibrant winterberry, yellow twig dogwood, luminous paper birch branches, spiky sugar pinecones, and fragrant incense cedar, this arrangement is a fast, long-lasting way to add sparkle for weeks of celebrating.

HOW THE DESIGN GROWS

Winter is the prime focus for these freshly cut greens, as they will hold in the moist soil of this container for weeks on end. When spring is on your mind, switch a few of the key elements for boughs of rose-like quince, fragrant witch hazel, or viburnum. Or try using trimmings of boxwood, euonymus, salal, pittosporum, or laurel. For spring aromas, scent your doorway with eucalyptus, daphne, or sweet box.

FOLIAGE FRAMEWORK

- >

Noble fir (*Abies procera*) The noble fir is a large, vigorous conifer with a broad conical crown that makes it a popular option for cut Christmas trees. Its branches bear up-curved blue-green needles with light undersides and large purple-brown cones. Prefers moist but well-drained soil in full sun. Grows to 150–200 feet tall and 50–60 feet wide in zones 5–7.

- >

Incense cedar (*Calocedrus decurrens*) Native to western North America, this low-maintenance evergreen tree is prized for its wonderfully intense cedar aroma and narrow growth habit. The flat, fern-like branches are soft and deep green. Prefers full sun to partial shade. Grows to 30–50 feet tall and 8–10 feet wide in zones 5–8.

FINISHING TOUCH

- >

Paper birch (*Betula papyrifera*) This tree is popular for its white exfoliating bark and clear gold foliage. Spring brings an abundance of drooping catkins that can be as long as 4 inches. As either a single or multitrunk tree, it will be a large specimen that loves cold climates and cool moist soils. Grows to 50–70 feet tall and 25–50 feet wide in zones 2–7.

continued on next page

Contemporary Holiday continued

Winterberry (*Ilex verticillata*) An excellent hedge or foundation plant, the winterberry shrub provides year-round interest. Also popular for moist soils and low spots, this deciduous shrub provides showy red winterberries that birds and designers love equally. Grows to 3–12 feet tall and 3–12 feet wide in zones 3–9.

Sugar cone pine (*Pinus lambertiana*) This tree is not only the largest pine, but it also provides the biggest cones, many of which are up to 20 inches. Best suited for full sun and moist but well-drained soil. Grows to 200 feet tall with a trunk that can reach 7 feet in diameter in zones 6–9.

Yellow twig dogwood (*Cornus sericea* 'Flaviramea') Tolerating clay soils and wet conditions, this deciduous suckering shrub brings beauty to tough spots in the garden but may be too vigorous for small areas. Prune out one third of the stems each spring, as the best color is always on the youngest canes. Foliage color is medium green in summer and yellow in fall, and the plant prefers full sun to partial shade. Grows to 5–6 feet tall and wide in zones 3–8; spreads aggressively.

Metric Conversions

INCHES	CM
1	2.5
2	5.1
3	7.6
4	10
5	13
6	15
7	18
8	20
9	23
10	25
20	51
30	76
40	100
50	130

FEET	M
1	0.3
2	0.6
3	0.9
4	1.2
5	1.5
6	1.8
7	2.1
8	2.4
9	2.7
10	3
20	6
30	9
40	12
50	15

TEMPERATURES
$°C = \frac{5}{9} \times (°F - 32)$
$°F = (\frac{9}{5} \times °C) + 32$

Further Reading

Calhoun, Scott. 2008. *Designer Plant Combinations*. North Adams, MA: Storey Publishing.

Chapman, Karen and Christina Salwitz. 2013. *Fine Foliage*. Pittsburgh, PA: St. Lynn's Press.

Clausen, Ruth Rogers and Thomas Christopher. 2015. *Essential Perennials: The Complete Reference to 2700 Perennials for the Home Garden*. Portland, OR: Timber Press.

Cohen, Stephanie and Jennifer Benner. 2010. *The Nonstop Garden: A Step-by-Step Guide to Smart Plant Choices and Four-Season Designs*. Portland, OR: Timber Press.

Cohen, Stephanie and Nancy Ondra. 2005. *The Perennial Gardener's Design Primer*. North Adams, MA: Storey Publishing.

DiSabato-Aust, Tracy. 2009. *The Well-Designed Mixed Garden*. Portland, OR: Timber Press.

Hobbs, Thomas. 2004. *The Jewel Box Garden*. Portland, OR: Timber Press.

Lord, Tony. 2002. *The Encyclopedia of Planting Combinations*. Richmond Hill, ON: Firefly Books.

Lloyd, Christopher. 2007. *Exotic Planting for Adventurous Gardeners*. Portland, OR: Timber Press.

Ondra, Nancy. 2007. *Foliage: Astonishing Color and Texture Beyond Flowers*. North Adams, MA: Storey Publishing.

Acknowledgments

We foolishly thought this was going to be easy. With one coauthored book under our belts we naively embarked on this second adventure together with the assumption that we could "whip this out in no time." The reality is that we set the bar incredibly high so that neither of us would accept anything less than outstanding. After more than a year of writing, photographing, and editing we have brought you what we believe is the best of the best. It has not gone unnoticed that our local stores have had record sales of wine and chocolate, but the extra calories are collateral damage for the greater good.

This book is far more than the photo journals of two garden writers, however. It is the result of collaboration between dozens of individuals, many of whom may never meet except through these pages. Our profound thanks to the talented team at Timber Press for translating our ideas into this beautiful book. Tom Fischer, senior acquisitions editor, has been our advocate and cheerleader from the beginning, and our manuscript editor, Sarah Rutledge, coordinated, corrected, and cajoled our words and images with humor and grace.

It takes a very special person to be willing to oversee the editing of all the photography for a book of this nature, especially when you are the daughter of one author and pseudo-adopted daughter of the other. Katie Pond managed to balance diplomacy with a remarkable sense of humor as we asked her to magically make irrigation heads and slug holes disappear from our images or somehow adjust the color of a leaf that we had photographed in less-than-perfect lighting. Yet those were the least of her challenges. Taking hundreds of images from two different photographers with an eye to achieving an overall cohesive layout required a mind-boggling array of spreadsheets and an artist's eye for detail. Katie, you have made our images come to life and helped create a book we are proud of—thank you.

We relied heavily on friends, colleagues, and garden clubs to help us find these gardens across the country, but one lady went far above and beyond what we asked. Joan Looy of Victorian Garden Tours Ltd. not only sought out almost a dozen hidden gems in Victoria, British Columbia, but she also researched ahead of time the best angles for photography, tracked down plant names, and acted as guide, chauffeur, local historian, and lunch procurer (we frequently got too excited to eat). Our book is richer for her enthusiasm and dedication.

Shooting pictures for this book required tiptoeing through gardens at daybreak, dashing across the street with camera bag flying as we spotted dreamy light for an evening shot, twisting ourselves into pretzels, and clambering precariously onto boulders to get a unique angle while deflecting the sun's rays and simultaneously releasing the shutter cable. At times we even photographed in the rain while a homeowner held the umbrella; the glamour of it all was endless. Somehow we managed to write and photograph this book without being arrested and with minimal cuts and bruises.

To the generous homeowners that allowed us to share their private oases—and designers Daniel Mount, Gavin Martin, and Elaine Michaelides, who took time to visit their clients with us—our sincere thanks. Your creativity will inspire many, and indeed without you this book would not exist. We especially wish to acknowledge the following who generously shared their expertise, helping us to identify numerous mystery plants or suggesting suitable substitutions: Tony Avent, Heather Little Bradley, Mitch Evans, Harold Greer, Dan Heims, Judith Jones, Cynthia Meems, Naylor Creek Nursery, Kathy Norsworthy, Mary Palmer, Qualitree Propagators, Jessica Robertson, Jacqueline Soule, T&L Nursery, and Walters Gardens. A special thank-you to Molbak's Garden + Home and Duvall Garden Nursery for allowing us to dismantle your displays and borrow pots for emergency photo shoots, and for generally cheering us on throughout this process.

Finally, my greatest thanks and love to my ever-patient husband, Andy. You have always been my biggest cheerleader. Thank you for all that you do and all that you are.

Karen

Between our smart, funny, grown-up daughter that we lovingly nicknamed "The Girl" and one recently passed, incredibly ancient Pug, my creative musician husband has had his hands full. In addition to sharing the spotlight he still makes me laugh every day. Thank you, honey—I love you.

Christina

Photo Credits

Alyson Ross Markley *Robinia pseudoacacia* 'Frisia' (portrait)

Christina Salwitz A Queen and Her Court, All the Right Notes, Blues with a Feeling, Color and Cut, Contemporary Holiday, Cool Cola, Delicate Details, Dipped in Rosé, Dripping with Jewels, Emerald Isle, Mise en Place, Mixed-up Mosaic, Puzzle Me Perfect, Rich and Robust, Rainless Rocky and Restful, Secret Weapon, Sharing the Spotlight, Sitting Pretty, Stalwart Standouts, Sunrise Sunset, The Bells of Spring, The New Black, The Green Light, The Gilded Age, The Long View, Vivid Vivacious and Violet, Welcome to the Party, Whipped Cream on Lemon Mousse

Dan Heims *Athyrium felix-femina* 'Dre's Dagger' (portrait)

Karen Chapman A Plum Opportunity, A Point in Time, A Vertical Twist, A Warm Embrace, A Winter Romance, A Woodland Romance, Abstract Art, Aging Gracefully, Almost Native, Aquascapes, Bad Hair Day, Balance, Beauty Without the Beast, Bee Happy, Bejeweled, Berries Blades and Branches, Berry Fiesta, Cabbage Queen, Calculated Risk, Casual Sophistication, Cherry Garcia, Citrus Splash, Classics Ablaze, Color Carousel, Color Play, Connect the Dots, Contained Excitement, Dinosaur Soup, Double Duty, Dreamsicle, Easy Breezy, Fall Symphony, Final Flourish, Fire and Ice, Fit for a King, Flavor of the Month, Focal Point Formula, Foliage Explosion, Frills and Fronds, Fuss-free Drama, Golden Moments, Golden Threads, Gone Fishing, Hanky Panky in the Shade, Ice Cream Sandwich, In the Spotlight, Incredible Edibles, Jurassic Moment, Lemon Drop Martini, Lemon Layer Cake, Limited Edition, Lovable Rogue, Make a Wish, Midas Touch, Mix and Match, Naughty But Nice, Nesting Instincts, Pizzazz with Palms, Petite Beauty, Picture of Innocence, Pineapple Crush, Pocket Prairie, Portable Portrait, Pretty in Pink, Pumpkin Spice Latte, Pure Indulgence, Purple Passion, Ring of Fire, Rustic with a Twist, Sassitude, Savvy Solution, Scentsational, Sculptures and Skeletons, Serendipity, Shadows and Silhouettes, Silver Dust, Smoke Signals, Soup for the Soul, Spring Fever, Star Struck, Starburst, Summer Crunch, Summer Galaxy, Swimming with Succulents, The Magpie Effect, The Ticklish Porcupine, Tickled Pink, Traffic Alert, Treasure Hunt, Triptych, Tropical Staycation, Tropical Tapestry, Twist and Shout, Understated Opulence, Unexpected Prize, Unlikely Trio, Will-O'-the-Wisp, Winter Sparklers, Winter Whites

Qualitree Propagators *Thuja occidentalis* 'Mirjam' (portrait)

Design and Location Credits

Designer

Christina Salwitz (Renton, WA): Blues with a Feeling, Contemporary Holiday, Dipped in Rosé, Rich and Robust, Sunrise Sunset, The New Black

Daniel Mount / Daniel Mount Gardens (Seattle, WA): A Woodland Romance, Abstract Art, Color Play, Fit for a King, Pineapple Crush, Star Struck, Summer Galaxy, Unlikely Trio

Deborah Smith / Deborah Smith Landscape Design (Greenbank, WA): A Plum Opportunity, Easy Breezy

Gavin Martin and Daniel Mount (Seattle, WA): Aquascapes

Joan Bentley / Magnolia Garden Design (Surrey, BC): Color and Cut, Delicate Details

Karen Chapman (Duvall, WA): A Point in Time, A Winter Romance, Berries Blades and Branches, Cabbage Queen, Casual Sophistication, Color Carousel, Dinosaur Soup, Dreamsicle, Fall Symphony, Fuss-free Drama, Golden Threads, In the Spotlight, Limited Edition, Lovable Rogue, Make a Wish, Petite Beauty, Pretty in Pink, Pumpkin Spice Latte, Pure Indulgence, Rustic with a Twist, Sassitude, Sculptures and Skeletons, Silver Dust, Soup for the Soul, Tickled Pink

Karen Steeb (Woodinville, WA): Portable Portrait

Paul and Gwen Odermatt / Petals and Butterflies Nursery (Surrey, BC): Sitting Pretty, The Long View

Vi Kono / Creative Designs (Redmond, WA): Calculated Risk, Connect the Dots

Location

Alan Richards (Tucson, AZ): Shadows and Silhouettes

Bellevue Botanical Garden (Bellevue, WA): All the Right Notes, Ice Cream Sandwich, The Green Light, Vivid Vivacious and Violet, Whipped Cream on Lemon Mousse

Birgit Piskor (Victoria, BC): Cherry Garcia, Smoke Signals

Carol Ager (Woodinville, WA): A Warm Embrace, Flavor of the Month, Midas Touch, Traffic Alert

Chanticleer Garden (Wayne, PA): Secret Weapon, Stalwart Standouts

Claudia and Jonathan Fast (Woodinville, WA): Focal Point Formula, Incredible Edibles, Twist and Shout

Craig Quirk and Larry Nell (Portland, OR): Dripping with Jewels

Debra Lee Baldwin (Escondido, CA): Scentsational

Denver Botanic Gardens (Denver, CO): Serendipity, The Ticklish Porcupine

Diane and Gary West (Coupeville, WA): Contained Excitement

Dunn Gardens (Seattle, WA): Sharing the Spotlight

Edith and Bernie Silbert (Woodinville, WA): The Magpie Effect, Unexpected Prize

Government House (Victoria, BC): Double Duty, Hanky Panky in the Shade, Mix and Match, Naughty But Nice

Graham Smyth (Victoria, BC): Foliage Explosion, Winter Whites

Harry P. Leu Gardens (Orlando, FL): Tropical Tapestry

Highline SeaTac Botanical Gardens (SeaTac, WA): The Bells of Spring

Horticulture Centre of the Pacific (Victoria, BC): Bejeweled, Berry Fiesta, Citrus Splash, Understated Opulence

Ivor Soric (Escondido, CA): Swimming with Succulents

Jeff and Pam Coney (Woodinville, WA): Aging Gracefully

Jim Guthrie (Woodinville, WA): Balance

Joanne White (Redmond, WA): A Vertical Twist, Pizzazz with Palms

Kubota Garden (Seattle, WA): Mixed-up Mosaic

Langley streetside planting (Langley, WA): Summer Crunch

Lily Maxwell (Victoria, BC): Bad Hair Day, Lemon Layer Cake, Will-O'-the-Wisp

Longwood Gardens (Kennett Square, PA): The Gilded Age

Lucien and Joanne Guthrie (Redmond, WA): Purple Passion, Starburst

Margaret Andersen and Bob Wolters (Langley, WA): Bee Happy

Mary Jo Stansbury (Greenbank, WA): Pocket Prairie

Mary Palmer (Snohomish, WA): Almost Native, Final Flourish, Golden Moments, Jurassic Moment, Nesting Instincts, Savvy Solution, Treasure Hunt

McComb Gardens (Sequim, WA): Beauty Without the Beast

McMenamin's Chapel Pub (Portland, OR): Emerald Isle

Mitch Evans (Kirkland, WA): Classics Ablaze, Ring of Fire

Molbak's Garden + Home (Woodinville, WA): Tropical Staycation

NBC Universal, Orlando (Orlando, FL): Welcome to the Party

Peggy and Al Shelley (Woodinville, WA): Picture of Innocence

PowellsWood Garden (Federal Way, WA): Puzzle Me Perfect

Ruth and Gary Hough (Woodinville, WA): Gone Fishing

Seattle Arboretum (Seattle, WA): Fire and Ice, Frills and Fronds, Mise en Place, Rainless Rocky and Restful, Winter Sparklers

Swansons Nursery (Seattle, WA): A Queen and Her Court, Cool Cola

Terra Nova Nurseries Inc. (Canby, OR): Lemon Drop Martini, Spring Fever, Triptych

INDEX

About the Authors

Karen Chapman's love of gardening led her to establish her container and landscape design business, Le Jardinet, in 2006. She writes regular garden-related articles for online and print publications and her work has been featured in numerous national magazines, including *Fine Gardening* and *Better Homes & Gardens* titles. Karen is also an instructor for *Craftsy* and a popular speaker at garden clubs, nurseries, and Flower and Garden Shows across the country. She lives on five rural acres in Duvall, Washington, where she is trying to create her dream garden—despite the deer. www.lejardinetdesigns.com

Christina Salwitz is a horticulturist with a passion for the use of color in design, and she uses simple tips and tricks to make container design and gardening easy to understand. Her Seattle-area business, The Personal Garden Coach, helps gardeners of all skill levels achieve their gardening dreams with flair and originality. Christina's containers and writing have been featured in *Better Homes & Gardens* and *Fine Gardening*, among many other publications, and she is a regular speaker at garden clubs, horticultural shows, botanic gardens, and nurseries all over North America. She tests out her crazy design ideas in her Renton, Washington, garden, and is determined to perfect the art of "cramscaping" as many luscious leaves as possible into a small suburban lot. www.personalgardencoach.wordpress.com